Honor and the American Dream

A Volume in the Crime, Law, and Deviance *Series*

Ruth Horowitz

HONOR
AND THE
AMERICAN
DREAM

Culture and Identity in a Chicano Community

Rutgers University Press *New Brunswick, New Jersey*

Parts of Chapters 4 and 5 have previously been published in Horowitz and Schwartz, "Honor, Normative Ambiguity and Gang Violence," *American Sociological Review 1974* 39 (April):238–251; and Horowitz, "Passion, Submission and Motherhood: The Negotiation of Identity by Unmarried Innercity Chicanas," *The Sociological Quarterly* Spring, 1981:241–252.

Library of Congress Cataloging in Publication Data

Horowitz, Ruth, 1947—
  Honor and the American dream.

  (Crime, law, and deviance)
  Bibliography: p.
  Includes index.
  1. Mexican American youth—Illinois—Chicago.
2. Chicago (Ill.)—Social conditions. I. Title.
II. Series.
F548.9.M5H67   305.8′6872′077311   82–7642
ISBN 0-8135-0966-1   AACR2
 ISBN 0-8135-0991-2 (pbk.)

To Maria, Diana, and their families,
to the Lions, and to the residents of 32nd Street,
without whose cooperation and friendship
this book could not have been written

Contents

Preface

This book continues, and I hope enhances, the intellectual tradition of urban community participant-observation studies that early came to be identified with the Chicago school of sociology and finds perhaps its earliest expressions in the work of Harvey Zorbaugh and W. I. Thomas. Carried forward by a number of able and sometimes brilliant studies, this tradition includes among its most recent examples works by Gerald Suttles, William Kornblum, and Eli Anderson.

Community studies are ambitious, perhaps hopelessly so, seeking as they do to explain a complex social world. Community studies are demanding, requiring the almost total submersion of the observer for great lengths of time in the community being studied, for it is only through such a commitment that an observer may understand the meanings of the observed behaviors and may pointillistically portray that social world. But community studies can provide insights and explanations that less systemic analyses might not provide. I hope this book reflects that special attribute.

This study of an inner-city Chicano community in Chicago focuses on the community's youth and on the process of growing up. I have been particularly interested in discerning and describing the process by which the community and its youthful members negotiate the meanings of particular kinds of conduct and relationships. This community provides fertile ground for such an inquiry. Because it exists within, is affected by, and to some extent adopts the larger Anglo culture, community members are sometimes provided with alternative, culturally approved meanings or interpretations of situations or behaviors. Thus, these materials should provide a clear (but by no means unique) example of the negotiation of social meanings and the flexibility inherent in that congeries of meanings and evaluations we call culture.

The study of 32nd Street is of general interest because it examines the complex interweaving of structural, ecological, situational, and cultural elements in the local urban community. For example, the appraisal and evaluation of some behavioral patterns clearly are not derived simply from the lack of political power and economic opportunities but are also an affirmation of a cultural tradition. Other patterns reflect class-based and fundamentally American ways of life, while still others are rooted in the social ecology of the inner city.

The early field work for this study (1971–1974) was carried out while I was an ethnographer for the "Youth in Illinois" study at the Institute for Juvenile Research, which was funded by Illinois Law Enforcement Grant No. 2–09–25–0410–03. My return to the community in 1977 was funded by the National Institute of Juvenile Justice and Delinquency Prevention, United States Department of Justice, Grant No. 77–N1–99–0066.

Parts of Chapters 4 and 5 have previously been published in Horowitz and Schwartz, "Honor, Normative Ambiguity and Gang Violence," *American Sociological Review 1974* 39 (April): 238–251; and Horowitz, "Passion, Submission and Motherhood: The Negotiation of Identity by Unmarried Innercity Chicanas," *The Sociological Quarterly* (Spring, 1981) 241–252.

Without the support of many people this project might never have been realized. Without the encouragement of both Morris Janowitz and Milton Singer, I might never have entered the field and learned to see what was to be seen. Gary Schwartz of the Institute for Juvenile Research has been a constant source of support and ideas. His insights into the community and his astute and detailed comments on my work were invaluable. Likewise, the perceptive criticisms and sound advice of Peter K. Manning were essential to the completion of this book.

Jane Davidson and Susan Parker helped edit this book and remained my friends throughout. Janet Bruno, my teaching assistant, helped me untangle many phases and kept me "well humored" in the preparation of the manuscript. Joan Bothell handled the difficult task of editing the final version of this book with great skill.

Many people contributed to the typing of this book, particularly Carol Anderson, Claire Blessing, Marie Gregg, and Meg Oakes.

I must also thank my great-aunt Fan Grob, who has always been my model of a modern professional woman, and my husband, William Allen, who encouraged and supported me throughout.

Honor and the American Dream

Introduction

On a warm summer evening more than five hundred Chicano[1] community residents of all ages gathered in Pancho Villa Park in the 32nd Street[2] Chicago community to celebrate the opening of a new basketball court with stadium benches as well as a new mural painted by community residents on a wall separating the park from an alley. It had taken two years to obtain funds from the city to turn the garbage-strewn lot into a park, but now everyone could enjoy the rock music emanating from two local bands.

Several young women got up to dance and were joined by small children hopping up and down. The music was so infectious that several young men were coaxed to dance. One small girl wet her pants in the excitement and everyone laughed as her mother took her home to change. Young women paraded up and down in threes and fours wearing summer outfits of pastel pants and halter tops, pretending to be unaware that they were being scrutinized by the young men dressed in sleeveless T-shirts and dark pants. Lounging easily on cars and on the bleachers, the young men freely passed around bottles of Boone's Farm Strawberry Wine and quart bottles of Schlitz. Others, in groups of threes and fours, meandered around, stopping now and then to talk with friends.

It was the first big concert of the summer and everyone was there, including many members of different gangs.[3] There was gossip to exchange: new babies, pregnancies, marriages, and deaths. Frequently young children broke away from their mothers or their friends and ran to their fathers for a hug, a pat on the head, or a nickel. Hardly any young men and women conversed in mixed

3

groups, with the exception of a few teenage couples who stood or walked arm and arm, listening to the music.

One woman opened her apartment so that everyone could use her bathroom and another donated electricity for the speakers. Many people sat on lounge chairs, which filled the back wooden fire escapes facing the park. One family was cooking outside and made a taco for anyone who asked. When the meat ran out, a friend dashed over to a corner grocery and brought back more meat and several six-packs of cold beer.

A policeman tried to drive through the area, but cars blocked the street. He looked as if he might try to get the cars moved but changed his mind and returned to his cruiser. At midnight, after a noisy but tranquil evening's fun, the crowd started to disperse.

Several months earlier, these same people had thrown bricks at policemen (injuring eight of them and damaging two squad cars) when the members of the Board of Education, the mayor, and the press had refused to listen to their demands for better education. In the same year, a twenty-four-year-old man was shot and killed when he tried to negotiate peace between two antagonistic gangs. Four others were wounded.

Those youths who wear black or gray sweaters with contrasting trim and who congregate in parks and on street corners are members not of social clubs but of fighting gangs who kill each other sometimes at a rate of almost ten per year.[4] An increasing number of community youths who are not themselves gang members are also killed every year. As they grow older, marry, and have children and get jobs, many youths turn away from the fighting and violence, though others maintain these concerns.

The contradiction between conventional behavior and brutal violence is part of everyday life in the 32nd Street community. While the economic, political, and educational success of community residents has been limited, they still have not given up the American dream that working hard will lead to an improved future. On the one hand, residents make great efforts to help each other, both financially and socially. On the other hand, young men are shot on street corners while discussing peace among gangs. While community residents write proposals for aid from governmental agencies, violence is used to demand help when proposals fail. A few programs have helped to increase educational opportunities and a new high school was built, yet schools are frequently dangerous for the uninitiated.

It is easy to see why 32nd Street might appear chaotic to an outsider. Do these people have any morals? Do their parents teach them right from wrong? Why don't they become "good law-abiding citizens" who work hard, come home, have a drink, discipline their kids, watch television, and aspire to move to the suburbs? Isn't that what all "Americans" want? These are questions that often arise when outsiders read about the gang fights, the high school dropout rates, the violent protests about inadequate services and opportunities, and the number of illegitimate births in inner-city areas. Why are these people not like us? outsiders ask. Are they forced by circumstances to act as they do, or do they like to act as they do?

The cultural life of this Chicano community is organized around several pivotal themes: violence and convention, public life and private identity, honor and the American dream, close personal ties and academic or financial success, and passion and virginity. The actions of community members in many situations can be understood as attempts to mediate between these often conflicting themes. Despite the fact that all the youths live and interact in the same social settings and experience the same barriers to educational and economic achievement, they develop a variety of orientations toward each other and the world in which they live. Some are more concerned with the excitement and violence of the streets, while others are more concerned with family, school, and convention.

Getting In

At times I have tended to romanticize my fieldwork experience. That tendency helped sustain me from 1971 through 1974 and brought me back to 32nd Street in 1977 to find out what had happened to the youths I first met in 1971. Attending local dances, parties, weddings, and cotillions was exciting. Sitting on a park bench or walking around the neighborhood talking and watching was an adventure. Many families made me feel at home by inviting me to family functions and letting me know that I was always welcome. They celebrated my birthday and spent long hours making tamales, which they knew were among my favorite foods. The romantic adventure image helped me overcome my fears and bear the tedium of dictating notes at two or three in the morning, often six nights a week, and made my fellow students' talk of Durkheim, Weber, Mead, Simmel, and Marx pale by comparison.

The adventure was often overshadowed by the fears and drudgery of doing fieldwork alone. Some of the problems I encountered were typical of all fieldwork, others stemmed from the nature of the community I had chosen. All previous problems seemed minor compared with entering an unknown setting with no set status or identity, introducing myself to many people, and remembering names and their pseudonyms used in my notes and this book. I regarded every resident as critical to my research and thought that offending any one of them would compel me to leave the field.

Though I was fluent in Spanish, life in Spain, Mexico, and North Philadelphia had not prepared me for doing research and moving to 32nd Street in 1972. I quickly learned to distinguish between the sounds of gunfire and firecrackers and to block out the noise and music emanating from the pool hall below my apartment. However, I found the world of the streets sometimes a frightening place. Watching guns being passed through washroom windows to young women at public dances rattled me, particularly when we returned to the dark, noisy dance floor, where a bystander could as easily have been shot as the intended victim.

Readers may wonder how a woman could possibly have joined gang members as they loitered on street corners and around park benches and developed relationships that allowed her to gather sufficient and reliable data. In fact, the manner of conducting research was influenced by my personal characteristics: I am Jewish, educated, small, fairly dark, a woman, dressed slightly sloppily but not *too* sloppily, and only a few years older than most of those I observed (Shaffir, 1974; Wax, 1971). These attributes did make a difference in how people appraised and evaluated me and my actions, and the activities and thoughts to which I was privy. Careful observation of what kind of information was available to me and how different groups perceived and evaluated me allowed me to see not only what categories were important to each of the local groups but how I should try to negotiate my identity, as I started with only the vague outline of one.

I had little choice but to acknowledge publicly the reasons for my presence on 32nd Street; not only do I differ in background from the 32nd Street residents but I had to violate many local expectations to gather the data I needed. For example, women do not spend time alone with male gangs as I did. Because I was an outsider I had to ask a lot of "stupid" questions—"Who are the guys in the black and red sweaters?" or "Why do you fight?" As anything but an acknowledged outsider I would have had a difficult time asking them. Moreover, while my appearance allowed me to blend into a youthful crowd, I sounded and looked sufficiently different so that most people who did not know me realized that I was not from the neighborhood.

While I spent time with students and teachers in several schools, with many families in their homes, and with political activists in several community organizations, I spent most of my time with youths in the streets and at their other hangouts.

As examples of my initial meetings, the variety of identities I negotiated, and the changes I had to make over time, I will briefly characterize my relationships with some of the groups of youths with whom I interacted: the Lions (a gang), the young women who sometimes went out with the Lions, and some of the upwardly mobile youths.

My decision to leave the definition of my identity partly up to the 32nd Street residents and to enter without local sponsorship presented problems, particularly with the Lions and other street-oriented males whom I met. I chose to sit on a bench in a park where many youths gathered from noon until midnight. On the third afternoon of sitting on the bench, as I dropped a softball that had rolled toward me, a young man came over and said, "You can't catch" (which I acknowledged) and "You're not from the hood [neighborhood], are you?"[5] This was a statement, not a question. He was Gilberto, the Lions' president. When I told him I wanted to write a book on Chicano youth, he said I should meet the other young men and took me over to shake hands with eight members of the Lions.

The park became my hangout every day after that, but it was several months, several bottles of Boone's Farm Strawberry Wine, and a number of rumors about my being a narcotics agent before gang members would give me intimate information about their girlfriends, families, and feelings about themselves and the future.

The facility with which I entered the community and eased into a fairly comfortable relationship with the Lions went to my head, and I nearly pushed my acceptance too far by not exercising a reasonable degree of caution. During my second month in the field, I heard about a gang peace meeting that was to take place on a Sunday afternoon at the park. All area gangs had been invited to attend. A perfect situation, I thought, a superb piece of data. On Sunday it was drizzling but I hurried down to 32nd Street. By 1:30 about one hundred and twenty gang members had gathered under the porch of the park gym. Although I noticed that all the young women had disappeared from the park, I thought nothing of it.

The meeting began. A man in his late twenties started talking. I could not identify him as he was not wearing his "colors." He spoke for almost ten minutes about how the Chicano gangs had to stop fighting each other and instead get together for political purposes.

Suddenly, the speaker stopped and turned toward me, as did everyone else. My heart started doing triple time. He demanded, "Who are you?" I managed to say, "Hi! I'm Ruth and I'm writing a book on how the gangs are really together around here." Gilberto grabbed my arm, pulled me behind him, and said, "She's cool, she's been hanging with us." Another whispered to me to get out.

The gang member who challenged me at the gang peace conference was a Senior Greek. After the meeting I came back to the area where all the gangs were standing around. The speaker came toward me and invited me to join him and some other Senior Greeks at the corner tavern. They had already been drinking heavily. Frightened, but thinking only of the research opportunity, I followed them to the tavern. There they proceeded to tell me a story that sounded like the song "Officer Krupke" from *West Side Story*: they were "sick" and losers, the system was corrupt, and their parents had many problems. Over the next few years I got to know them much better, both how cruel and dangerous and how polite and thoughtful they could be.

My relationship with the male gang members never was easy. They felt more comfortable after they found I was not a social worker (I came on weekends), and one of the Lions decided I was like a reporter and began to call me "Lois Lane." While as a woman I was not invited to attend fights or to go out after other gangs, I was taken along to buy guns and as a reporter was told about all the fights, which I could verify with individual gang members and outside observers. I did have to be extremely careful not to develop a sexual identity. My lack of care with appearance, which both males and females continually remarked upon, helped, but I was very careful not to spend too much time alone with any one male and not to dance with them at the many parties and dances I attended.

A group of young women with whom I spent much time congregated in the same park as the Lions and some of them went out with the Lions. I did not meet these young women until the fourth week of research, as many of them did not arrive until early evening. During the first two weeks I left the community well before sundown. It was not until I got to know enough residents and felt secure changing buses on the ride home that I began to stay in the park until eleven or twelve at night.

My identity as negotiated with these young women was ambiguous: I was neither a reporter nor quite an equal. There were few events in their lives that they thought would be interesting to a reporter, and I rarely asked pointed questions, as a reporter might. They began to talk with me more openly when they found that I went on trips abroad without a chaperone, lived with women my own age, and sat around talking about men with them. I had a "shallow cover" (Kleinman, 1980); that is, what I was actually researching was not entirely obvious to the young women, though I told them many times that they too were going to appear in the book.

Though I became more or less an equal, my status was to some degree marginal to the young women. I had no interest in "styling" (dressing in the latest fashions) or finding a husband. These traits proved to be an advantage, explicitly indicating that I was not interested in their men. No matter how much they pleaded, I never took up their offers to lend me outfits or cut and set my hair. My constant willingness to accompany them to the bathroom at all the dances and parties and my general unwillingness to dance further confirmed my lack of interest in obtaining a husband, yet made my presence useful.

I did not meet any of the upwardly mobile youths until two months after I met the Lions, and it was they who sought me out. My first meeting with two of these young women illustrates the differential importance given to personal attributes by various local groups. I was approached by two sixteen year olds whom I had seen before but did not know. Their dress was similar to my own "sloppy" dress. One young woman said, "You work in the park?" (knowing that I did not). Then the other asked, "Which university are you from?" When I replied, "Chicago," she said, "Oh yes, Hyde Park. What are you majoring in?" When I replied, "Sociology," the other said, "Oh, yes, the study of groups and cities and delinquents and things, right?" They went into consultation. I saw one curl her finger over her nose and the other nodded and asked, "You're Jewish, aren't you?" This was one of the few times anyone expressed concern with my religion and heritage. These young women asked me hundreds of questions about my life and my family and gave me only a few opportunities to question them. That night and many nights during the first year, they and a group of their friends walked me the five blocks to the bus stop. By the third time I saw them at the park they invited me to their homes to meet their families and to eat. In one family I was immediately adopted and included in all the family celebrations and holiday dinners.

While I never hid the fact that I was doing research, from their perspective, my demeanor did not generally reflect that activity, nor did these young men and women define my identity as a researcher. I was seen as a big sister and good friend who had been out in the wider society and would understand their problems and help them obtain their goals. Because I was able to obtain all the data I wanted in casual conversation, I rarely needed to remind them of their status as research subjects, and they did not view themselves as subjects.

One evening I was sitting with two young women in the bedroom of one of them and asking a series of very pointed questions about school, who was friendly with whom, whether friendship networks in the school and street overlapped, and whether they ever had been friends with any of the more street-oriented youths. They both jumped on me, saying that I was just a researcher and not there because I liked them. One of them ran out of the house crying that she never wanted to see me again. I had a long talk about field-work with the other young woman, who was equally hurt but willing to listen. She understood or at least valued her relationship with me more than she disliked the research role. It took me more than two weeks to rebuild an understanding with the second young woman, but she remained wary of our relationship for a long time afterward. I felt uncomfortable and worried also.

I had expected some problems with the parents of the youths because my behavior violated local standards for young women. What kind of identity could be negotiated with parents? I feared that parents of the upwardly mobile girls would think that I was influencing them to break away from their families as I had done, but no such problem developed. Though the parents were often upset that their daughters wanted to go away to school, they did not find it troubling that I had done so. I was a stranger from a different world, and they were aware that in that world it was acceptable for a woman to move out on her own. The mothers even let their daughters stay with me. The mothers also took me along to talk with their *comadres* (their children's godmothers) and other relatives. On these occasions my ability to speak Spanish was critical. I was often treated as a slightly strange member of the family. They worried about my eating habits, my health, and my exams. They also worried increasingly about my "catching a good man." However, they did not judge my actions by the local standards. Because I was an outsider, it was acceptable that, though a single woman, I lived almost a thousand miles from my parents.

After a year and a half, I began to spend less time on the streets and more time with the political activists and a small group of Chicano feminists. I attended regional and local political meetings and demonstrations. My identity was significantly different from the one that I had negotiated on the streets. Many times I was included because I had needed skills. I was able to help write successful proposals for funding and to teach in a local college program. Moreover, working with people gave me an additional perspective on the lives of 32nd Street residents.

When I returned in 1977, I did not expect to find easily so many people I had known. Most people acted as though I had been away several months instead of years. The Lions were playing softball in their park, many of their girlfriends had become their wives, and only a few had moved away. Some youths had graduated from college and others had started, but nearly everyone I had known either lived on 32nd Street or came to visit relatives and friends there.

Scope of This Study

To grasp the broad cultural pattern of the residents of 32nd Street, this study focuses on two periods in the lives of young people in the community. The first phase of the study considers teenagers as they interact and develop identities in various social settings: in the adult world, in their homes, on the streets, and in the schools. The second phase of the study examines the process by which the transition from teenager to older community member is made, following some of the same individuals as many of them start families of their own and begin to support themselves.

The first phase employs a largely ahistorical perspective, analyzing variations in social identities within different peer groups and different settings. It also analyzes the meanings that similar symbols have in different contexts (situational and institutional) and among different groups. The second phase deals with changes: the movement of youths into new social settings and the reevaluation (either change or reaffirmation) of social identities.

Chapter 2 explicates the debates over the relative importance of structure, ecology, and culture in the study of urban communities. It begins to develop the two cultural themes that are intertwined in the lives of 32nd Street residents: honor and the American dream.

Chapter 3 discusses the socioeconomic and political marginality of the 32nd Street community within the wider society and its pursuit of the American dream. It compares the attributes that identify the community's status in the wider society and the community's own view of the attributes that distinguish the members from others, that is, their social identity.

Chapter 4 investigates the role of the family in the persistence of the code of honor, including the high evaluation of men who are independent, dominant, and self-supporting, of women who remain virgins until marriage and then become mothers, and of family units that retain close ties. However, the meanings of traditional social relationships within the family context are affected by the economic and ecological realities of everyday life.

Chapter 5 examines the male world of the streets and the relationship between honor and status among the different male peer groups. Several different styles of identity are constructed. Some young men join tough fighting gangs. Others, while they remain tied to the excitement of the streets, engage in fights only if directly provoked. Still others would be content to avoid much of the excitement of the streets, if they could. The situations in which these different groups fight are explored.

Young women are concerned with their status as virgins and mothers rather than with the acts of prowess that reaffirm male status. Chapter 6 discusses young women's efforts to construct a sexual identity around the cultural symbols of motherhood, virginity, and male domination. For young women the critical situation for establishing their sexual identities occurs when these symbols cannot be translated readily into nonconflicting expectations: whether to maintain their virginity or to give in to the demands of their boyfriends. The modes of resolving this conflict and others' evaluations of it also serve to change their collective appraisal and evaluation of motherhood and virginity.

The issues arising in chapters 7 and 8 are the continual tension between the individualistic success ethic as taught and expected in the schools and on the job and peer group solidarity. The tension is experienced with particular intensity within the local schools. Although education is valued in the abstract, the schools attended are not seen as helpful to expanding economic opportunities or increasing self-esteem. Moreover, peer group expectations develop that encourage both dropping out and violence, making the atmosphere worse for learning.

With chapter 8, the book turns toward the movement of youths into new social settings and explores why new roles have affected the lives of some while not affecting others. The meaning of work to both men and women and its impact on changing other facets of their lives are analyzed. Most jobs are in the secondary labor market, and local residents, like members of the wider society, do not value highly their specific jobs.

The question of why gangs remain fighting gangs even when many of their members marry, hold full-time jobs, and no longer like to fight is the subject of chapter 9. The adult gang members continue to waver between street life and convention and to lean toward peer group solidarity over individualistic attempts at economic achievement.

Chapter 10 explores how family and peer group relations give way to the pursuit of the American dream of individualism and worldly success. For some this means moving out of the community, developing entirely new definitions of social relationships, and often having difficulty in developing new ties. Others return to or stay in the community as community activists, developing new locally based solidarities.

Chapter 11 explores the question of why residents of 32nd Street are different from mainstream Americans and why they desire to remain so even if they are able to obtain increased economic and political resources. It uses the concept of community culture to explore the linkages and conflicts between honor and the American dream and the economic realities of everyday life.

2

Culture and Inner-City Neighborhoods

The study of "problem" youth and poor inner-city communities has
a long history in sociology, originating in the 1920's at the University of Chicago. Studies by Anderson (1923), Shaw (1931, 1966),
Thomas and Znaniecki (1918), Thrasher (1927), Zorbaugh (1929),
and others stimulated discussion of the relative importance of
cultural, situational, structural, and ecological variables in explaining the way of life of the poor, the deviant, the urbanites, and the
minorities.

The relative importance of social structure, ecology, and culture
in modern society has been debated periodically.[1] Janowitz (1967:
xx) wrote that "the question must still be asked whether symbolic
and cultural content is being adequately considered as a system of
'action' and influence." Recent studies in several areas have viewed
culture as static and abstract and have minimized its importance in
maintaining today's industrialized urban social order. Suttles (1968,
1972) and Kornblum (1974) in studying poor and working-class
ethnic neighborhoods agreed that structural and ecological factors
are the major bases of social order. In reexamining the contemporary persistence of ethnicity in the United States, Yancey, Ericksen,
and Juliani (1976) attributed this continuity to structural variables.
Kornhauser (1978) in her analysis of delinquency studies argued
that structural problems, not subcultures, are causes of delinquency. In all these studies culture is said now to play a minimal role
in the ordering of social relationships. There is, in Stein's (1960)
phrase, an "eclipse of community."[2]

Suttles (1968, 1972) downplays the importance of culture in
understanding life in an inner-city community. He sees the local

social order as created by structural and ecological variables and by the manner in which the local community is linked to or cut off from the wider society. Culture, in Suttles's (1978) view, is largely a product of those same variables. He argues that though values of the wider society must be attenuated or suspended for a number of reasons, slum residents are able to establish a predictable social basis upon which to construct a moral order. For example, the high-crime area he studied includes residents with a variety of ethnic backgrounds and with few institutionalized or conventional indicators of respectability. The residents tend to perceive each other as the wider society perceives them—as untrustworthy. They are able, however, to establish a social order to ensure safety in interaction. While this social order is not complete, it is sufficient to meet many of the situations faced by community residents.

To establish a social order under these conditions, residents must gather personal information about the people closest to them and must associate with others of similar characteristics. Social order is possible by limiting interactions to "safe" relationships such as those based on similar age, sex, ethnicity, and territory. This process of limiting social relationships is called ordered segmentation. Groups based on these criteria combine into larger units but not one sufficiently comprehensive to provide a basis of unity for the community as a whole. Suttles (1968: 229) argues that "moral" order is based on individualistic evaluations rather than on some normative ideal, that is, "a personalistic morality in which individual precedent is the major standard for evaluation. . . . Judgments of worth and social sanctions are individuated and tailored to past commitments."

Adhering to this ecological and structural argument, Suttles (1972: 190–191) concludes that gang violence arises not out of a "delinquent subculture" but out of the failure of the wider society's agencies of social control to do their own policing. "Intra- and inter-group fears of invasion in one form or another are so general that the street corner gang and defended neighborhood develop naturally without any conscious or intentional effort on the part of anyone" (ibid., p. 65). Gangs become meaningful in neighborhood conflict when the solidarity of the groups depends upon adversarial relations rather than upon common values and a shared "sense of community" (ibid., p. 98).

In this view the group culture may provide solutions to cognitive problems but plays a minimal role in the overall ordering and evaluation of social relationships, particularly in poor neighborhoods. Moreover, the meaning of being a member of a given ethnic group, expressed in symbols that connote affiliation, is largely determined by the degree of "provincialism" of the group. By "provincialism" Suttles (1968: 225) refers to a balance between the group's linkages to the wider society and its degree of control over local institutions, that is, "the balance between involvement in the wider community and continued participation in the local neighborhood." According to Suttles, a group needs connections in the wider society to protect and control local investments. However, these connections become detrimental to community solidarity when they motivate movement out of the local community and the termination of local relationships. The more provincial residents are, the better they can control their lives, because they are less susceptible to believing others' evaluations of them. While a few ethnic differences are attributable to variations in expressive symbols,[3] such as language, gestures, some public demeanor, and clothing style, other ethnic differences are attributable to degrees of provincialism. The extent of provincialism creates differences in the extent to which relationships are well ordered by territory, ethnicity, sex, age, and personal reputation.

In his later writing Suttles places greater emphasis on the process of creating and communicating a life-style through the development of expressive symbols among people who have "shared in the disgrace of poverty" (Gronbjerg, Street, and Suttles, 1978: 93). This process allows such individuals to develop a social order that insulates them "from the destructive stereotypes of the wider society" (ibid., p. 96). However, the meaning of the expressive symbols and life-styles, Suttles argues, is located in the group's position in society, that is, "how their members have been separated from the mainstream of American culture—whether they have been 'left behind,' 'kept in their place' [for example, hillbillies], or experienced partial acceptance as 'hyphenated-Americans' [for example, Polish-Americans]" (ibid., p. 95). Moreover, members of these groups frequently move between their own traditions and those of the wider society when the economic situation changes.

Culture for Suttles is a product of ecological and structural forces operating in the wider society; a strong moral order can result only if the social order is complete. Moreover, he conceives of the content of culture as primarily social-psychological, such as the perception of the trustworthiness of community residents. Culture is seen ultimately as *reflecting* social relationships, not determining them.

Kornhauser (1978) more strongly rejects the use of subculture to explain delinquent activities. Emphasizing the variable strength of culture in a highly urbanized, industrialized, and mobile society, Kornhauser views culture as a limited force in determining behavior in poor communities and an inadequate explanation of delinquency.[4] This view can partially be explained by her definition of culture as autonomous, that is, neither dependent on outside forces to retain its incumbents[5] nor a reaction to situational exigencies.[6] Moreover, she considers completeness—that is, cognitive, expressive, and evaluative orientations, harmoniously and clearly articulated values, and a balanced variety of valued goals—necessary for an enduring culture (ibid., pp. 124–125). Unless culture can meet these stringent criteria, it is a weak explanatory variable in Kornhauser's view. On this basis, she dismisses culture and subculture as potential explanations in the study of the delinquency because delinquency-ridden communities have little normative, exchange, or coercive control and consequently little social order.

—While Kornhauser has taken a particularly strong position in rejecting delinquent norms as an explanation of delinquent actions, others have argued over the degree to which local norms or beliefs are determined by the position of a group in society. For example, some scholars argue that structural conditions (such as status or class) that persist over an extended period create a distinct culture that reflects behavioral differences. Miller (1958, 1969, 1971), for example, argues that lower-class male culture becomes self-perpetuating and generates behavior among male juveniles that the wider society views as delinquent but that members of the subculture consider proper. A moral order distinct from that of the wider society evolves.

Gans (1962, 1968) sees "true culture" as static and abstract. Lower-class populations generally accept the criteria of the American dream of social and economic success, but because of their class position (a situational exigency) individuals develop a set of beliefs (Gans), or a shadow culture (Liebow, 1967), that makes their present behavior patterns more acceptable. If their economic positions change, these beliefs will disappear and the individual will be able to adhere to the overreaching moral order of society.

Taking a moderate position, Hannerz (1969), in his study of a black inner-city neighborhood, criticizes the extreme views that lower-class values are self-perpetuating or situationally adaptive. Some characteristics of "ghetto-specific" life are determined by structural constraints—for example, "economic problems form one of the foundations of male-female conflict as generated within the ghetto household" (ibid., p. 182)—while others are learned and cultural. Hannerz's view of culture as learned behavior is less abstract and more flexible than, for example, Gans's (1968) conception of culture. For Hannerz, "the learning and maintenance of modes of behavior within the community [constitute] the fundamental criterion of culturalness" (ibid., p. 185). He argues that to be viewed as cultural, behavior must be viewed as morally acceptable. Culture is adaptive and "largely situational" (ibid., p. 183), that is, both constrained by the macrostructure and learned through interaction with others.

Hannerz adopts a much more flexible view of culture than Gans, Liebow, or Kornhauser, who conceptualize "true culture" as deterministic and autonomous. When a culture is not autonomous, it becomes a weak or partial one, in which the content of a life-style is determined by the structural position of the group and situational factors. These arguments tend to be too extreme—on the one hand in discounting the role of cultural context, and on the other in making it paramount. The apparent contradiction between these positions may be resolved if one sees the role of culture not as uniform and stable, or present or absent, but as situationally relevant to action. Moreover, its relationship to structure should be seen as complex and dynamic rather than mechanical. This perspective is a two-dimensional view of culture. It is not a new one. Its origins can be found in the early Chicago school, particularly in the works of W. I. Thomas, G. H. Mead, and Clifford Shaw.

A Two-Dimensional View of Culture

While acknowledging the variable strength of culture and its problematic relationship to a system of action and social structure, one need not disregard culture entirely in the study of delinquency and poverty-ridden communities. Nor is culture necessarily absent if the social order is not complete. The one-dimensional Parsonian notion of culture is utilized by both the structural perspective (Gans, 1962; Kornhauser, 1978; Liebow, 1967) and the cultural perspective (Miller, 1958). Parsons (1951) views culture as a quasi-objective entity in which values and norms are objects and invariant points of reference toward which people orient their behavior. Such values and norms give everyday interaction its *stable* qualities. These values give moral and affective meaning to social relationships and role performances, and control choices by indicating the relative merit of particular courses of action. Parsons conceives of culture as the most general factor in a hierarchy of control or social action, that is, the least variable analytic component of action. His notion of culture, because of its abstract nature, limits the importance of culture in a system of social action.

The concept of culture adopted in my study is more flexible and less abstract than the model proposed by Parsons. In my model culture consists of the meaning of behavioral patterns. The uniqueness of a subculture rests in its symbols, that is, in the cognitive and moral categories through which group members appraise and evaluate their behavior and that of others. Cultural symbols acquire meaning when people talk about something, when they agree or disagree about the definition of a situation. People not only use meanings to make sense out of situations[7] but change or reinforce prior meanings in interaction.[8] Consequently, culture is neither static nor necessarily the most stable component of social action, but constantly evolves.[9]

> We can say that the culture "speaks" the person. On the
> other hand, it is equally true that individuals draw upon the
> meanings of those cultural forms in ways which enrich or
> alter their significance. In this sense, we can say that the
> individual "creates" the culture. The place where the "ob-
> jective" and "subjective" aspects of cultural form come
> into direct contact is the intersubjective realm of social
> interaction and communication. (Schwartz, n.d.: 38)

Behavior, then, must be carefully observed because it is "through
the flow of behavior—or, more precisely, social action that cultural
forms find articulation" (Geertz, 1973: 17). It is the meanings of
behavior patterns, the way people interpret and evaluate their relationships, that constitute the data presented here. Culture in this
sense determines the meaning of social relationships; it does not
just reflect them, as Suttles (1968) argues. Cohen (1974: 30) states,
"We can observe individuals objectively in concrete reality, but the
relationships between them are abstractions that can be observed
only through symbols." Social relationships develop through and
are maintained by symbols and are objectified by them.

The lives of 32nd Street residents are shaped in part by two
distinct but intertwined normative codes. (Codes as used in this
study are not a set of rigid, unchanging rules but a flexible, often
ambiguous set of expectations about what one should do and how
one will be evaluated.) The first code is expressive, concerned with
the maintenance of personal and family honor. Interactions
involving this code dramatically signal community membership and
moral boundaries. While the form of the code has its origin in Latin
American and Mediterranean traditions, its content as expressed
among 32nd Street community residents is not necessarily
identical.[10] The second code is largely instrumental, concerned with
achieving the American dream of social and financial success
through hard work and education. This code has its origin in the
Protestant work ethic. Its content is constantly evolving as it is
shaped through the local institutional context. Both codes—though
not necessarily to the same extent, or in the same manner—provide
symbols by which community members orient their lives.

Honor: An Expressive Code

Honor as a cultural system is not unique to this community and has traditionally been found in many Latin and Mediterranean societies. The notion of Berger, Berger, and Kellner (1973) that honor is obsolete in contemporary societies is not borne out by my observations of 32nd Street or by contemporary studies of Mediterranean societies (Peristiany, 1966).

The structural prerequisites of an honor-based subculture include face-to-face personal relations rather than impersonal relations and the importance of character within the local community over roles in the wider society (Peristiany, 1966). Honor cannot be measured by tests or money. Under this code individuals are dependent on others' *public* evaluations of their actions, but it is the *style* of those actions and not their effectiveness in achieving a particular goal that is judged.

Moreover, since these actions reflect on the self and their validity can always be challenged, individuals must constantly be ready to assert and reassert their claims. This makes a person extremely vulnerable to others' claims to personal precedence, to status superiority (Peristiany, 1966). The self, not a job or financial resources, is the currency of status. The characteristics of an honorable person—those characteristics that have local value—provide the bond between self and community (Campbell, 1966).

Pitt-Rivers (1966) observed that honor among men is an issue that arises solely between social equals. Under a code of honor, refusing to grant precedence amounts to an insult, while accepting another's claim to superiority is tantamount to dishonor. Almost any act may be interpreted as a possible sign of disrespect for the other person's character. When men are not exempt from contests of honor because they are "partners" (two men tied by close friendship) or kin (blood or fictive), they must make a continuous effort to maintain the respect they think they deserve.

Honor touches the person directly in that it is an attribute of the individual. Yet according to Pitt-Rivers, any aspersion cast on an individual as a group member reflects upon the honor or moral worth of the group as a whole and is perceived as a public test of the group's status. Moreover, honor adheres to those actions that reflect personal decisions and judgments and here is concerned with the integrity of one's physical being. Dishonor is experienced as a failure of manliness or the physical capacity to maintain claims to precedence among peers.

Honor sensitizes an individual to violations of his person that are interpreted as derogations of fundamental properties of self. Any incursions on the personal territories of self that signal attempts to deny "due respect" may be seen as "an incursion, intrusion, encroachment, presumption, defilement, besmearing, contamination—in short a violation" (Goffman, 1971: 44). An action such as failing to shake hands or staring may be interpreted, from a conventional middle-class perspective, simply as a violation of good manners; however, within the honor framework violations of the common rules of etiquette may be seen as attempts to demean an individual.

Moreover, a man of honor should avoid placing himself in a position subordinate to another by incurring extensive debts. Any man who is in debt cannot support his claims of dominance and superiority in interpersonal relations. A debtor is by definition in an inferior position and consequently dishonored.

The honor of a man is linked not only to his own actions and perhaps to the honor of his peer group, but also to that of his family. A woman's "shame" (an unmarried woman's loss of virginity or a married woman's extramarital affair) reflects on the male family members. It indicates a man's inability to control the lives of his women and a failure to maintain his dominant position over them. A woman can maintain her honor only by remaining chaste and, should she not do so, it is up to a male relative to take revenge to maintain the family honor.

Because the evaluation of an individual rests entirely upon a public dialogue, it depends upon continual subjective evaluation by others. Honor, as Berger, Berger, and Kellner (1973) argue, is distinct from the more modern concept of dignity. Dignity "always relates to the intrinsic humanity divested of all socially imposed roles or norms" (ibid., p. 89); honor can be maintained only by following particular norms and being evaluated by others as having done so successfully.

The American Dream: An Instrumental Code

Community members give a high value to achieving the American dream and to using the expected methods to attain these goals.[11] They wish to be esteemed by others for their occupational mobility and success. This code is different from the honor-based code. Its measures of achievement and respect can be applied to all uniformly without face-to-face interaction and yet are based mainly on individual achievement. Beyond rather vague formulations this code specifies very little about what is valued and thus who is respectable.

For young people, the school is supposed to be the focal institution where they spend much of their time. Although staying in school and moving from one grade to the next are generally understood as the proper mode of ensuring future success in the job market, it is unclear exactly how this success occurs. Academic success does not necessarily lead to job success, nor does high job status or financial success necessarily imply academic success. Teachers, parents, students, and sociologists frequently disagree about the connection between schooling and the world of work. Moreover, the meaning of success in school and its measurement are often debated. Success is often measured by school authorities in terms of the smooth movement of students from one grade to the next and one school level to the next, by standardized test scores, and by grades given by teachers. An "A" student should be able to succeed in the world. Success, however, is generally not measured in terms of the intrinsic value of learning and cognitive development unless it is reflected in grades. Coleman (1961) voices the fears of many American parents when he suggests that academic success is being replaced by popularity and athletics as student measures of school success and respect. Others argue that the competitive skills learned in athletic competition and the social skills acquired in the popularity contests provide a strong basis for later economic success in the business world.[12] Thus academic success is not necessarily congruent with peer group respect and individual self-esteem; nor do respectability as perceived by peers and respectability as perceived by adults necessarily coincide.

Adults are also concerned about whether a particular youth will turn out to be a "decent" member of the community. Decency is more than a question of not violating the expectations of the community or the laws of society. What is morally acceptable in the pursuit of success is often difficult to define. It is also difficult to appraise just when an individual becomes viewed as a failure, as someone who is no longer respectable and who may have given up the possibility of success or gone beyond the bounds of decency.

Respect and success do not necessarily occur simultaneously. One can be an academic success and not be considered respectable because one has been arrested too often, has been inconsiderate to one's family, or has been an outcast among one's peers. Or a youth may achieve respect by following interpersonal peer group expectations and being nice while nevertheless failing in school. Consequently, a young person must discover the balance between being respectable and attempting to become successful. Moreover, local institutions frequently do not clearly articulate what is actually meant by success and whether efforts toward future success in the job world are worth investing in now.

Institutions and Values

Values, for the purpose of this study, are not highly abstract analytical constructs but are incorporated within people's daily interactions with local and national institutions. Contact may be direct, as in the school, the job, the family, and the church, or noninteractive, as in the media, through which symbols and ideas are filtered. All of these institutions in which youths participate are controlled by adults (Matza, 1964). Some are managed by local adults (the family and some community organizations), though most are dominated by the wider society with few local personnel to incorporate local values. Young people negotiate their own way through these institutions by appraising and evaluating the goals of the institutions from their own perspectives.

Norms and values, whether those of the family or those of the wider society, are also shaped and reinterpreted by the demands the youths place on the institutions. Thus, a dialectical process emerges in which the norms and values of the youths are continually reaffirmed or reshaped in the interaction between their experience of the adult norms and values as filtered through institutions and their previously objectified moral categories.

Messages concerning appropriate and valued actions thus arise from many sources, creating the possibility of conflict between messages received from different institutions. Some of these messages are consistent with the American dream, while others are more consistent with the traditional code of honor.

Because the two codes apply to specific settings, some of the potential conflict is avoided. While at times the codes seem to require the application of different meanings to similar situations, the setting may define the appropriate choices. The code of honor generally applies to situations on the streets and at home; the code of the American dream, in the abstract, structures social relationships in the school, outside the community, and on the job. Behavior that is highly valued in one setting may be denigrated in others.

Setting is not the basis for all code selections. The two codes are understood, applied, and intertwined with the social structure in various ways. It is necessary to examine vacillations between codes, ambiguous choices, possible conflicts, and the resolution and evaluation of potential dilemmas.

Goffman (1963: 2) states, "Social settings establish the categories of persons likely to be encountered there. The routine social intercourse in established settings allows us to deal with anticipated others without special attention or thought." According to this view, interaction is unproblematic; that is, if the situation is structurally ordered, one should know the kinds of people and the kinds of behavior to expect in particular social settings. This posits a rather mechanical relationship between structure and meaning. From the perspective presented in this book, in any setting the identification of one's relationship with another is potentially problematic and also potentially very dramatic. Though expectations about the nature of proper conduct are to some degree established by setting, they are not always determined for everyone on all occasions.

In some situations the meaning of actions may be unclear to any of the participants. For example, which norm should govern the action may be ambiguous, or norms may conflict in a particular situation. Following one norm may mean violating the other. At other

times economic or political realities and changes may make new adaptations necessary. The meaning of actions, particularly in these situations, must be negotiated.

The tension between instrumental and expressive codes is revealed through various cultural dilemmas, which in turn reflect the disparities between economic and social aspirations and the realities of everyday life in the inner city. Through these cultural dilemmas and continuities people experience the contradictions and inconsistencies of their positions relative to the wider society.

Triggering Situations and Social Identities

During adolescent years, peer groups take on particular importance in the development of an individual's self-image. Peer group membership is among the few means available for youths to define who they are to themselves and others; the role repertories and activities of adults are largely unavailable or demand little involvement of the self to fill these roles. Adolescents are extremely sensitive to peer judgments about who they are and how well they fulfill that image.[13] Consequently, peer groups and peer activities become the major arenas in which the dramas of constructing identities are staged.

The concept of culture as collective appraisals and evaluations developed in peer group interaction is consistent with the finding of group differences that extend beyond distinctions attributable to historical and socioeconomic variations.[14] Perspectives on group ties, demeanor and dress, sexual identity, authority, education, and future life-styles all may vary. If meanings and evaluations are shaped in interaction with others, it is conceivable that significant cultural variations can occur among people with similar socioeconomic positions and histories.[15] Therefore, structural explanations of variations are insufficient to the extent that they cannot explain cultural differences among groups who occupy almost the same socioeconomic status.

Not only would one expect to find a variety of symbolic orders among diverse communities and ethnic groups, for example, but one would also expect to find some normative variations among different networks within an ethnically and economically homogeneous community. Variations among youthful peer groups in this community can be explained in part by an intertwining of the honor and American dream codes, by differential ordering and evaluating of particular social relationships, and by varying interpretations of these codes developed in interaction. When the normative codes provide different definitions of the situation, or when structural limitations or situational contingencies make it difficult to act in accordance with either code, variations in meanings between groups are likely to occur. Different groups may resolve these critical situations in different ways, and, in doing so, may develop their own variations of the shared meanings of the situation.

Where dilemmas exist, the drama of the situation becomes acute. Neither the meaning of the situation nor its appropriate resolution is clear or universally accepted. When existing rules fail to govern or articulate the meaning of a situation, the actors must then negotiate the meaning every time the situation occurs or negotiate to establish a new meaning. There are few ways of anticipating the outcome. These dramatic situations of choice serve as potential triggering situations, revealing the types of persons the actors perceive themselves as being. By defining a situation in a particular light and then pursuing a course of action predicated on that definition, individuals call attention publicly to their social identity. Such individuals are negotiating (actively or sometimes unknowingly) with their audiences in order to be appraised and evaluated as being a certain kind of person.

It may be particularly difficult to negotiate the meaning of another's actions without knowledge of that person's social identity, because neither actor can anticipate how the other will interpret his/her own actions. There are few obvious distinguishing characteristics among the youths because all youth groups share and participate in the same institutions. Most seem, at least superficially, to share a single, undifferentiated identity. For example, many different groups, including gang members and those who rarely fight, spend time in the parks. Unless a gang member happens to be wearing his gang sweater or colors, there may be no way to distinguish him from anyone else. Therefore there are few indications of how he will interpret the actions of others, creating many potentially dramatic situations.

Social settings and social situations within these settings are where important social relationships are negotiated and where crucial decisions are made.[16] There is also a processual aspect to these settings and situations. Individuals change as they move into new or different social settings, situations, or institutions. In these new contexts relationships may have to be redefined. Under other conditions the old evaluations may be reaffirmed despite structural differences.

This book asserts that there is an order in the 32nd Street community where, according to many sociologists, little order should exist. An analysis of the processes and situations through which youths create, change, or maintain social identities as they take on new roles and move into new situations reveals a precarious order. This order depends not only on the class position or social ecology of inner-city life but also on the traditions of the honor code and the American dream code. Residents face many dilemmas in which the cultural order becomes problematic and is sometimes transformed for people who try to live according to both codes. But a cultural order exists, and at times it may have more impact on social action than do structural variables. It is through an analysis of problematic situations that the relationships between structure, situation, ecology, and culture are revealed.[17] Using this perspective, one may explore why many young women become pregnant before marriage, why many young men join gangs and continue their membership into adulthood, and why and how locally rooted solidarities differentiate 32nd Street from similar inner-city communities and remain salient in the lives of the residents.

3

Marginality and the American Dream

Nearly three hundred community residents, including local gang members, college students, small babies carried in their mothers' arms, and a few women old enough to be those babies' great-grandmothers, gathered on 32nd Street for the two-mile walk to the Board of Education offices downtown. The march marshals wore arm bands and several carried water bottles to quench the marchers' thirst, as the sun was hot.

This march was part of an effort to secure a new high school for the community. Elaborately developed proposals and attempts to voice community views at public meetings had failed to convince the board of local needs. The committee for a new high school had voted to hold this march because earlier marches for more city transit jobs at least had received some good publicity.

Education in general is a major concern for many community members. The academic success of 32nd Street youths has been well below the nation's average, with an estimated 70 percent of the youths never completing high school. Education is sufficiently important that meetings on this issue are well attended by adults who are not involved in other protest or community groups. The educational issues have ranged from concern over decrepit facilities, to the removal of principals and teachers viewed as insensitive to the needs of their students, to a new community-requested high school within the boundaries of the 32nd Street community. That school (for grades ten through twelve) would replace a building that had been constructed at the turn of the century and never remodeled, and where the security system was fortified with locked doors and guards.

The publicity gained by the march did little good. The board members would not speak with community leaders. Later a group of protesters entered the ninth grade extension of the high school (condemned ten years earlier) and requested that a board member or someone from the district supervisor's office come and listen to their grievances. When only the police arrived at the school, bricks were thrown at them. Several protesters were hurt and others were arrested. Only then did the school board agree to build a high school within the community. Several years later the new school was built, but not without conflicts between the community and the board over the program, the principal, the staff, and the building architect.

This series of events illustrates some of the ways in which the 32nd Street residents experience their position in the urban stratification system and react collectively to those experiences. Of all Chicago communities, 32nd Street ranks very close to the bottom on a socioeconomic hierarchy.[1] Outsiders base their judgments about the community on this status ranking and its inner-city location.

Most sociologists would agree that position on a socioeconomic status hierarchy is critical to individual and collective experiences in a society. But how are inequalities experienced and what are their effects on the behavior and expectations of people? How and to what extent is the sociocultural world affected by position in the wider society?

By examining the community's social identity—those attributes that members of the wider society use to identify and evaluate it and those attributes that residents use to distinguish themselves from other communities—the links between the socioeconomic position of the community and the residents' expectations become clearer. The terms in which the wider society appraises and evaluates 32nd Street and the resulting identity are inconsistent with many of the categories local residents use to evaluate themselves, with the community's objective position, and with the community residents' evaluations of themselves and of their prospects for achieving the American dream. People and institutions in the wider society use the inner-city location to conclude that the 32nd Street residents are poor, helpless, and undesiring of education, and that the area is deteriorated beyond restoration and infested with uncontrollable social problems. The residents, in turn, perceive community members and the community in terms of personal attributes, ethnic identity, and the strength of local social relationships. What concerns local residents is their social honor, which Weber (1964) defines as the cultural standard through which a group states and defends its self-worth relative to other groups. Through their lifestyles, residents publicly indicate the kind of persons they think they are (Schwartz, 1972).

The perceptions of members of the wider society not only differ from those of the local community residents but also mask the diversity within 32nd Street and ignore the inconsistency between status indicators and the residents' continued desire for a better future despite limited success so far. Though never abandoning the American dream and its dominant ideology, the residents continue to hold their own notion of social honor, which distinguishes them from other groups in similar circumstances. Chicanos intensely value the importance of local social relationships while actively struggling, both collectively and individually, for increased educational and economic success.

Community Boundaries, the People, and Population Movement

Like most Chicago inner-city neighborhoods, 32nd Street has historically been a location of first residence for immigrants. Factories are located throughout the community, frequently providing more filth and ugliness than employment. The community also suffers from poor housing, crowding, and lack of recreational space. The one hundred and thirty square block area is only a few miles from the downtown area and a new state university. It can be reached by several bus routes, by an elevated train that has one stop in the community, and by two major elevated highways. Despite its proximity to the downtown, the 32nd Street neighborhood is isolated from the surrounding communities by a canal, a river, and railroads.

Only a small section of the present community was included in the city in 1837 when Chicago was incorporated, but with the construction of a major canal, working men began to settle along the river. Most of the land remained devoted to truck farms, and most of the families were of native American, Irish, or German heritage. A major fire in 1871 destroyed much of Chicago but did not touch this area. As a consequence, industries moved in and workers began the construction of wooden frame homes. While the number of Irish and German settlers continued to increase, a large number of immigrants from Poland and Czechoslovakia settled in the area. By 1895, when Czechoslovakians and Lithuanians became the predominant ethnic groups in the community, the older homes were beginning to deteriorate. At the turn of the century Italians settled in one corner and that section has largely maintained its character to the present date. The population reached 85,680 by 1920, when the Poles became the dominant ethnic group, remaining so until the mid 1960's. By 1970 the population had declined to 44,500.

While some Mexicans, who came to work on the railroads, moved into the community in the 1930's, the majority did not arrive until the late 1950's and 1960's, when urban renewal destroyed the neighborhood where many had resided. In the 1950's approximately 30 percent of the community were Spanish speaking. By 1970, 55 percent, most of whom were of Mexican heritage (though a small percentage were Puerto Rican), were Spanish speakers. If the largely Italian section of the community is excluded, as it is in this study, the Spanish-speaking population reaches 61 percent (of a total population of 37,000).[2] A 1972 survey found close to 70 percent to be Spanish speaking.[3] There is, however, a significant difference between the census figures and estimates by local residents of the entire area (including the Italian section), some of which place the population as high as 70,000. While this estimate may be too high, Spanish speakers seem to be systematically undercounted throughout the United States.[4]

As Burgess's (1967) concentric zone analysis of Chicago suggests, the greater the distance from the central business district, the nicer the homes and the less crowded the area. The 32nd Street area does change slightly as distance from the center city increases: there are increasing numbers of persons of Middle European ancestry and fewer foreign-born residents, more open spaces and trees, higher rents, and more owner-occupied dwellings. These differences are reflected in the community's official names, which are used by government agencies and sometimes the media but rarely by the residents.

The residents generally refer to the entire area, excluding the Italian section, by its major shopping street, which I have called 32nd Street. This is consistent with their views of the area. They all experience the same problems: poor medical care, lack of garbage pickup, poor press, poor schools, lack of political clout, and minimal recreational facilities. The gangs are everywhere.

Chicano gangs have been around on 32nd Street since the late 1950's. Several individuals who were living in the community then describe the Chicano gangs as evolving out of the need to protect Chicanos from other ethnic groups in the neighborhood who opposed the Mexican influx. A number of young men formed a group called the Sons of Azteca for this purpose. Fifteen years later residents recalled that there were constant scuffles between the ethnically based gangs. The Sons of Azteca divided into four gangs, two of which remain dominant today. As the community changed from an ethnically mixed area to one of relative homogeneity, the Chicano gangs turned on each other within the community, on the Chicano groups to the north in the old neighborhood, and on the Chicano gangs to the west.

Residents feel that the western part of the community is a nicer place to live because of the nicer homes, though violence is everywhere. A Chicana who lives on the west side but frequents El Pueblo Park on the east side with her boyfriend (a member of one of El Pueblo Park gangs) said, "I know why my parents moved to the west. It's much nicer there. There aren't so many *cucarachas* [roaches] and rats, besides we got a yard, but we got clubs too. Did you hear that a Noble [a gang member] got shot by my house last week?" In fact, more gangs congregate around the park in the western section than in El Pueblo Park. There is no way to escape violence on 32nd Street.

As in most inner-city areas, there are few parks and much activity takes place outdoors. Until 1973, there were only two parks in the neighborhood. El Pueblo Park, in the east, is one square block, and Western Park, in the west, covers two square blocks. All the parks are continuously and simultaneously utilized by different groups and for different activities. The users range from gangs to old people to mothers with babies. The activities include sports, doing homework, listening to music, drinking, flirting, conversation, and intergang conflicts.[5] The pool in El Pueblo is used mainly after it closes in the evening as none of the teenagers will wear the bathing suits required during the day. At ten everyone climbs the fence and jumps in, fully clothed. The site of much of my research was El Pueblo Park, where I met many of my informants and spent much of my time. It is the hangout for the Lions and Senior Greeks gangs; the Red Shirts, a marijuana-smoking group; a female gang; mothers and their babies; and several other groups.

A Typical Slum: The Outsiders' Views

The ecological setting of this community gives the impression that it differs little from other poor inner-city areas, and it is this impression and the community's low socioeconomic status that outsiders use to make decisions about the community and its residents. Most outsiders see no reason to assume that 32nd Street is anything but a poor community. The media portray the violence and the social problems of the residents, the political actors ignore the area, the general public avoids entering the community, the school board does little to improve its deteriorating schools, the local banks and food stores charge high prices for goods and services, and the city urban renewal plan designated many of its buildings for destruction and its residents for removal.

Because of its proximity to the downtown, a large state university campus, and a large medical complex, much of the area was scheduled for development in the late 1970's and 1980's as a middle-income, high-rise area in order to make it attractive to the professionals who work in these institutions. The plans were not revealed to the residents who would have been dislocated by the renewal efforts. After the city's plans became known to several individuals who were sympathetic to the needs of the residents, a protest was mounted. It was only at this point that an architectual firm working on the plans agreed to consider present residents. No major renewal effort has taken place almost a decade after the plan was initiated.

Not only are the 32nd Street residents viewed as powerless and their homes ready for destruction, but the media, when they report on 32nd Street, emphasize social problems: the violence, the low level of education, the dirty alleys, and the large numbers of illegal immigrants living in the area. Articles in metropolitan newspapers about protests for better schools emphasize the momentary violence of a protest rather than the year-long peaceful struggle with school authorities who refuse to listen. Headlines, for example, read "8 Cops Hurt in Melee" rather than "School Board Ignores Struggle for Better Schools." News accounts do not mention that residents were prohibited from speaking at several board meetings. Pictorial essays show "enchanting" Mexican children posed against the "stark reality" of a crumbling building, and other articles discuss illegal residents in crowded, miserable conditions living in fear of being sent back to Mexico.

The school board's seeming disregard of educational needs in this community also indicates the "slum" label given to the area by institutions. Slum residents are perceived as lacking interest in education, so the school board does not feel the need to provide college preparatory classes or to improve the poor physical conditions of local schools. The facilities are some of the oldest and most dismal in the city. All but one were built around 1900. According to the *Chicago Daily News* (February 1974) most city schools were to receive face-lifts if the school board found enough money. Of the seventeen schools mentioned as too dilapidated to renovate, four were used by 32nd Street students. Many of the teachers leave as soon as they can get other jobs. Even the Catholic church does little to keep up the physical facilities of some of its elementary schools, and several have been closed for lack of funding.

Even if the youths should graduate from the Marsh Upper Grades Center (the seventh and eighth grade school for the area), the choice of high schools is dismal. Few 32nd Street students ever graduate from Tudor, the comprehensive high school, and most who do have been directed into the lower tracks. The technical schools are located some distance from the neighborhood, and some have entrance requirements that many eighth grade graduates cannot meet. Leslie's Commercial High, which attracts a number of young women from 32nd Street, has courses in cosmetology, secretarial skills, and prenursing but lacks the classes necessary for college entrance: foreign languages, science, and mathematics.

Public institutions are not alone in treating the community as an impoverished and powerless slum area. The private sector contributes by charging more for services provided in this community than in other parts of the city. The excuse usually is that it costs more to operate a business here. Banking, for example, was an expensive service in this area. A $500 balance was necessary to maintain a checking account with no service charge at a local bank, while many other banks in the city required only a $200 balance. The banks have been accused by many community residents of taking the people's money and investing it elsewhere instead of lending it to community residents to buy or remodel homes (redlining).[6] Many people, particularly those without cars, used one of the many currency exchanges for cashing their checks and paying bills, but charges for check cashing were high.

The local stores added to the already large expense of feeding a big family. The one large grocery chain store, located in the eastern section, was difficult to reach for those without a car, did not give credit, did not keep its shelves stocked, and was often more expensive than better chain stores in other areas.[7] Small corner stores maintained their importance and popularity because they gave credit, were more convenient, and were friendly. Tiny groceries occupy almost every corner in the community, each typically belonging to the dominant ethnic group on the block. One local resident, a frequent user of a corner store, explained in Spanish, "I like to shop there. It's close and I know what I'm getting. Sometimes we run out of money before my husband gets paid. I pay them when I get the cash. They always help out. We've been going there for years." The prices are frequently higher than at chain supermarkets, but in addition to giving credit, they also serve as a center of gossip, reinforcing local ties.

The residents are perceived as untrustworthy and the area as dangerous both by outsiders who work in the community and by others who might potentially use the available facilities. Few city residents drive through after dark. Many teachers who work in the area do not venture far beyond the school property and do not remain in the community after school hours. Few teachers ever

attend local community functions or local church festivals. Even
with the increasing popularity of Mexican food, not many outsiders
venture into the many inexpensive local restaurants, while the few
downtown Mexican restaurants that serve essentially the same food
at double the price are crowded with non-Mexicans. Members of the
wider society perceive 32nd Street as a slum community, and the
actions of those nonresidents both reaffirm and help create that
image.

A Close Community: The Insiders' Views

Residents do not employ ecological variables when discussing the
value of living in the community. While some community members
do worry about the children, and no one likes to live in a crowded,
deteriorating home, other, more important aspects of community
life make 32nd Street a desirable place to live and bring up a family.
The many close ties with friends and relatives and the "Mexican-
ness" of the area are the reasons many residents will not leave the
area when they can afford to do so.

The extensive personal network of friends and family is important to most residents. It is impossible to walk or drive on block
without meeting a relative or friend. Even after being in the field for
only a month or two, I could not walk between two points in the
community without stopping several times to talk with acquaint-
ances. People know where their friends spend their time and who the
friends of their friends are. Since all seventh and eighth graders
attend Marsh school, young people meet each other there.
Commonly, when two young people from the community meet for
the first time, one asks about the relatives of the other. The conversation may go like this:

> First person: "Do you have a sister Maria, about nineteen
>   years old?"
> Second person: "Yes."
> First person: "I went to school with her in the eighth
>   grade ...."

The lack of indoor space encourages street interaction and informal meetings. When the weather is warm enough, everyone is out in the streets from afternoon until late at night, seated on kitchen and deck chairs that are scattered over the well-swept sidewalks. Apartments are too small for entertaining. The typical larger apartment has only a living room, dining room, kitchen, and three bedrooms. The bedrooms are large enough for a bed and sometimes a dresser. There are few closets, and often only curtains separate rooms.

The close ties with large numbers of people are the basis of positive evaluations of the community, but for the young people they sometimes produce negative evaluations of the smaller unit, the neighborhood. For most people a supportive network is crucial and those without one are pitied, but some young people feel that the extensive social network of their parents confines their social activities. If a young girl comes in "too late," an "old gossip" may tell everyone what transpired. One young woman, walking with her boyfriend in the western area, was spotted by an uncle, who reported it within minutes to her mother in the far eastern end of the area. The uncle embellished the tale: "He was kissing her in public." The mother was waiting for the young woman and, upon her return, forbade her to leave the house for a month except to go to school. The fifteen year old declared that she wanted to move away from home but not out of the community.

But one nineteen-year-old wife felt better after she moved eight blocks back to where most of her family lived:

> I've always lived close to my family. My married sister
> lives around the corner, my parents live on the next block,
> I have six aunts and uncles within five blocks, and my
> husband's family mostly lives around the corner. I'm glad
> we moved back here. It was nice over there. I got to know
> a different place, but it's better over here.

Affirming the importance of close ties is the fact that many of those who can afford to move to a "nicer" area do not. They stay and repair their homes, reasserting the image of the community as a good place to live. One mother of six explained in Spanish:

All my friends are here. The kids don't want to move
because their friends are here. They say they want to go to
Tudor [high school] but Junior cut classes all last year and
failed. I don't know what to do.

This family had looked several times for a home farther from
the center city but had decided against it each time. One mother of
nine explained that her husband and an older son wanted to buy her
a house in the suburbs, but she liked the area, with all its problems.
Both she and her husband were born in the United States and spoke
English at home, but she was excited when two of her daughters
began to learn Spanish. She felt that most of her children had grown
up successfully; all still lived in the area. The common culture and
support of kin outweighed all problems of the community.

Residents feel most comfortable in their own community
whether they leave the area rarely or frequently. "I like to go to
clubs downtown but I don't ever really get the bread [money]," one
of the gang members claimed. When he did have the money, he took
his girlfriend to dinner downtown. Many teenagers skip school to go
shopping downtown or to the movies, but some residents, especially
the very young and the older residents who do not work outside
the neighborhood, rarely venture downtown. There are cheaper
discount stores, convenient to reach by bus, and less expensive
movies elsewhere. "I don't like to go downtown. When I do go, I
take one of my older daughters because my English isn't too good
and there are too many people. Besides it's much too expensive,"
explained Mrs. Mendoza in Spanish, a mother of seven, whose
daughter attended a state university and rode her ten-speed bike
around the city. One youth who worked for a community social
service agency and who traveled all over the city told me, "Sure I go
all over the city, but you know, I just feel more comfortable where
my people are. Of course I can act any way I want." Though most
residents leave the community for entertainment, work, or shopping
trips, 32nd Street is home and the place where its residents feel
most comfortable.

Young people like knowing many people as well as the constant
potential for excitement. One gang member described why he

visited his gang every weekend after his parents moved to the suburbs.

> We want to stay here. It's where things are happening, where my people are. It's dead out in the suburbs and there's the same problems all over the city, maybe just west on 40th Street they got nicer houses but they got clubs [gangs] there too—worse than here. I come in to be with the guys [his gang] every weekend. There ain't nothing to do in the suburbs. Here there's always some action.

There is a dance, a wedding, or a cotillion in the area every Friday and Saturday night; though these are not officially "open" affairs, everyone is admitted. People often run back and forth to seek the best parties and dances. If nothing else is happening, everyone goes to the park to drink; young people frequently remark that something is bound to happen.

While residents, using the traditionally close social relationships and a common ethnic culture as criteria rather than the ecological and economic criteria used by the wider society, usually evaluate 32nd Street as a reasonable place to live, they are not satisfied with their limited socioeconomic success. They consider themselves the hard-working and respectable poor who must struggle with the institutions of the wider society to improve their opportunities.

Persistence of the American Dream

The composite index of socioeconomic rank obscures much of the reality of 32nd Street. Closer observation reveals a community that is struggling to overcome its image by working hard, attempting to better the educational opportunities and gain political power, and affirming the moral validity of being Chicanos. Institutions, however, provide few resources and little aid in facilitating the strivings of the Chicano 32nd Street residents toward the American dream. Clearly, it is a community whose members expect to work hard but have discovered that it is extremely difficult to equal the educational attainment, political clout, and social status of Anglos.

Economics

The median family income in the 32nd Street community was $8,560 in 1970,[8] higher than 18 percent of Chicago communities that ranked above 32nd Street in the overall socioeconomic ranking of eighty-five communities. A surprising 24 percent of the families made from $10,000 to $14,999, but only 12 percent earned over $15,000.[9] While 18 percent of the communities that ranked above 32nd Street on the overall index had a higher percentage of families below the poverty level, 17 percent of the families on 32nd Street had incomes below the poverty level, according to the *Chicago Sun-Times* (October 22, 1972). Of the 32nd Street families below the poverty level, approximately 23 percent were receiving public aid.[10]

Several factors contributed to the relatively high family income and the significant percentage below the poverty level. In over 40 percent of the households, a female member was employed, which contributed both to the relatively high family income in families where both adults worked and to the high percentage below the poverty line in families where the woman was the sole wage earner,[11] as Spanish-speaking women tend to earn less than non-Spanish-speaking women.[12] Also contributing to the number of families below the poverty level was the significant number of large families in the community.

The employment situation on 32nd Street was not quite as good as it may seem at first glance. In 1970, of the males over sixteen and under sixty-five who were not in school, about 5 percent were unemployed and 12 percent were not looking for work.[13] Of those employed, 29 percent were operatives, 16 percent craftsmen, and 11 percent laborers (nonfarm).[14] Women were largely employed as operatives and clerical help. Their unemployment rate was 2.7 percent, lower than Spanish-speaking (7.5 percent) and non-Spanish-speaking (4.6 percent) women of Chicago.

The housing picture was mixed: some units were badly deteriorated, while others were well maintained by residents. Even many renters spent money to maintain their units. Many of the brick facades were freshly painted in bright reds and trimmed in white, and many interiors had been remodeled. Other homes were in poor condition because the absentee landlords refused to do any repair work. The people who lived in those homes did their best by constantly cleaning, plastering, and painting, but it is difficult to keep a home presentable if the pipes leak badly and the bathroom needs new fixtures. Major investment in rented homes seemed futile to many renters, and obtaining a mortgage was difficult, as 32nd Street was considered a high-risk area by the banks. There has been almost no new construction in the area in over twenty years.

Though their income may not be high and their jobs may be largely unskilled, most residents view themselves as hard working, and their actions demonstrate their desires to improve their position. A married man with one child said:

> We are the respectable poor. We work hard for what we earn. We are always clean. My mother, even when we only had beans to eat, when we were small, always kept us clean. Lots more of us could be on welfare, but we don't beg from anyone.

One father of seven was upset because his salary as an assistant machinist would not go as far as he wished. He worked on the night shift to earn more per hour and often worked overtime. "I know if I had gotten more than a third grade education, I could have done better. I really know a lot about machines but I can't be a Machinist Union member without a high school diploma." He wanted skilled or professional jobs for all his children and helped to send one son to the most expensive parochial school in the city.

Collective efforts have been made to ameliorate the future job situation. Protests have been mounted against restrictive practices in labor unions, against the Chicago Transit Authority, and against the police force, which had only 178 Latins out of 13,000 officers in 1972. Local organizations have established training programs and job development agencies. One program had a union carpenter train youths whom the union promised to hire as apprentices when the program was completed. Several such programs were run by community residents. Unsatisfied with their relatively low level of attainment, community members desire an improved future. The image that arises is not of the "disreputable" poor but of hard, consistent workers who believe that through concerted, sometimes collective effort their position will improve if they are given the opportunities.

Education

The educational achievement of community members presents a generally dismal image and is among the strongest indicators of slum status. Only 21 percent of those residents over twenty-five years old were graduated from high school. This is the lowest percentage in the city. The dropout rate prior to high school graduation is close to 70 percent.[15] Only 65 percent of the fourteen-to-eighteen age group is enrolled in school, and the reading levels are among the lowest in the country.[16] At Tudor High School, which services about twenty-one hundred students, approximately 60 percent black and 32 percent Latin, of a sophomore class of more than eight hundred, four hundred began their senior year and approximately three hundred were graduated. For a marking period at Tudor High in March 1973, only a handful of students had "A" averages and just over a hundred students had "B" averages. The rest had "C" averages or below. According to the 1970 census, very few residents were enrolled in colleges. The community residents, on the average, have not succeeded educationally.[17]

The numbers of parents who have joined organizations concerned with education and who have tried to obtain a better education for their children by paying to send them to parochial schools leave little doubt concerning the importance given education. For example, the parents of one gang member wanted to send him to cadet school so that he would finish high school, although this would mean a significant financial sacrifice for them with their six other children. Some 22 percent of school-age children attend parochial schools, and the reasons for sending females and males differ. Parents want their sons to have a better chance in the economic world and their daughters to avoid pregnancy, delay marriage, and eventually marry men with greater economic potential. One young, uneducated mother planned to send her daughter to Catholic school starting in the seventh grade so "she won't get into no trouble with guys too early." She claimed that the public schools were too rough and too many girls became pregnant. Mr. Mendoza declared that he would pay anything so that his sons could get good educations and make careers for themselves, an opportunity he felt he never had. For his daughters, education was not as important, though he willingly helped to support his eldest daughter while she attended the state university as long as she lived at home.

Many parents worry that their children will not be sufficiently prepared if they are placed in "special education" classes. One father refused to sign the papers to place his daughter in a special school for handicapped children because of an eye problem. Her parents felt that the diagnosis was incorrect and that going to a special school would not benefit their daughter.[18] Another family was distressed to find that their son had been in "educationally and mentally handicapped" (EMH) classes for three years without their knowledge. They took their case to a lawyer and after several months of testing, the child was placed into a normal class. The mother explained to me that he would never be able to succeed in the world if he came from an EMH class. His intelligence quotient was within the normal range. She said:

> I never went very far in school 'cause I got married when I was fourteen but my daughters . . . I got them in school now. The younger one is in honors and wanted to drop out but she won't, I talked her out of it. My older daughter got into trouble, she went to parental school [for problem youths] for a while and then decided to go to Tudor. She said she wasn't learning nothing and a teacher told me to get her out of there and into a good school. She needs one more credit and then will go to that downtown commercial school. It's supposed to be real good.

Though many parents feel there is little they can do as individuals about the quality of public education, residents have organized into community action groups, which have been successful in bringing about educational changes through proposals and protest. During the summer of 1972, the principal of one elementary school was removed in response to parents' protests over her inability to deal with Latin students (90 percent of the school). Nearly two hundred parents demonstrated day and night until she was removed and replaced by someone more acceptable. A community action group set up an alternative high school for dropouts, three of whom were accepted at major universities after the program's second year. While achievement has been limited, community residents continually reassert the importance of education for gaining success in the wider society and try to change the outsiders' views of them as educational failures.

Ethnicity

The positioning of Chicanos on an ethnic status hierarchy is difficult, not only because of the problems of actual measurement, but also because of the ambiguous nature of their status, as a large percentage are not physically distinct from the majority population (Peñalosa, 1973).[19] They do not appear to be a distinct social group and are generally viewed as neither black nor white.[20] Historically, Chicanos, except for the very dark-skinned members, have not been discriminated against as much as blacks, yet neither are they considered by the majority to be equal to white ethnic groups (ibid.). In Chicago, some Chicano families moved into a neighborhood where blacks had been burned out of their homes, yet Chicanos have been denied access to other neighborhoods.

This ambivalence of the wider society toward Chicanos is partially revealed in their exclusion when concessions are made to minorities. For example, the police department was forced by law to hire more minority members, but until they subsequently lowered the height requirement, many Chicanos were too short to qualify. When minority programs are developed, Chicanos are rarely included. The city opened a junior college, developed around the concept of ethnic studies, for those interested in black studies. Only after the enrollment declined was a Chicano studies program started and were Chicano students actively recruited.

The Chicanos perceive themselves as socially and culturally distinct from other urban groups, their Mexican traditions separating them from non-Latins and other Latin groups. Walking along 32nd Street, one is aware that it is a Mexican community. The signs are often in Spanish. The restaurants advertise tacos, enchiladas, and *menudo* (a tripe soup), while the groceries sell fresh tortillas, dried, fresh, or canned chilies, pork rinds, and the ingredients for tamales. The bakeries sell Mexican *pan dulces* (sweet rolls). Many families eat mostly Mexican food. "Boy, after three days of American food I get a real taste for Mexican food," claimed a fifteen year old who had been away from home for three days. Driving lessons can be obtained in Spanish. Several of the stores sell goods from Mexico such as books, magazines, records, and *piñatas*.

The traditional culture, however, is often modified. The sounds of a band practicing Mexican music may reach the street, but so do the sounds of standard American rock music or the music of Santana and El Chicano (two popular Latin rock groups in the United States). Some of the clothing stores are owned by Chicanos but sell trendy United States styles of clothing. Farther west along 32nd Street there are more Anglo faces and many more stores with Polish and Czechoslovakian names. The Spanish- and Slovakian-language newspaper offices stand opposite each other on 32nd Street. Two funeral homes are owned by Chicanos, the rest by Middle Europeans.

Efforts are made to continue Mexican traditions. Area residents celebrate Mexican holidays, and the Chicano-staffed social service organizations have vacation days for Mexican rather than United States holidays. September 16, Mexican Independence Day, is one of the area's largest celebrations, with an elaborate parade that marches for about forty blocks from the center of downtown through 32nd Street to Western Park. The Mexican flags hung throughout the neighborhood give the area a festive look. Parties continue until the early morning hours.

Chicanos themselves vary in how they perceive their status relative to other groups in this country. Peñalosa (1973) characterizes different groups as "Americans of Mexican ancestry," "Mexican-Americans," and "Chicanos." For the first group, ancestry is generally unimportant. Members of the second group are conscious of their ethnicity, which for them has "an ambiguous blend" of positive and negative values (ibid., p. 65). The third group is committed to the defense of Mexican-American values. It is the most

active and political and claims to view its culture as the better of
the two.

Chicanos feel that they differ socially and culturally from blacks
and from other Latins, such as Puerto Ricans. They wish to maintain some of those cultural differences. While they are not subject to
the same derogations as either group, they are well aware that they
are still not regarded as social equals to the Anglos. Although
ethnicity does not scale as easily as income or education, Chicanos
seem to fit somewhere on the bottom half of a vague ethnic status
hierarchy. While unsatisfied with their evaluation, residents wish to
maintain their Chicano identity.

Politics

The city political system is so well immersed in traditional arrangements that new groups have little opportunity to become involved
in the system. The Chicanos are no exception. They have been
unable to infiltrate ward politics to elect a representative, and although someone is appointed by the mayor to represent Latin interests, the position has not been one of power. The one Latin school
board member maintains a distance from the local community and
frequently, in the view of some community members, votes against
their interests.

Inroads into local politics and positions of influence have been
minimal but not because of lack of interest or effort. The city political machine is organized so that the precinct captains obtain favors
to dispense according to the number of voters they turn out on election day. Because many of the Chicanos are not citizens or are not
registered to vote, they cannot vote, which partially accounts for
the few Chicano precinct captains and the few desirable city jobs
they receive as election spoils.[21] Attempts to obtain representation
are made more futile by the division of the 32nd Street community
into two city wards, each of which is still controlled by the ethnic
group that was predominant fifty years ago and neither of which
has a significant proportion of Chicanos. The aldermen from these
two wards have been in office longer than those from other wards.
Nonetheless some residents are trying to launch one community
activist into city politics.

Past failure in the local political arena has been partially counterbalanced by efforts to obtain federal grants for resources that might otherwise be obtained through local political sources.[22] Because the city and state have not provided the necessary services, several former gang members and street people have written proposals for federal funding for an alternative college program, supplementary educational programs, recreational programs, a bilingual library, a social service program, a contracting and skill-training agency, a methadone maintenance clinic, a drug program for youths, and a health clinic. All proposals were funded and the programs were developed and staffed by community members, who also controlled the boards of directors.

These programs were all started and are run by residents who saw the need for services that were not being provided by outside agencies.[23] A number of Catholic priests have helped to organize both protests and proposals and have served as middlemen in dealing with institutions of the wider society. Fernando and Alfie are among the best-known local residents for dealing with the Washington federal bureaucracies. Fernando plays the "heavy" and Alfie plays the "straight man." Fernando wears no tie and often puts on some "typical Mexican" clothing. His hair appears uncombed, his manners are rough, and he intersperses militant street language into his talk. Alfie wears an expensive suit and tie, has his hair well groomed, and uses a sophisticated vocabulary to demonstrate his sympathy for the "establishment." The two men grew up together on the street. In meetings with outsiders Fernando "threatens" the officials and Alfie appears to calm him down. Many officials give in to their demands.

In order to create a youth center Fernando and Alfie walked in and took over an unused Catholic school in December 1971, although they had already been denied use of that building. Within a few months the school housed several community service programs with community residents as staff.

In addition to programs initiated by members of the community, several other programs have come under local control. There are two settlement houses in the community. The one in the west serves only youths under fourteen, as does the Boys Club nearby. Many of their personnel are from outside the community. An externally funded settlement house in the eastern area was taken over by community members to house the Free Health Clinic (developed by community residents and staffed by volunteers), the Brown Berets,[24] and a newspaper run by some of the community's politically active youths. A neighborhood association became a troubleshooting group, helped to organize many of the educational protests, and was instrumental in the plan for the new high school.

Though members of the community have failed to secure resources through traditional political channels, they have been quick to procure necessary resources through the federal government. These organizations provide important links to the institutions of the wider society as well as linking residents at the community level. While not all the organizations persevere or accomplish all their goals, the local staffs have become a core of socially active and politically aware people who remain in the community. While political clout through traditional channels is low, community members have actively and successfully pursued alternative paths.

Community members fulfill the wider society's definitions of working-class social respectability: most community members hold steady jobs, most families are two-parent families, most families make a marginally decent living through hard work if not good jobs, and few families are on welfare. Moreover, the adults clearly support the notion that education is the best means for their children to achieve upward mobility. The American dream is embedded in the lives of most residents, and their achievements, though limited, encourage the pursuit of greater success. Success, however, has been hindered by outsiders' appraisals and evaluations of the residents as poverty-stricken, untrustworthy, lazy, and dangerous, for their treatment is based on these attributes, contributing to the gap between the limited success of residents and their desire to achieve and be respected.

There are attributes that community members perceive as distinguishing them from others in similar positions in the wider society and as identifying them as members of a distinct ethnic group. This self-identity includes not only individual economic achievements but also moral character. The distinguishing attributes concern family and personal honor, which are characteristic of both Mexican and some Mediterranean societies, and are generalized local standards of self-worth. To many of the residents, maintenance of locally rooted moral character is more important than economic success, such as moving to the suburbs. It is not that residents do not wish to achieve economic success, for they do keep working, but they do not hold the "melting pot" as an ideal. Residents see their ethnically rooted standards as desirable, distinguishing them from others and having overriding importance.

Youths experience others' evaluations of them in interaction with school personnel, with youth-serving agencies, and later with coworkers and bosses. On the one hand, they are told to work hard in school and to behave properly in order to get a good job, while on the other hand, they are often told that they are a drain on the welfare system, ill prepared for school and work, and lazy. Throughout locally based institutions and relationships such as the nuclear family, the expanded family network, and peer groups, estimations of worth are based on more traditional criteria of social honor. These social relationships are also affected by experiences in the wider society, so that traditions must be reassessed and either reaffirmed or altered. Within the family setting, youths are exposed both to the standard of economic success and to the standards that distinguish them from other groups. The following chapter analyzes the impact of the Chicago urban context on traditional family relationships.

4

The Expanded Family and Family Honor

Three months prior to Ana's cotillion, or *quincecañera* (fifteenth birthday celebration),[1] everything appeared to be ready. Sponsors to pay for almost all aspects of the religious ceremony and the party afterward had been found. Relatives, *compadres* (godparents), and friends had been enlisted to help: an uncle was paying for the food, an aunt was paying for the liquor, a grandmother was buying her dress, baptismal godparents were buying the cake, and two of their daughters were going to "stand up" (serve as an attendant) for the church procession. Other relatives and friends were enlisted as godparents to pay for the flowers, a *cojín* (pillow) to kneel on in the church, a *diadema* (diadem or tiara), the bands, the photographs, and several other incidentals. As Ana had chosen to have the dinner and dance in the gym of the local community center, she did not have to rent a hall. An order for two hundred invitations had been placed at the engravers with the names of all the attendants printed on an inserted sheet.

In addition to finding enough relatives and friends of the family to pay for the affair, Ana had found the requisite fourteen young couples, *damas* (women) and *chambelaones* (men), to stand up in matching dresses and tuxedos. This is frequently a difficult task, as each of the young women has to buy her own dress (generally $45 to $100), which Ana, like most celebrants, picked out of a catalog of bridesmaid dresses. The cost of the rented tuxedo is often $40. A cotillion is an expense for everyone. Ana had already stood up for two of the young women, who were returning the favor, and she was scheduled to participate in four more. Finding fourteen couples who could afford and would agree to stand up for the affair was diffi-

cult. In addition, she wanted to exclude from the males any potential troublemakers. As it was, two of the young women were standing up with their brothers, who were in different gangs, and
another's escort was in a rival gang, but none were known as troublemakers at parties.

Problems began several weeks before the affair. An aunt's
family dropped out, claiming they could not afford to pay for the
band because they had to attend the funeral of a relative in Mexico.
Excuses such as this are common, but the day was rescued when
Ana's mother agreed to try to pay for the band herself.

One week prior to the cotillion Ana discovered that her mother
had hired only a Mexican *ranchera* (Mexican country music) band
and not a rock group. Ana did not want a cotillion without a rock
group, and a local band was finally located forty-eight hours before
the party. Then one of the couples decided that they could not afford
to pay for the clothes and dropped out. Another couple broke up and
an escort had to be found on short notice. While anxious about
having only thirteen couples, Ana claimed it was better than seven
or eight, as some had. Her problems were not over. An aunt informed her mother that she had seen Ana kissing her boyfriend, and
her mother threatened to cancel the event because she did not want
to endure the questions about Ana's virginity that public knowledge of her activities might engender. If the affair had been can-
celled, the strength of the family network might have been questioned.

A cotillion is a public affirmation both of a young woman's
virginity and of her kin's ability to work together to pay for such an
event. Not all fifteen year olds have cotillions. Many families cannot
afford them. Moreover, rumors often claim that a young woman
holding a cotillion is trying to prove that she is still a virgin when
she no longer is one. On the other hand, failing to have a cotillion is
frequently considered a good indication that the young woman is no
longer a virgin and may even be pregnant.

The evening before the affair required major organization, as
beans and rice had to be prepared for two to three hundred guests
and the gym had to be decorated. Retiring at two in the morning,
everyone was awake by six. Clothes had to be ironed for her six
brothers and sisters and both Ana and her older sister had to buy

shoes the day of the affair. Her family congratulated themselves for having chosen to buy fried chicken rather than spending the considerable effort to cook the more traditional *mole* (a spicy baked chicken in sauce), though a few guests later commented on its absence.

Ana marched down the church aisle in her long white dress and veil on the arm of her uncle, following the thirteen couples and the new godparents. As she knelt with her boyfriend before the priest, Ana and the others resembled a wedding party. She did not kiss him but quietly left her flowers at a side altar and prayed there to the Virgin Mary. Her mother was pleased that seventy-five guests attended the church ceremony and that close to two hundred attended the party, many of whom brought presents. Wandering around the room while the photographer took pictures, one could hear compliments about the open bar, the dresses Ana had chosen, and the Mexican band.

Several of the members of the Lions gang arrived after dinner, having learned of the party from their member Ten Pen, whose sister stood up for Ana. On their best behavior and wearing their good clothes, they sat quietly drinking and, when the rock band played slow tunes, got up to dance. No incidents occurred, unlike several weeks before, when a groom fought at his own wedding and was arrested when the fight continued outside the hall. Ana's cotillion was dubbed a success by all. After the party, the photographs were admired over and over.

This event symbolizes much of what is valued in the Chicano family: the close, interdependent family network and the family's success in finances, in containing the sexual activities of the daughter so that she not only remains a virgin but is perceived as such, and in following the proper forms of social interaction. Expectations based on symbols of the expanded family, male domination, virginity, motherhood, and formalism determine the meanings of social relationships within and outside the family. The family relationships should be strong, the males should be dominant, the unmarried women must remain virgins, and the married women should center their lives around motherhood. Courtesy toward and respect for others, particularly elders, is expected of everyone. Some expectations closely resemble those found in Mexican villages;[2]

others are affected by United States institutions. In either case, situations of normative ambiguity create dilemmas for concrete action, and the economic status of community residents creates problems for which new cultural resolutions are constantly devised and tested.

While familial social relationships have been somewhat altered, traditional arrangements remain strong. According to Bott (1971: 265) "geographical mobility *alone* should be enough to disrupt the sort of close-knit networks one finds in homogeneous working-class areas, and such disruption should be accompanied by greater jointness in the husband-wife relationship."[3] On 32nd Street the move from other areas of the United States or from Mexico has not greatly altered traditional arrangements. The worlds of the men and the women remain largely segregated and traditionally oriented yet interdependent. This is attributable to a number of factors: relatives often came together or followed one another; close networks were expanded to include *compadres* (children's godparents), who were often friends and/or neighbors; and the cultural symbols that give meaning to social relationships were frequently stronger than many of the forces of change. It is situations where the circumstances (ecological, social, or economic) have changed that highlight the strengths and weakness of the collective expectations. What *should* be done may become unclear, be revised, or be reaffirmed. Let us look at these dilemmas and the evolving solutions.

A Cohesive Family

The kinship network on 32nd Street can best be termed an "expanded family" in the model described by Gans (1962). While many relatives of varying generations tend to live nearby and interact continuously, each household is comprised of a nuclear family unit. A similar structure is found throughout the Chicano population regardless of social class and is the expected standard for families.[4] In Mexico, particularly among the urban poor, the ties of kinship have been augmented to include *compadres* (fictive kin) through treating the godparents of the children as part of the expanded family network.[5] While there is some indication that the importance

of fictive kin as an extension of family relationships is lessening in
some areas of the United States today,[6] in other communities it
remains important.[7] On 32nd Street, the relationship between the
godparents of a child's baptism and the child's parents remains particularly important for many families. *Padrinos* (godfathers) and
madrinas (godmothers) are remembered on mother's and father's
day and celebrate birthdays and many holidays with their godchil-
dren. The interaction among generations and the closeness among
age groups serve in part to maintain cultural continuity in Mexico
and in the United States.

—The expanded family is the normative familial form for all
classes, whether or not it includes fictive kin in the United States as
in Mexico. An important aspect of the expanded family network is
one of continuous exchanges that are not governed by laws of
supply and demand. Not only is the relationship with friends who
have engaged in these exchanges strengthened by being named
compadres, but the mutual obligations further strengthen the
relationship of the entire expanded family unit both as a symbol of
their cohesiveness and because they need each other. The content of
the exchanges varies slightly by social class among Chicanos (Sena-
Rivera, 1979). While the extent of economic interdependence and
the exchange of personal services vary by social class, the family in
all social classes remains the primary source of emotional and social
support and is a major source for feelings of self-worth.[9] Sena-
Rivera argues that economic interdependence is strongest for the
most affluent and the least affluent families, that "interdependence
in personal services is universal . . . but . . . follows socio-economic
class lines (actual necessity rather than performance as an end in
itself)" (ibid., p. 127). On 32nd Street the exchange of economic and
personal services is frequently necessary for survival. Exchanges of
money and individual skills are frequently made among kin and
fictive kin. Turning for help to outside agencies such as public welfare or a public employment agency is regarded as a failure of a
family's solidarity and worth. Ana's mother, for example, feared a
public disgrace for the family when an aunt's family could not assist
by paying for the band at the cotillion.

Having a large, close family that can be augmented by *compadres* who can and will readily help in time of need is very highly

valued. Being seen as a cohesive family transcends economic success.[9] In such a family on 32nd Street and in other Chicano communities members lend each other money, locate a car mechanic, and help
out in innumerable other situations.[10] "We can hardly keep track of
all the money that goes around between us anymore. We just assume it's about equal," a young couple declared while discussing
the state of their finances and their families' aid.

Much tension and weight are placed on the family relationship,
which sometimes cannot support the demands made on it. At times
these demands may lead to conflicts. With the lack of economic
resources available to a nuclear family unit, its financial situation
can easily become overextended, as when Ana's uncle dropped out,
leaving her mother with additional expenses that were more than
she could afford. This situation strained the family's relationship
for several months until Ana's uncle was again able to help them.
Economic pressures can disrupt the ongoing flow of resources and
social relationships.

Being a cohesive family does not mean that members do not
have problems. Amelia's family is close and they help each other frequently by exchanging favors and with mutual social and emotional
support. Amelia is one of nine children (aged eight to thirty).
Though her mother frequently drinks heavily, which embarrasses
her, the children were very close to their mother and were upset at
her first absence, when, as a local representative, she went to
Washington for a conference. When one of the daughters married
and moved into the basement apartment, her sister felt the double
bed was too large for one person and had a younger sister sleep with
her. A second married sister lives upstairs, another lives ten blocks
away, and the sons all live within a few blocks. All the sons and
daughters congregate almost daily at their mother's home. Amelia
considers her family to be a cohesive one. They constantly help each
other, just as Ana's family did in providing aid to make her cotillion
successful, and reaffirming their image as a strong family.

Those families who do not have relatives or *compadres* on whom
to rely must turn to public welfare in time of financial problems or
must ask for support, thereby publicly acknowledging their humiliation. The neighborhood is atuned to such events, and news of them
is quickly shared.[11] One of the members of the Lions gang fre-

quently attempted to invite himself to dinner at other homes. The
other gang members often refused and laughed at his attempts,
ridiculing him for his inability to obtain readily a meal from the
usual sources—relatives. While eating at relatives' homes is common, no one *asks* to do so; relatives or *compadres* are expected to
offer meals to anyone at their homes at mealtime. A person who can
survive without money for a long period by going from relative to
relative, is viewed as having a cohesive family. A responsible individual does make some attempt to reciprocate, though no accounting is kept and the help received may not be reciprocated for a long
period of time. However, even within the family, overdependence
can lead to tension, as there is little money to go around.

    Compadres and relatives usually make up an emotional and social
support group. Women move freely back and forth between homes
—cooking together, talking, taking care of one another's children,
shopping, and going out together for entertainment. They have frequent Tupperware, makeup, toy, and clothes demonstrations at
relatives' or *compadres'* homes. A young woman described once
such party:

> They're lots of fun. We girls get together and play lots of
> games, talk, laugh a lot, and buy too many things. Our hus-
> bands don't always like that when we have to pay up.
> Everyone dresses up to come and we laugh and gossip a lot.

    Holidays, birthdays, and other special occasions are usually
celebrated with *compadres*, relatives, and their children. A special
dinner is prepared, and people eat in several shifts if no table is large
enough to accommodate all the guests. Attending a Thanksgiving
dinner, which includes not only turkey and sweet potatoes but rice,
beans, and chili sauce, at the Mendoza home with two sets of *compadres* (each of the three families had seven children, then all below
seventeen years old), guests ate in three of four shifts. The children
played and ran in and out, while the women discussed problems of
child rearing in the kitchen and then joined the men to dance to
Latin music.

    Not everyone is pleased with the close familial ties. For those
who wish to do things differently, close ties may be viewed as prying,

not helpful. Tina, a twenty-five-year-old mother of two boys, explained:

> I hate living around the corner from my mother-in-law. She
> always wants to know what's happening over here. It's
> my family and I'll run it as I choose. I like some of my
> relatives but having them all over here asking for things
> constantly is too much.

Several months later I bumped into Tina after she had moved from the eastern to the western side of the community. She declared that living so near her mother-in-law had become too unpleasant and she had moved at the first opportunity. Tina gave her sister-in-law all her old dishes and furniture when she moved into the downstairs apartment. Both declared that they were happier in their new apartments in the same building. While a close family is highly valued, privately it displeases those who wish to be different.

The strong network of intergenerational relationships provides a means by which traditions can be readily passed on. Few child-rearing manuals are used, and intergenerational aid encourages traditional practices. Young girls spend time helping their mothers and learning the mothering role. Girls frequently take on household responsibilities and care for their younger siblings before becoming mothers themselves.[12] At ten or twelve, girls frequently are party to discussions among their mothers' friends and between their mothers and grandmothers about family life and relationships. The intergenerational interaction and the strong emotional support these relationships provide are a solid basis for the maintenance of traditional sex role relationships within the family, upon which the code of honor is based.

Manhood

Manhood is expressed through independence, personal strength, control over situations, and domination. This image of manhood, particularly in relationship to femininity, has been traced by some scholars to the culture of Spain, where the desire for precedence in interpersonal relationships and authority over the family are important symbols of manliness.[13] Others trace it to the culture of the Aztecs, where women were expected to be subordinate and submissive to men, while a third group argues that male domination was a result of colonialism.[14] Though the traditional symbols of manhood have not changed substantially in the transition to 32nd Street and have significant implications for men's relationships as fathers, husbands, sons, and brothers,[15] male domination as worked out within the family does not weaken the critical position of the mother.

The role of the Mexican father/husband has been described as one of domination and control over his wife and daughters. Studies of Mexican towns demonstrate that men are seen as people who cannot be "gotten around."[16] Fathers are seen as rigid, closed, and distant.[17] Sons become independent at an early age.[18] Some of these descriptions are similar to those of relationships for fathers and husbands in the 32nd Street community while others are not. The symbols of manhood articulate many of the salient meanings of social relationships within the family. The father/husband, as the dominant member of the household, must maintain the honor of his wife and daughters. To dishonor them reflects not only on them but also on his ability to maintain his self-respect as an independent and dominant individual. He alone must be responsible for supporting his family and must not publicly appear to become dependent on a working wife. The husband/father as the family head and the son as an independent young man both expect to be served by the women in the household and to come and go as they please. Sara, an eighteen year old, explained:

> My brother, he comes rushing in and sits down at the table
> expecting a hot dinner no matter what time it is, just like
> my father . . . . You know he gets it every time and we have
> to make it.

No one found it extraordinary that one wife, who worked an early shift (7:00 A.M. to 3:00 P.M.), was expected to prepare dinner for her husband, who finished his shift at 11 P.M. and arrived home to eat at 4:00 A.M., after several hours of drinking. If she was asleep he woke her, and she had to cook and still get their seven children ready for school and be at work by 7:00 A.M. A spotless house was also expected and provided.

Though the men can demand and usually receive services (cooking, cleaning, and so forth) of the women when they want, the men are dependent on the women to provide these services. Men are taught that cooking, washing clothes, and cleaning are women's and *not* men's work. For example, when one male youth pulled out the ironing board to iron his pants, his sisters took it away from him and laughed and teased him for wanting to do "woman's work." They all thought him strange and talked about him behind his back. His father even gave him a lecture. A man who does "woman's work" must be unable to find a woman to do that work, and therefore less than a man, or must be unduly controlled by his woman. This male dependence actually gives a woman a significant source of power.

Husbands

While a husband may have extramarital affairs, he should not publicly flaunt them because it would demonstrate lack of respect for his wife.[19] In one family with seven children the mother caught her husband three times with the same fifteen-year-old woman. The oldest son beat his father. "It was OK, my mother doesn't like him either. He tricks [goes out with other women] on her all the time." This man could barely support his family, making the situation worse for him. His wife frequently said she would leave him but she never did. Though this is not typical, similar situations exist.

Moreover, some wives argue that men are "free spirits." A scene at a large community dance illustrated some of the manipulations and interactions that occur between husbands, wives, lovers, and friends. The rock music emanating from the packed gym could be heard several blocks away and eliminated conversation. Margie sat at a table with a girlfriend and a friend of her new husband, Dino, trying not to follow Dino's movements as he wandered around the room. He stopped to slap palms every few feet and pulled a young woman out to the floor to dance a fast dance. Walking by me he complained to a female friend that Margie did not care for him or their new baby properly. He stopped by another young woman and invited her out after the dance. He then sauntered over to his wife and pulled her out to the floor for a slow number. Her expression was sulky as they walked back to the table, where he told her that if they had any money left he was going out with his male friends later. She silently found a few bills. He handed half of them back and wandered away.

Many people were aware of what was going on, but no one said anything. Finally, Dino came back and asked me to take him and his wife to get their baby at his sister's. Margie really did not want to leave yet and was silent in the car. When Dino claimed it was Margie's job to get the baby from his sister, she told him that it was his baby too. Dino got out and said that taking care of the baby was her responsibility; he worked. Looking depressed, Margie said she wished Dino would come home with her.

Dino told me to hurry to take him back to the dance after we dropped off Margie. At the discothèque downtown Dino spent the few dollars he had. Afterward he and his girlfriend went to a married couple's house. When he went home the next day he told his wife that he had passed out at a male friend's. She understood, he said. I heard later from friends that she threw several pots at him. Two years later she left him and went back to school.

While not all husbands have girlfriends, many wives believe that as long as their men come home to them, husbands should be allowed to do what they want. Christina, a friend of Margie's, claimed that Dino left Margie for six months because she tried to keep too many tabs on him.

> You can't control what a man does and you got to accept
> him the way he is. Men are free spirits and as long as they
> come home to you, why should you worry? If they bring in
> some money and you cook, clean, sew, and are ready for
> them, why should they leave? Margie made a mistake that
> night at their party. She shouldn't have left when they
> had that fight, because she should have known that
> Dino would just stay there with one of his girlfriends. She
> holds him in too tight.

While wives may not like the fact that their husbands leave them home, many believe men must be free to roam.

As the person who must maintain his dominance and control the household, the husband is responsible for supporting the family without the help of his wife. Given the poorly paid jobs available, the wages of a working wife or daughter frequently become an economic necessity. Over 40 percent of the community women work, though many of them have working husbands or fathers (Schensul, 1972).

Within this cultural context, men are caught in what appears to be an unresolvable dilemma. A working wife is a public indication that the husband is unable to support his family and therefore lacks control in the family and dominance over his wife, who could become economically independent. But the alternatives to an employed wife are few and not much better. A hungry and poorly clothed family does not enhance a man's reputation, nor does depending on support from the expanded family for any length of time without reciprocation. Caught in this dilemma, many husbands prefer to let their wives work and explain their actions within the traditional cultural context. By stating that they are still in control, that they *let* their wives work, and then only to pay for incidental expenses while the men remain the main breadwinners, their actions are legitimized. For example, while two men in their thirties were sitting in a bar discussing whether wives should work, one said to the other, "I would never let my wife work while I got this good job, but a lot of guys are getting laid off now and my wife didn't get bad money before we got married." The second responded, "I got her working now 'cause we need a new washer and dryer to help her out. Now she has to go to the laundromat." Both men criticized another man whose wife was working though he had a well-paying job and the couple had a "good home." Only if a man explains that he is still in control is a working wife considered legitimate. The fact that women work is still articulated in terms of male domination, and the women infrequently use their employment to change the husband-wife relationship.

Fathers and Sons

A son, like any man, is expected to be independent and dominant in any social relationship with women. In the family this means he

should come and go as he pleases, as his father does. Staying near
home is not regarded as proper. One eleven year old who always
remained on his front steps was told by his father to "go hang somewhere else." What he does outside with his peers is seen largely as
his own business. Some parents do not know that their sons are
gang members and may know little of their sons' lives outside the
home, to the point of not recognizing their "street names." One
gang member told me to tell his parents that I met him in a settlement house because they did not know he was a Lion. Should a son
begin to jeopardize his job potential by getting into too much
trouble, his parents are faced with a dilemma. To interfere is to
question his autonomy and threaten his manhood. Paradoxically, a
father who refuses to control his son's behavior fails to fulfill his role
as dominant family member. A situation of normative ambiguity
exists: if he interferes, he violates his son's independence; if he does
not, he demonstrates his lack of control. There is no higher order of
rules to resolve this striking moral incongruity. Each situation
must be negotiated.

The youths are aware of their parents' dilemma. One son expressed the dilemma in the following manner:

> My old lady [mother] gets really upset with me running
> around in the street 'til real late 'cause she's got so many
> things to worry about. I shouldn't do it 'cause of my
> old lady but can't help it; besides my old man he's out
> a lot anyways doin' his thing.

Felipe at fifteen was rarely punished, though he was often
absent from school. He was a man, according to his father, and
should be granted independence outside the home. The father felt
that he had no authority over his sons and could not tell them how
to organize their lives. Only inside the walls of his home did he feel
he had a right to control his sons' activities. If Felipe talked back to
his father or mother, or came in noisy and drunk, then his father felt
he had a right to act. As a man, he had a right to maintain order in
his home; otherwise, he felt he had no say. Another father felt
similarly about his son. After trying for a long time to encourage his
son to continue his education, the father decided that he could not

use punishment to force his sixteen-year-old son to attend school.[20]

> I know my son is real smart, his teachers told me that many times, but he and his friends leave school every day before they finish. He says its boring. He's a good artist—I told him he could go to art school but he says the teachers are all fags [homosexuals]. He has to finish school to get anywhere, but I can't force him. He's a man.

Other fathers put their sons in military schools or send them to Mexico, resolving the dilemma. The father remains in control and the son retains some independence by living away from home.

This dilemma is a triggering situation in that either solution carries implications for the parents' (largely the father's) identity in the eyes of their sons and other people in the community. If the father tries to control his son's activities, he will become known as a strict disciplinarian who is denying his son's independence. Community members will see him as someone who takes the American dream seriously but may be making his son into less of a man. If he leaves his son on his own, the son may perceive his father as distant and tough but allowing him to pursue his activities as he sees fit, as an independent man. In that case, community residents may see the father as helping to develop an independent, honorable man but failing to maintain his own manhood by losing control over his son's activities.

Neither resolution is entirely successful and both may add to the distance between the father and his children. Fathers are generally marginally involved in the care of older children except as disciplinarians. This does not mean that there is a lack of mutual respect, only that the relationship is perceived to some degree in terms of discipline and control.[21] "During the week we have fun, but when my father's home on Sunday we can't go nowhere or do anything. He just plays his lousy music," claimed a fifteen-year-old boy. His father works the afternoon shift (he makes more money doing so) and is rarely home and awake when his children are. "When we were young my father always took us places, now he takes us nowhere," explained a twelve-year-old boy. Fathers play with babies and hug their young sons and daughters but remain at some distance from their older children. A fourteen-year-old girl complained:

> My father hardly does anything with us. He gives the little kids anything they want and he lets my oldest brother do anything he wants, but we can't go anyplace and he never takes us anywhere. He doesn't even talk to us and he only talks to my oldest brother at night sometimes.

Faced with a number of dilemmas as fathers, husbands, or sons, men must negotiate situational solutions. As a husband, a man must support his family and not allow his wife to work in order to remain dominant, but he is frequently faced with poor job prospects and an insufficient paycheck. New rationalizations and norms legitimate a wife's work and maintain the man's honor. The father-son relationship is replete with dilemmas of independence and domination, with no culturally acceptable solution to the situation of normative ambiguity. The father must decide in each situation whether to discipline his son or encourage the son's autonomy. His choice affects not only his relationship with his son but how he is viewed publicly. Moreover, most fathers realize the importance of education and the potential for getting into trouble in the streets while they also see the importance of the male peer group and male independence.

Virginity

The Virgin Mother is among the most salient religious symbols in Mexico. She is more important than the adult Christ in many Mexican religious ceremonies. For example, *el día de la Virgen de Guadalupe* (December 12) is an important celebration both in Mexico and on 32nd Street, when even men who rarely attend church go to mass.[22] In Mexico City women walk on their knees the several miles from the downtown to the Virgin in Guadalupe's shrine. The sexual purity of women—the faithfulness of a wife to her husband or the virginity of an unmarried woman—is symbolized by the Virgin Mother. The honor of a man is besmirched if a daughter is not a virgin at marriage or a wife is unfaithful. His honor is inexorably tied to that of his family. In Mexican villages, the role of an honorable woman, both as a mother and as a daughter, is that of a *mujer abnegada*, a self-sacrificing, dutiful woman (Diaz, 1966: 78). While the symbol of the Virgin Mother is used in evaluating women's relationships on 32nd Street, some expectations have changed from those of the traditional Mexican village.

According to Mexican tradition, maintaining a young woman's public image as a virgin requires that she be accompanied on social occasions by a chaperone (usually an older or younger relative). On 32nd Street, chaperonage of unmarried women has largely been eliminated though wives are often accompanied by their young children when visiting or shopping. The result is that everyone is aware that most women can escape the watchful eyes of their kin. Consequently, maintenance both of a woman's virginity or faithfulness and of community perception of that state are difficult. Most families are concerned with the movements of their daughters but cannot completely restrict their activities, though a few families do attempt to retain tight control.

Brothers and other relatives act as unofficial chaperones for young women. They will often stop young women from drinking, watch their sisters if they are with young men, or tell all their friends to stay away. For example, at a party sixteen-year-old Sara asked me:

> Please tell me if you see my brother because I can't drink
> with him around, he'll beat me. Me and my sisters are not
> supposed to drink, he doesn't like that. You know when
> we go to dances on the north side, we got to sneak 'cause
> if he ever found out he would follow us around and we'd
> never get to go anywhere.

The importance that parents give to a daughter's identity as a virgin is revealed in the following example. Alicia, when she was fourteen, hid her pregnancy from her parents until her sixth month. Her parents sent her to an aunt and uncle in Mexico to whom she was supposed to give the child. Realizing how much she wanted to keep the baby, her aunt persuaded Alicia's parents to let her keep the child. When she returned home seven months pregnant, Alicia was not permitted to leave the house. Anytime a visitor arrived, she

hid, first under the bed and then, when she became too big, under
the sink in the kitchen. Labor pains started when she was hiding in
the garage. Later her parents almost took over the upbringing of her
son, taking him as a deduction on their income tax even after
Alicia went to work and referring to him as their son, though
everyone knew who the parents were.

Parents are faced with what seems to many an unresolvable
dilemma. If they follow the traditional honor-based code and refuse
to allow their daughter to go out unsupervised, then her virginity
remains publicly unquestioned and the honor of her family is
upheld. The wider society and many of the local institutions,
whether organized by members of the wider society or by local residents, provide legitimation for allowing a young woman some
degree of freedom. Both the schools and the churches sponsor
dances that are sparsely supervised. Local community groups also
sponsor dances with American rock bands. Parents are invited to
attend yet discouraged from participating or actually attending by
the type of music and the dim lighting. This local legitimation of
more freedom for young women places parents in a problematic situation. Freedom heightens the risk of the daughter losing her
virginity or being perceived as having lost it. But if they closely
supervise her activities, they risk alienating her. Again a situation
of normative ambiguity exists and the resolution must be situationally negotiated between parents and their daughters.

The parental dilemma is exacerbated by the expectation that
men will take what they can from women. Men are defined as
dominant and women defined as submissive; consequently, only
male relatives can be trusted with women. One father succinctly expressed these views:

> You know what all men are after . . . . It's natural for them
> to go out and get it anyway they can. I don't trust any of
> the young punks around here. They take it and run. There
> are too many unmarried pregnant girls around here. The
> young girls don't know how to handle themselves.

Parents are confronted directly with the dilemma when young
women ask permission to attend a party or dance with friends.
Parents often employ the tactic of nondecision. They postpone any

decision until the last moment. Then, when their daughter is ready to go out, they deny her permission. Other times the responsibility is shifted back and forth between mother and father and then changed again at the last moment. This lack of resolution can result in dissatisfaction on both sides. Many young women stop asking. "I just go where I please without asking permission. She [her mother] would just stare at me in silence when I asked, so what's the point in asking?" a nineteen year old explained. By going out on their own, young women risk being appraised as nonvirgins.

Some families are able to retain strict control over their daughters. Lana, for example, must ask permission to sit in front of her house and rarely is allowed to go anywhere. She was particularly upset when she was not permitted to go anywhere or do anything on her birthday.

> I don't ever get anything, like one time my father gave me ten dollars five days after my birthday and I threw it back at him and I told him that I don't want his ten dollars. I didn't ask you for money. He said this was a way to pay me back for what I'd done for them. I told them that they didn't owe me anything. All I wanted for my birthday was some fun like a picnic at the beach. I didn't want any money. I just wanted someone to remember and have some fun. I'm never allowed to go to the movies. I do all the cooking and cleaning. My mother comes in and takes a bath and watches TV.

Another mother timed her daughter's return from school every day; it took eight minutes to walk home and if her daughter was not home within twelve minutes after the last bell, the mother went out looking for her. While this case is extreme, other families only allow their daughters to attend parties or dances under the supervision of a mature older relative. Most of the young women, however, have enough freedom to do what they want during the hours they are permitted outside the house. Many skip school to attend parties or be alone with their boyfriends.

Unable to resolve the dilemma with their parents, many young women marry in order to leave home. Marriage is one of the few culturally legitimate means for young women to leave home and still maintain their honor and that of their families. For example, Mita's parents did not approve of the man she wanted to marry. She resented the fact that they physically restrained her from going out with him. At one point they threatened to send her to Texas to stay with her relatives. They followed through on the threat as far as taking her to the station but did not actually send her. Mita later moved out of her house to live with a married girlfriend and planned a wedding on her own. The week before the wedding her parents took her to Mexico on a false pretext and kept her there for a month. Finally, a few months later they gave up their efforts and let the couple marry. Mita explained:

> They want me to marry a doctor or something but I want to get married now. . . . I can't stand my parents telling me do this, do that. At night my mother makes sure we're [Mita and her younger sister] in bed and if we get up for a drink of water, she starts following us around and tells us to get back to bed. We have to sneak anything we do.

Parental permission for their daughter to go out affects the public evaluation not only of the parents but of their daughter. If she is permitted to attend parties, she is at a much greater risk of being appraised as a nonvirgin even if she actually retains her virginity. Parents frequently increase the risk of such erroneous perceptions by failing to take a strong stand if their daughter sneaks out. It is the public perception of her sexual purity that reflects upon the parents. If she is perceived as a nonvirgin, then her family's honor is questioned. Only complete parental control over her behavior minimizes the risk of her being perceived as a nonvirgin or of actually losing her virginity. As such control is difficult to maintain in modern urban society, it is more an ideal than a reality.

Motherhood

Motherhood is the most culturally acceptable identity available to women. The role of independent career woman is not culturally acceptable. Women must be either wives, sisters, or mothers to men. Motherhood is seen not as a last resort but rather as a highly honored role. The Mexican image of the Virgin Mother, loving and dependable, the person with whom the child satisfies desires for nurturing and acceptance, is the 32nd Street model of motherhood.[23] Motherhood is the basis of the strongest bonds of blood ties.[24] These bonds are much stronger than those of husbands and wives or fathers and children.

The husband-wife bond is based on procreation and expression of love but little on companionship. The expectation that men will dominate in all situations makes it difficult to develop companionable relationships between men and women even in marriage, as sociability usually develops between equals. (Moreover, any time a man and a woman who are not related through blood ties are together, it is expected that they will become sexually involved, because men dominate women and, lacking equality and the possibility of friendship, the only reason they would be together is as sexual partners.)[25] Most socializing occurs in single-sex groups, and the expanded family network fulfills companionship functions. But children's ties with their mothers are natural and lifelong:[26] they never become distant with age, as do ties with their fathers, who discipline and control them. While the dynamics of the father-child interaction is in part determined by the child's willingness to obey him and demonstrate respect for him, mothering places no such conditions on the parent-child relationship.

Loyalty and support for his mother was demonstrated by a young man who had become addicted to heroin and entered a methadone program only after stealing from his mother:

> I used to steal all the time from my brothers and sisters
> and went through my old man's coat pockets many
> times . . . even stole his watch once and pawned it, but
> you know when I took some bread [money] from my
> old lady, then I knew I had to do something. Taking
> from your old lady's real bad.

The mother remains the central and most stable feature in a son's life. He depends on her for nurture and emotional support and she on him for support and the ultimate protection of her honor. As a son his honor is dependent on hers; any aspersion cast on her honor reflects on his own.

In an extreme case of maintaining a mother's honor, a son killed his father after repeatedly catching him with teenage women. Some community residents felt the murder was justifiable, that the father's behavior was dishonorable and the resolution culturally acceptable. But the community was not unanimous in defining the situation as one where the family honor was at stake. Some residents felt that murder was not a necessary or legitimate resolution and that the son was a criminal who deserved to be jailed. His mother, though, worked continuously for his release. Sentenced as a juvenile, he was out in less than three years.

Young women vicariously experience the mother role through their continual associations with relatives and *comadres* and their babies. They are frequently enthusiastic about their own mother having additional children. Fifteen-year-old Celia, one of seven children declared:

> Man, I want my mother to have a kid so I can take care
> of it. I love babies. I like to baby-sit for the little kid
> next door, she's so smart. Now my mother's *comadre* is
> having a kid so maybe I'll be able to help, but they live all
> the way by 40th Street, but then maybe I can stay by
> their house sometimes.

At sixteen, Celia became pregnant and married.

The traditional expectation that a woman's unique role is to be a mother with many children creates a conflict for those young women who have interests outside the home. Some reject motherhood. One nineteen-year-old college student, the eldest of seven, despised the traditional female role of daughter and mother:

> I had to change diapers for my three youngest brothers
> and sisters. They were such a mess and were so much
> trouble. I hate them for it. I wish my mother didn't have
> them. What did she need so many kids for anyway? It
> would have been a lot better without the last two. They
> were always crying and wanting attention . . . comb their
> hair, wash them, feed them, change their diapers, and
> put them to sleep. . . . They're my mother's kids. She
> should be responsible for them. I'm not their mother . . .
> if my mother gets married again and has another kid I'll

die. One time I told her I wasn't going to have any
kids. She really got angry and said God will punish me.
It was up to Him, not me. She didn't speak to me for
a week. I'm not going to have any kids. They're just trouble.

Celia's oldest sister, a student, added another problem to the list:

It wouldn't be good for my mother to have more kids.
They cost money and it would be like the dog; everyone
would get excited for a while and then bored and not want
to take care of it. [Celia objected here.] I don't
want to take care of it. I'd move out.

The views of the two students are not generally accepted and
often considered immoral. They violate all expectations of
femininity and the family. Though it is becoming more common for
young women to desire to limit family size, in part because of the
expense of bringing up children, older people and many younger
ones see this not only as tampering with "God's will" but also as
comparing things that cannot be compared: economics and family.
These young women are openly denying the importance of motherhood and appear to equate the family's worth with that of money.
For most, social and economic success are not valued above motherhood. Problems arise only for those young women who are beginning to strive for success in the wider society. The exclusion of
motherhood is still regarded as deviant.

Chivalry and Respect

Chivalry and etiquette are not regarded as critical for most of
American society today. Except for some fictional British detectives, such as Dorothy Sayres's Lord Peter Wimsey, symbols of etiquette and chivalry are rare today, but the precise form of social
relationships remains important for the residents of 32nd Street.
The formalities of social interaction are essential in an honor-based
subculture, where even the slightest word or movement may be seen
as placing a person in a demeaning situation.[27] Etiquette "sets
limits and protects us from having to expose ourselves in ways
which may be detrimental to our public image" (Goodenough, 1963:

197). Formal rules provide order for everyday social interactions, creating some sense of security and stability in potentially problematic situations. Rules channel impulse, passion, and desire into ways of acting that are recognized as having a particular social meaning in a particular social setting. "Form surrounds and sets bounds to our privacy, limiting its excesses, curbing its explosions, isolating and preserving it" (Paz, 1961: 32). Formal rules of etiquette create a distance between actors, minimizing the potential for questions about precedence and the need to prove invulnerability in a situation. For example, following rules against staring at others can prevent a person from defining a situation as a challenge to his claim to precedence.[28]

Following an elaborate set of formal rules of etiquette is expected in both Chicano and Mexican families. Foster (1967: 96), describing a Mexican village, states, "From early childhood one learns to be 'correct'. Children when confronted with a family friend or a stranger are told *dále la mano* [step up and shake hands]." On 32nd Street swearing is not tolerated in the home by either females or males. Swearing often results in a slap or a belt across the seat, administered by a mother, father, or older sister or brother. Nor is insolence or rudeness tolerated in the home. Doors must be closed nicely. An older person must be greeted and taken leave of with a courtesy that would please Emily Post. The following exchange took place when I brought a male friend to meet the ·Lions at the park. After I introduced him, each of the Lions greeted my friend with "I'm very glad to meet you" as they shook hands. Courtesies such as taking a woman's arm when walking in the street and always walking on the curb side are performed by most men. The first time one of the Lions held my arm as we crossed an icy patch on the sidewalk, I turned to him astounded and asked if he always did such things. He replied that he usually did, as he had been instructed to do so since he was a child. Similar behavior was frequently demonstrated at weddings and cotillions.

Adherence to the rules of etiquette is a sign of respect when dealing with persons older than oneself. Punishment is expected if these rules are not followed. Ronny, a member of the Lions gang, was made to lean over the edge of the bathtub by his mother and was beaten with a belt when he arrived home drunk and telling wild stories. "She only does that when I come home real drunk. I usually sober up before I go home. I deserve it when I come in high." His mother felt she had no control over his drinking, but when he demonstrated a lack of respect by coming inside her home drunk and disorderly, she would and could discipline him.

Not only do formal interactions help youths to maintain order between generations, between the sexes, and between men, but youths who successfully employ the rules of etiquette at home are well received by all adults, while those who demonstrate a lack of manners within the home are denigrated by the community regardless of behavior outside the home. Those who know when to use their manners are those who gain the respect of others, even among gang members. Consequently, the use of common rules of etiquette not only demonstrates respect for others and channels behavior but is also highly valued by others in the community.

It is clear what the important symbols of family life are: solidarity, male domination, virginity, motherhood, and respect. In the context of an urban community within a highly industrialized and educated society, some of the expectations derived from these symbols become distorted, are ambiguous, or are in conflict. While some of the problematic situations can be resolved within the traditional culture, for other situations all solutions seem less than perfect. Much of the ambiguity and conflict is found in the expectations concerning sex role behavior and child-parent relationships.

In the urban context youths are granted many freedoms and hold few responsibilities. These expectations are validated and supported by the media, by the schools, and even to some extent by the Catholic church. The situation places continual pressure on parents to allow their children more freedom while encouraging youths to demand those freedoms. Moreover, women are encouraged to work, particularly because of financial need.

The cohesive family with its strong network of relatives and *compadres* provides economic supports to help deal with financial realities, emotional supports to deal with normative ambiguity and conflict, and social supports and mechanisms to maintain the traditional symbols of sex role relationships and nearly traditional behavior patterns. With the support of the expanded family, actors negotiate difficult situations of normative ambiguity and conflict. Sometimes the process is painful, emotionally charged, and the consequence unsatisfactory to both parties; a son is physically punished or a daughter is locked in her room. Members of the expanded family may provide advice and emotional support or may invite the unruly son or daughter of a relative or *compadre* to live with them. Families do their best to keep members out of the social welfare and justice systems.

Youths are caught between the traditional model of social relationships and the Chicago urban reality: the streets, the school, the media, and the job scene. With the freedom they take or are given, the youths are faced with many dilemmas as they venture beyond the confines of the communal and familial order. The subsequent chapters explore their attempts to resolve a variety of dilemmas as they interact outside their homes.

5

Young Men in the Streets: Honor and Reputation

Sam screeched to a halt on his younger brother's small bike in front of the bench where a number of the Lions regularly congregated. Out of breath, he informed those around him that the Junior Greeks had been found with one of the Lions' sweaters. Tiger readily acknowledged that the sweater was his. They argued heatedly about whether they should wait until the rest of the gang showed up or whether the twelve members present should take the Junior Greeks by surprise. Then someone remembered that Rat Man, who was not around, had one of the guns, and Sal, who had the other one, had left it at home. Sal, always ready to fight especially if he could do so without risking physical contact, rushed off to get his gun while someone else went off to look for Rat Man. Within forty-five minutes both guns were located, four more Lions joined the group, and a number of bats and knives appeared. Most of the Lions walked toward where the Junior Greeks had been spotted, while three joined Pierre in his brother's car. Alicia, Pierre's girlfriend at the time, tried to stop him by declaring that she would break up with him if he went. He completely ignored her entreaties.

I remained at the park with the Lions' girlfriends, who patiently awaited their return. There had been no doubt in their minds from the very beginning that the Lions and Greeks would fight today over the sweater. Taking another gang's sweater was an explicit insult and had to be redressed immediately for the Lions to maintain their image as some of the toughest gang members of 32nd Street. No one seemed particularly excited, though Alicia was fuming because Pierre had ignored her wishes. Most of the discussion among the young women centered on what to wear to the upcoming dance on Saturday night.

About an hour later the Lions began to filter back into the park. They had found the Junior Greeks and had had a good fight but had not gotten the sweater back yet. No one had been seriously wounded and only one or two cuts looked as though they might need stitches. Going to a doctor was out of the question because, according to Rat Man, the police might locate them. Plans were already afoot to mount a surprise attack later that evening in order to rescue the sweater.[1]

Not every situation that could be appraised as an insult is so interpreted, and not every insult evokes a violent response. Gilberto, leader of the Lions at twenty and known as one of the "toughest dudes" on 32nd Street, did not frequently miss an opportunity to fight. However, even he discounted many potentially explosive situations as social blunders rather than insults requiring immediate redress. For instance, at one dance in the basement of a local church there were well over three hundred young people in a room the size of a basketball court, drinking beer and hard liquor and dancing the latest steps to a live band. Gilberto's wife was not there but Alicia, the mother of one of his sons, was present and so were most of the Lions and their girlfriends. Members of four other gangs wore their "colors" (gang sweaters or other garments with their colors). Gilberto was standing near the door, waiting for Alicia to pass his gun through the bathroom window to one of her girlfriends. He could not bring it in himself because all males were frisked at the door before they could pay their four-dollar entrance fee. A member of the Nobles came toward him, looked him in the eye, and bumped into his shoulder. Gilberto said, "Excuse me," and moved slightly away from the offender. That was the end of the incident.[2] Gilberto got into no fights that evening. In fact, the only excitement was when an unidentified person threw a tear gas bomb into the crowd, ending the dance.

When they were not in school, most of the male youths spent most of their time outdoors whatever the time of the year or the weather. Even when the temperature dropped below freezing, many could be found huddled in one of the parks until eight or nine in the evening. There were few places to go indoors: their homes were too crowded, the drinking age was twenty-one, and one settlement house prohibited anyone over fourteen from entering. The only public indoor facilities were the community-run social service center, the park building (from which the Lions were often expelled), and the second settlement house, which had been taken over by local activists and sometimes stayed open late. With the limited park space and the densely populated neighborhood, there was insufficient territory for any one group to "own" much except for a bench or a single corner. Several gangs congregated at each park, and many unaffiliated youths associated with the gangs. There was little way for different groups to segregate themselves spatially and not constantly be crossing borders.

Gangs play a major role in the lives of many area males. Approximately 70 percent join one for at least a short period between the ages of twelve and seventeen,[3] though not all tough young men join gangs. There are eight major gangs in the area, each of which is segmented by age: miniatures (ages eleven to twelve), midgets (thirteen to fourteen), littles (fifteen to seventeen), juniors (eighteen to twenty-one), and seniors (twenty-one and over). Each section has between fifteen and forty members. Not every gang has members in each category throughout its history. In addition, many short-lived gangs developed rapidly and disappeared just as fast. While different age groups may bear the same name, they are not necessarily allied on all occasions. For example, in one situation the Senior Greeks helped the Little and Junior Lions against the Junior Greeks.

It is usually possible to identify an individual as a member of a particular gang by his hangout and his official jacket sweater with the gang's emblem and its color on a stripe on the shoulder, the collar, and the belt. Sometimes they wear shoes or shirts in their colors. Neither method of identification is infallible. Many nonmembers associate with members, and members do not necessarily wear their colors all the time. Most young men in gangs wear similar clothing styles but many other youths dress like them. Most take great care with their clothes. Len of the Lions told several other members of the gang, "I wouldn't ever wear jeans,

they don't keep a crease and bag at the knees." Only those outside
the street scene appear to be largely unconcerned with style and the
latest fashions.

Though many youths join gangs for approximately a year, the
majority of males (aged eleven to eighteen) are not in gangs at any
one time. This does not mean that they can avoid interpersonal
violence or even try to. In this chapter I examine the context in
which violence occurs among male youths on 32nd Street both as
individuals and as members of gangs, and the different meanings of
violence and its relationship to identity.[4]

Studies have postulated a variety of macrolevel causes for delinquent and violent behavior. A number of theories have tried to link
societal causes, usually mediated by norms that direct actions, to
the actual behavior of juveniles. Cultural conflict models view delinquents as adhering to norms that conflict with the norms of those in
power.[5] Structural strain models maintain that delinquency occurs
when there is a disjunction between goals and the means for
obtaining those goals.[6] Social disorganization or control models
explain delinquency as a breakdown in the controlling impact of
traditional institutions (school, church, family, and community.)[7]
The mediating norms may be conceived as subcultural, contracultural, opositional, or variants on the "American Way."[8] While
some models link behavior directly with normative codes, other explanations pay closer attention to situational exigencies and group
dynamics: group cohesion,[9] group status and social disabilities,[10] or
the "situation of company" and "shared misunderstandings."[11]

On 32nd Street a violent response to threats to self-esteem is
embedded in a code of personal honor. Honor is a normative code
that stresses the inviolability of one's manhood and defines
breaches of etiquette, violations of a female relative's sexual purity,
and accusations of dependency on others, in an adversarial idiom.
Honor sensitizes people to violations that are interpreted as
derogations of fundamental properties of the self. Within a more
conventional normative framework these same actions might be
appraised and evaluated as mere violations of etiquette that would
be ignored or excused, or as violations of the law that would require
the police. Young men tend to fluctuate between commitments to

conventional and to honor-bound responses. Normative ambiguity exists when it is unclear which norms should govern interpersonal relations. The lack of commitment to either code links interaction to the marginal position of the community in the wider society, to the tension between aspiring to succeed and the limited possibility of doing so.

All male youths experience the structural position of the community, though reactions to the tensions between the excitement of street life and conventional pursuits vary. Some drift toward gangs that expressly pursue excitement and develop a strong street identity, while others prefer to pursue more conventional careers. Yet no one avoids the tension between street life and convention on 32nd Street. The meaning of violence in the construction of identity and reputation among male youths and youth groups varies from one identity orientation to another, but it is always rooted in a concern for personal honor.

Insult, Honor, and Violence

Honor revolves around a person's ability to command deference in interpersonal relations. A person doubts his own efficacy or suspects that he is viewed as weak when he believes he has been publicly humiliated. This situation is particularly critical to men who do not have a history of personal accomplishments or who cannot draw on valued social roles to protect their self-esteem when they are confronted by an insulting action. In an honor-bound subculture that emphasizes manhood and defines violations of interpersonal etiquette in an adversarial manner, any action that challenges a person's right to deferential treatment in *public*—whether derogating a person, offering a favor that may be difficult to return, or demonstrating lack of respect for a female relative's sexual purity—can be interpreted as an insult and a potential threat to manhood. Honor demands that a man be able physically to back his claim to dominance and independence.

Sensitivity to Insult

A situation is defined as insulting when an actor believes another person intends to place him in a demeaning light. When he is placed in a position where he may be viewed as weak, an individual experiences a lack of self-esteem.[12] Sensitivity to a perceived insult is particularly keen in public situations, where judgments can be made readily by others and the actor perceives himself unable to neutralize or negate the intentions of the insulter.[13]

In a context where men believe it is important that an honorable man be in control of all situations, infringement of any rules of interpersonal etiquette may be perceived as insulting, casting doubt on a man's ability to control. How a person responds to perceived insult reflects directly on the kind of person he is and determines whether others will perceive him as admirable or contemptible. An insult is a challenge to his right to deferential treatment. His interpretation of others' intentions and his reactions to them have real consequences for his standing among his peers. Honor is not something that one has permanently; it can always be challenged and must therefore continually be reaffirmed before one's peers.

Responding to Perceived Insult

How should one respond to insult within the context of the code of honor? When actions are interpreted as insulting, honor compels an individual to take an unequivocal stand, to immediately enforce his claim to precedence no matter how small the incident may seem. Because honor concerns actions that reflect personal decisions and judgments, disputes over honor must be settled personally, not through the legal system. Direct action takes priority over legal judgments of right and wrong. One young man spent two years in jail for shooting and severely wounding the man who raped his sister. He did not even consider going to the police at the time. It was his duty, he said, to repair the affront. Some things cannot be left to the law. Dishonor is experienced as a loss of one's manhood, which is culturally defined as the ability to enforce claims to a dominant position in interpersonal relations and to resist similar claims by others. The response must be physical: violence is triggered by the norms of the code of personal honor.

The physical response must follow certain rules if this act is to contribute to an identity as an honorable man. Violence must be used only when an insult is appraised as intentional. Shooting someone in the back for fun is not following the rules, nor is beating someone while robbing him, unless the victim has failed to demonstrate sufficient deference to his captors.

Moreover, as in cowboy movies, the style violence takes is critical if others are to approve its use. Ronny, a member of the Lions gang, was chastised by another member for breaking a bottle over his opponent's head instead of beating him with his fists to win a fight. Winning a fight with an obviously weaker person is not evaluated as honorable. The bigger youth should not need to react because of his obvious superiority in strength. In certain situations, however, the inequality of sides may be justified. When a new member is being initiated into a gang, he may be jumped by three members. He will lose and by losing he does not change the status rankings of old members within the gang. All the new member must do is put up a good fight. Paulie's arm was broken but that was because he fought so well that the Lions "had to break it."

— The importance of the style and the situational legitimacy of violence is exemplified by the reactions to movies in which personal dominance is gained through violence. Gang discussions of these movies merged directly into discussions of gang fights. Gang members saw the violence as realistic, little different in style from violence in their own lives. Young men expressed their pleasure when personal dominance was expressed through violence. In one movie a married woman overtly flirted with another man. Her husband did nothing about it and continued to ignore his wife. The man with whom the wife had been flirting raped her, which the Lions thought was a legitimate action to maintain his honor because she was tempting him and acting as though she dominated his life. Raping her was domination of her by dishonoring her husband. Even youths who do not generally subscribe to a code of personal dominance through violence saw the rape as virtuous and honorable. The only way her husband could regain his honor was to kill the rapist; the Lions cheered when he did so.[14]

Justification of personal dominance through violence was disputed in the discussions of Lieutenant William Calley's guilt and the mass killings during the Vietnam War. Here the connection between violence in the streets and killing in war was debated. Several gang members approved of Lieutenant Calley's personal triumph in dominating the Vietnamese by killing all the men, women, and children of Mai Lai, but others were critical when one gang member failed to distinguish between personal honor and the military. "Did you know that they pay you for killing people in Nam and here man we got to go to jail for it. Man, I'd like to go to Nam and kill some," Sal said. Ronny explained to him, "Don't be dumb, you can only shoot who they tell you to—not just anyone. You see Calley ended in jail, just like us." Sal could not understand that Ronny did not equate Mai Lai with an affair of personal honor and that in the army there are rules about who should be killed. Vietnam had very little political meaning to many of the youths except as a place to fight and gain personal dominance. When they read newspapers, the stories of killings held their attention most. Veterans discussed how they shot Vietnamese, took drugs, and went out with women. Who was winning or what anyone was fighting for only rarely became an issue. Perhaps a word or two would emerge about communists, but most of the time it was weapons, tactics, killing, drugs, and women that interested them. Vietnam seemed to some of the younger males a glorified extension of their world on the streets. The youths find legitimation in the media and the world around them for their view of the proper response to intentional insults.

The Use of Guns

For the youths of 32nd Street, as for the cowboy, guns are an important symbol of a life-style. During the late 1960's the number of guns obtained illegally by young people, particularly gangs on 32nd Street, increased rapidly. Using guns to gain personal domination raises several problems. First, guns change the possibilities of gaining personal dominance through violence. Unlike a good fight with physical contact, using a gun does not test real skills—a twelve year old or a woman can shoot a grown man. Shooting someone does little to prove real superiority. Second, using a gun increases the possibility of getting into trouble with the law. Getting caught with an unregistered gun, particularly if the person is over sixteen, is a considerably more serious offense than beating up someone in a fist fight or getting caught with a bat or chain. Third, fighting with guns increases the possibility of a life-or-death encounter. Confronted by an armed person, the other may not even get a chance to react. One slight tug at the trigger may result in death.

The ready availability of .22's, .38's, .45's, and sawed-off shotguns has changed the form of gaining dominance, particularly among the gangs.[15] No longer are there prearranged fights, as in the 1950's, when large numbers of youths gathered to fight with bats, chains, and switchblades. While it was possible to kill with a knife, it took much more skill and an opponent had a much greater chance of protecting himself. Most conflicts now involve either a few armed youths who go out looking for the gang with whom they are warring or two individuals in a spur-of-the-moment fight. One young man was shot and killed by someone in a moving car. His companions could not identify the killer. Several other youths who were nearby did identify the killer, who received little approbation.

While most youths are aware of the legal ramifications of being caught with a gun, they feel that carrying a gun is necessary because they assume (often mistakenly) that everyone else has one. Enrique was dismissed from a job that he really enjoyed when his employers learned he had been arrested on a weapons charge. While the other Lions thought his dismissal unfair, they were well aware that the charge was serious and that Enrique was lucky to receive probation at age nineteen. If a youth is challenged by someone with a gun and if he does not have one, he is at a disadvantage. Sam of the Lions claimed, "I never go anywhere without my heat [gun]; you aren't anyone without one. It's dangerous." The feeling of being helpless without a gun is exacerbated by the knowledge that anyone could have one. Elaborate preparations are made to carry guns secretly. Portable radios are often fitted to carry the weapons. "We saw them carry guns in dictionaries on TV but it would look funny—us carrying dictionaries," Amos, another gang member, explained as he showed me the radio.

A number of older gang members say that it is better to have the younger members kill. One Senior Greek was quick to point out that a juvenile would be much less severely punished for the offense. When a twelve or fourteen year old kills someone in a gang fight, he is likely to receive a sentence of two years or less, whereas an adult might receive a life sentence.

Ambivalent feelings about the use of guns and those who use them is indicated by the fact that while gang sweaters are rarely lost, guns seems to be lost frequently. "The pigs were after me so when I came around the alley, I threw it in the garbage. I really looked for it after the pigs cut out, but it wasn't there. Now what am I going to do without a piece [gun]? I got two dudes after my ass," Len told the Lions when they chastised him for losing another gun. Amos explained, "Like one dude has one, then when we need heats cause we expect trouble, we can't find half of them. I guess we got six heats between all of us [about thirty-five youths]."

Further indications of ambivalence toward those who use guns to defend their honor are the stories told by older gang members of "good clean" fights between gangs, by which they mean there were no guns—only chains, bats, and knives. Face-to-face combat really indicated how strong a man and his gang were, they claimed. Now, one of the Senior Greeks told a young member of the Lions, a twelve-year-old "punk" can shoot and kill a strong and tough man. That does not change others' evaluations of the "punk." The young Lion nodded his agreement.

Yet these older men also carry and use guns. Alberto, who at twenty-five drove a public bus, was still a Senior Greek. He had responsibilities (a wife and two kids) and wanted the good things in life (a nice place to live, a stereo, a good time). He did not want to get killed; he said guns scared him. But he did fight and he did carry a gun sometimes. His sister said he punched a man who had been looking at his wife. The fight was broken up but Alberto chipped his tooth. Three weeks later he shot at someone who kept staring at him at a bar, but no one was hit.

Etiquette and Convention

There is no reason why a conventional response cannot be given in a situation that may be interpreted either as insulting or as inoffensive. Most young men have conventional social skills, in contrast to the gangs studied by Gordon (1967) and Short and Strodtbeck

(1965), who argue that lack of such skills is at the root of gang violence.[16] Most gang members have attended formal affairs in tuxedos and have behaved appropriately. While they do not go to downtown restaurants frequently because of the expense, they have all been there. With their knowledge of "polite" social skills and ability to use them, most youths can respond to situations as improprieties rather then as insults.

A conventional response in this situation can best be conceived as impression management (Goffman, 1959). Impression management implies that the actor maintains enough distance from the action to deflect any imputations of unworthiness away from himself and onto the properties of the situation. The necessary responses, then, are not violent. For example, if someone's foot is in my path and I trip, I can blame the crowded space and say "Excuse me." This places the onus on the situation or the setting which happens to bring the two people together, rather than on an intention to violate another's personal space. Alternatively, I could believe the person purposely stuck out his foot so that I would fall and make a fool of myself, which would call for an honor-bound response.

A second example concerns whether or not entry into another gang's territory is viewed as a violation of personal space. When a gang enters an area where rival gangs are located for a conventional purpose, its passage through that area is not viewed as offensive or intrusive, and rarely will foreign gang members confront the opposing gang members. Lions from 32nd Street frequently visited relatives on 40th Street, where several rival gangs were located, with no trepidation. But 40th Street is appraised as dangerous when the Lions evaluate their own behavior as intrusive. When they were out looking for rival Dukes to fight, the Dukes would view their actions as intentional violations of territory.

> If we go wandering around 40th Street then the Dukes know that we're out looking for them and we got to be careful 'cause its dangerous and we're likely to get shot at. They know who we are and they don't like us 'cause we got one of their sweaters.

"Coolness," which is much admired, may switch the onus onto the situation rather than the person. Coolness is the ability to stand back from certain situations and rationally evaluate others' actions. If, however, the offender is seen as *purposely* ignoring the other's feelings, then the victim's honor is being tampered with and the incident requires an immediate response.

Normative Ambiguity and Identity

Attributing meaning to others' intentions resolves a situation of normative ambiguity. Evaluating another's actions as intentionally insulting will tip this situation toward the code of honor, while evaluating the actions as unintentional will tip the situation toward convention. Both forms are considered proper modes of conduct and young males may choose between the two responses. An ambiguous situation becomes a critical triggering event for a male youth; for the manner in which he appraises and resolves the situation publicly reveals the type of person he perceives himself to be. Others' evaluations of the resolution then become part of his identity. On one extreme are those who rarely appraise situations as offenses to their honor. On the other extreme are those who frequently question others' claims to precedence in order to start a fight. Because most youths refuse to commit themselves wholeheartedly to conventional or honor-bound responses, the individual may invoke either set of norms to interpret the actions of others and to justify conduct. An individual may say on one occasion that killing is morally wrong and fighting over an infraction of the rules of etiquette is silly, and on another occasion the same person may say that it is necessary to defend one's honor, even by murder. There is a real tension between the rough-and-tumble excitement of street life and conventional behavior, and not all youths resolve it in a similar manner. Each decision made, however, can be critical to others' evaluations of a man's identity as an honorable person.

Orientations Toward Honor: Identity Types

Youths differ in both the number of violent actions in which they become involved and the way they negotiate potentially insulting situations, their orientations toward honor. Some youths frequently and intentionally provoke incidents, while others do not provoke incidents but are likely to appraise situations as insulting and respond accordingly. Still others define only a few situations as insulting to their honor, namely those in which the sexual purity of their sisters is threatened.

Toch (1969) points out that "self-image promoters" are sensitive to attempts to question their claims to precedence and habitually precipitate violent situations in which they can demonstrate their power, courage, and importance. "Self-image defenders" are sensitive to any actions that appear to discredit their image of themselves as persons with whom others do not trifle. On 32nd Street there are also "rep avoiders" (reputation avoiders) who are largely unconcerned with claims to precedence. They interpret most potential insults as unintentional and respond in a conventional manner. Only in situations where the honor of their mothers or sisters is questioned might they appraise the situation in terms of the code of honor and as a moral issue.

Violence and Reputation

Particularly for the image promoter, the outcome of a potentially insulting situation becomes an important criterion of reputation, the status ranking among image promoters. Status is achieved in part through the deference and appreciation others show a person about his fighting skills. The status ranking occurs not between identity types but within types.[17] The competition for honor among youths, unlike adults, results in a hierarchical ranking, a precarious and action-oriented ranking of reputation, or "rep," that depends on continuous confirmation by others of one's placement.[18] These young men measure themselves against a local code of personal honor. Whatever prestige or status they acquire through those means must be affirmed by their peers.

If a young man is concerned with the development of a reputation based on fighting skills and physical prowess, he not only must be ready to answer challenges to his claim to precedence but must actively challenge others, as his evaluation is related both to the magnitude of the challenge and response and to the number of challenges. He must be an image promoter. An image defender, on the other hand, is less concerned with fighting as a criterion for his reputation, and the rep avoider is entirely unconcerned with status as a warrior. For him honor and social status are unconnected.

Each identity category has distinct criteria (or varying emphases of the same criteria) for these rankings. The social order is negotiated differently among the three categories and among the peer groups within each category. While fighting skills are most important for self-image promoters, other skills are also important in the rankings for both the self-image promoters and the self-image defenders. Skills such as leadership, "cool" or impression management, seductive flirting with women, disparaging others, negotiating, knowing the streets (where to get guns, whom and when to fight), and dressing well are important in developing a strong reputation. Image defenders are also concerned with these skills and characteristics but not centrally concerned with fighting skills. The meaning of fighting for the two orientations is different. The rep avoiders, largely unconcerned with the street scene, are not ranked in terms of the skills and traits listed above.

The Biggest and Baddest

Not all of these with the biggest reputations are or were gang members. Reputation often depends on how far knowledge of a person's identity has spread through the grapevine. This is a good measure of how *big* his reputation is but not necessarily of how *highly* it is evaluated. When a person has become a myth and his story is constantly being told by many who have never met him, then his reputation is really extensive and highly evaluated as the "baddest."

Crazy Tom (the name is not derogatory), is one such myth. Though he was incarcerated for nearly twelve years, his story was well known among the youths and upon his release he was elevated to hero status. Every group has its own version of the Crazy Tom tale, varying in the number of people he was supposed to have killed and the way he ingeniously evaded the police for a long time. Shortly after I met the Lions, they told me about how he had hidden from the police in the trees of the park to avoid capture. After he was released he was able to move among all the gangs in an attempt to negotiate peace. Some young men were afraid of him and envious of his position. It would have been a great coup to challenge and beat him, a difficult job, but he was aware that someone might try. In addition, relatives and friends of those he had murdered might be plotting to take his life. He said that he must act first, not only for his own protection but so as not to appear to be running away from danger. After a little more than a year out of prison he disappeared from the community because he was too vulnerable to unpredictable attack and had few people to turn to for support.

Included on more or less the same level are several hustlers who do not belong to gangs and whose names and connections are known well beyond the confines of the community. These men rely on no one but themselves and perhaps one partner (best friend) for support. Mickey was a pool hustler who played all over the city and maintained relationships with many different groups within the community. He was able to communicate with many of the gangs and was admired for his impression management skills and leadership. "I don't need a gang. If I get into trouble, it's my trouble, but in a gang you're responsible for the trouble everyone gets in." Men with such wide and highly evaluated reputations are few.

Other individuals have reputations that go beyond their gang affiliation and are known by a wide range of youths both in and out of gangs. They are referred to as "really bad dudes." Most can be personally identified by other youths and most are over eighteen. One says "Ray of the Greeks," not "He's a Greek." They also feel they are known in other areas of the city. Several of the Senior Greeks refused to attend a baseball game in another community because they feared recognition by gangs affiliated with an enemy 40th Street gang. They claimed that the Latin Dukes had their pictures. These men have all committed their share of violent acts, which are talked about throughout the youth community. All have spent considerable time in jail, at least four as juveniles on murder charges (all were released after serving short sentences) and others on accumulated aggravated assault and battery charges. All these incidents took place among gang members. Due respect is granted these men. When any of them approach anyone of lesser status, all attention is focused on them.

One afternoon I was sitting on a bench talking with the Lions. Suddenly all conversation stopped and attention was focused on Spoof and Fidel, two Senior Nobles in their midtwenties. Spoof flipped his keys to the nearest Lion and told him to get his lounge chair from the trunk of his car. His orders were carried out silently. Spoof settled comfortably in his chair. He proudly produced three bullets: one had a cutoff head, one had a flattened head, and the third was unmodified. He carefully described just how each of the bullets reacted inside the body. Everyone listened quietly and a few asked technical questions. No one was allowed to hold the bullets. Fidel said that some men were after him and launched into a description of how he managed to escape every time but slept with his gun under the pillow. Then we were treated to a show and history of their scars while the Lions nodded their approval and were properly awed. Even after the two departed, the Lions discussed nothing else for the rest of the evening. Youths of nine or ten say "I want to be like Spoof." Unlike the "independents," Fidel and Spoof have fellow gang members who will help them out should they be challenged.

A reputation is always open to challenge. Because of the competitive nature of the status system (to gain status one must defeat someone else) and the action orientation of the claim to precedence, continual public certification of reputation is necessary. If anyone publicly fails to show proper deference, the situation must be addressed. It is through competition for deference that status is revealed; consequently, almost any behavior that could be regarded as lacking respect must be defined and responded to within the honor framework.

Collective Identity as Image Promoters: The Lions

For many who have chosen the image promoter path to an identity and a reputation, the perceived threats to their status seem constant. As they explain it, it is much easier to deal with threats if there are others who will help out. Most of the Lions, the gang known as one of the fiercest in the community, claim to have gotten into many fights before becoming members.[19] One afternoon Gilberto, the president of the Juniors, listed for me all the fights he had

had prior to joining the Lions and described how many youths had been chasing him because he had beaten them up. Most of the Lions had at least one big fight with more than one person just before joining the gang. Membership, they stated, was the only way to gain enough support to survive their complicated situation. While some of the Lions were relatives and others had grown up together, many others joined individually. Unable to handle all their business on their own, they became members of a collectivity, the gang, that augmented and protected their toughness.

Not all gangs form in this manner. The Junior Nobles claimed that they had been a softball team before becoming a gang with a name and colors. One day when they were at practice a gang started hanging around and heckling them. They took this to be a direct attack on their honor. Fighting back, they hurt several of the gang members enough so that they were perceived by other gangs as a potential threat to their status. From that point on they found themselves in many situations where they defined the behavior of others as insulting to the collectivity, as not properly deferential. The more they responded as a group concerned with its honor, the bigger their reputation became and the more it was challenged.

As a member of a gang, the basic parameters of an identity are laid out by membership. While some individual reputations extend beyond an identity as a gang member ("That's Gilberto, he's a Lion" rather than "That dude's a Lion"), many are known largely by their affiliations. As a member one *is* a Lion, and that group has a certain reputation as a gang. It becomes each member's responsibility to uphold that reputation. The collective reputation of the gang is potentially at stake in situations of normative ambiguity if the following three conditions are satisfied:

> First, at least one party to a face-to-face encounter must feel that the presence of the other party in this setting or his behavior on this occasion endangers his safety and impugns his dignity. In light of the actor's definition of the situation as threatening and provocative, he must make a decision on the spot. If he does not assume the role of an aggressor, he may play the part of a victim. Second, the actor must respond to this emotionally charged situation in a way that

visibly reveals his resolve (i.e., he feels his words, gestures or
actions express a definite intention) to inflict physical injury
on his antagonist or by actually doing so. Third, the actor
must account for his conduct on this occasion in terms of his
status as a member of a gang. (Horowitz and Schwartz,
1974: 238–239)

Not all incidents that involve gang members are defined by the
members as gang fights, and an individual member sometimes involves the group in an undesired conflict. If the member is a known
troublemaker like Sal, he might be left to defend himself. On one
occasion Ken, a Midget Lion, came running to the park yelling that
the Nobles had insulted him and he wanted help to protect the
name of the gang. Jim, a more prestigious Little, slowly turned
toward the others and explained that he had seen Ken trying to
provoke the Nobles; if Ken had succeeded, he ought to be able to
handle the situation himself. High status in the group leads to
greater assurance that the others will allow an insult to be defined
as a collective insult. Responsibility for defending the name of the
gang against collective insults becomes a criterion for continued
membership.

The Construction of Gang Reputations

In seeking to protect and promote their reputations, gangs often
engage in prolonged "wars," which are kept alive between larger
fights by many small incidents and threats of violence. Following
each incident one gang claims precedence, which means that the
other group must challenge them if they want to retain their honor
and reassert their reputation. On-the-spot insults are not always
necessary to provoke a fight and claims to precedence are carried
over from one incident to the next. If a group's desire to be treated
with deference is not honored, the group must claim precedence.
Members must also go out to claim deferential treatment and
superiority by demonstrating lack of respect for their enemies. For
example, the war between the Lions and Aces continued over three
years with intermittent claims to precedence by each side. Expectations of affronts and small skirmishes kept up the momentum of

the conflict. If either side had failed to respond publicly to the other's challenge, the challenging gang's reputation would have become increasingly formidable.

In one incident, when Rat Man thought he saw some Aces riding in a car, he shot at them but the .38 did not go off. "We are at war," he said, and that is what a gang member is supposed to do when he sees an enemy. After more incidents several Lions borrowed a car, took two guns, and went looking for the Aces. When they returned they claimed they had gotten off three shots but no one was hit. During this period, an Angel shot and killed an Ace, and the Lions expressed regret they had not done it. They criticized the Angel's method to avoid loss of respect in their own eyes. Later, Amos and two other Lions ran into the Ace who had thrown a brick through Amos's mother's window. Amos beat the Ace unconscious with the butt of his gun, but the Ace regained consciousness a few days later and identified Amos as his assailant. Amos claimed he would have killed him but he had no ammunition.

Several incidents in which no actual meeting occurred helped to perpetuate the war. Sometimes some of the Senior Greeks who congregated at El Pueblo Park joined the Lions. On one occasion I counted thirty Lions, six guns, numerous baseball bats, several chains, and many broken bottles ready for use. One of the Greeks was frightened enough to demand that another Greek leave his gun at the park when he had to leave for a few minutes. Everyone raced back and forth across the park and a lookout was posted at each corner. The darker it got, the louder and more violent the talk about the Aces became. By 9:30 people began to announce, "I've got to go home now." By 10:30 the park was almost empty. These no-show events help to maintain the fervor and momentum of the conflict. They allowed the waiting group to assert that the others were too frightened to show up and thereby to claim precedence over them.

These were only a few of the events that occurred between the Lions and the Aces over a two-year period of their war. The Lions also took several trips into the Ace's territory and the two gangs had a big fight over a sweater. There was roughly one major incident—which may or may not have ended in conflict—each month. After each incident someone loses and someone gains a claim to precedence over the other. The general feeling of the community in the year that most of these events occurred was that the Lions were the most violent and the least polished of any of the gangs.

When an incident is defined as a collective insult, all members must participate to ensure the continued reputation of the group or to better it. Participation also promotes group loyalty and solidarity. Members must participate even if they do not agree with a particular incident or the group is drawn into a situation by the irresponsible behavior of a member. If a person weakens the gang's right to claim deference from others by losing his sweater to another gang, someone has to get it back or the entire group suffers. The following incident illustrates what may happen to an individual who does not participate when an incident has been defined as a collective insult.

It was during a battle in the war between the Lions and the Aces. In the morning Jim, a Lion, had been jumped and beaten quite badly. At four that afternoon, fifteen members decided they ought to go out and retaliate. Lou was at work after school and could not be located before the Lions left the park. When the Lions returned at 7:30, someone remarked upon his absence and they started arguing about whether Lou could be trusted to fight with the group. Amos suggested that if he were to come around, they ought to challenge him and beat him up. There was a murmur of assent. The word got back to Lou and he stayed away for a week. By the time he returned, everyone seemed to have forgotten, but he told me he was furious about Amos's comment. His absence was not his fault, Lou claimed, because no one had called him at work and he had no idea there was a fight. The threat served its purpose to reinforce loyalty to the group and its reputation as tough and courageous, yet further conflict might have split the group. Nico also did not fight but his absence was no threat to the solidarity of the gang because he fought frequently with the group and had previously sustained two serious bullet wounds while supporting them. High status and consistent demonstration of loyalty can excuse a member from participation.

Having an identity as a Lion does not preclude membership in another type of group; however, to remain a Lion, loyalty must be demonstrated continually. Protecting the gang's claim to precedence from other gangs takes priority over any other affiliation. At one dance a Lion, Enrique, wearing a gang sweater, spoke for the Brown Berets during intermission. During the speech Enrique talked about peace among all Latinos, but as a Lion he was arming himself against the rumored invasion of the Aces. Several of the other Lions also started associating with the Brown Berets. Nico and Ronny were the first to join. Ronny said he joined because they had helped his retarded brother over Christmas. Several of the Brown Berets started to come to the park and several Lions drifted into the Brown Berets. They attended several meetings and Enrique and Jim started wearing the jacket of the Berets. The Lions who did not join called the ones who did "cop-outs" for their dual loyalty. Several of the new Brown Berets were assigned to be armed guards, which impressed them very much. But there was too much talk and too little action, and the Lions were demanding a demonstration of loyalty. Within three months they all dropped the Berets. The two identities were too difficult to retain. Their identities as Lions were too important to become secondary to that of the Brown Berets.

Gang Flexibility

There is a continuing debate among sociologists about the nature of gang organization. The conceptions range from an almost paramilitary organization to a pseudogroup. For example, on one extreme, Yablonsky (1950) regards the gang as a "near-group," with limited cohesion, disturbed leadership, impermanence, diffuse role definitions, shifting membership, minimal normative consensus, and limited definition of membership expectations. Taking a more moderate view, Klein (1971), while not including disturbed membership, views gangs as having low cohesion and a shifting role structure, with core and fringe membership and leadership as a function, not a position. Shaw and McKay (1966), with a view similar to Whyte's (1955) description of street corner groups, see the gang as a cohesive entity with an *esprit de corps*. The gang, according to Bloch and Niederhoffer (1958), is structured, has strong leadership, and is similar to all youth groups. On the other extreme, some, for example, the Welfare Council of New York City (1950), ascribe a much more rigid structure to gangs.

Group solidarity through commitment to the Lions' collective identity and reputation is reinforced by some sanctioned rules and regulations. These rules, however, are usually flexible, as is the organization of the group. Techniques of choosing leaders, their powers, and decision-making processes vary between groups; moreover, rules for joining and quitting and for the collection of dues are flexible. There are also differences in the way a group moves from one age segment to the next. Some groups move as a collectivity and must fight with an older group to move up. In other groups an individual moves up when he becomes of age and the older group thinks he is good enough. In 1971 the Lions were all one group. Later they decided to divide into the Littles and the Juniors and held separate official meetings. "It just happened, we didn't hassle it, the older dudes became the Juniors and the rest, Littles. We [Juniors] don't have any real officers, we're friends, and we can having meetings when we want," explained Enrique. Most members of both groups hung out at the park, though a few did not. Only on two occasions did the Littles become involved in an incident in which the Juniors did not. Age segments of other gangs are not necessarily this close.

In Klein's (1971) view gang leadership shifts with the needs and activities of the group. At times that was true of the Lions. During a period of war Gilberto was the leader, but Enrique was the one who calmed the group down and mediated both intragroup and inter-group conflicts. There were also other leadership positions, such as president and treasurer.

Gilberto, who has always maintained a position of leadership whether elected to office or not, organized an executive board of older members of which he was chairman in 1975. He claims he put Nico in as president of the Juniors. The Littles group elected officers and had discussions about who would make a good leader and what the procedures should be for an election. A good president, according to Sal, is one who can fight well, knows when to fight, is not hotheaded, and can tell the members what to do. They voted for a president, a vice-president, and a treasurer who collected dues.

Entering and leaving a gang are regulated but much variation occurs, usually depending on the needs of the group at the time and the individual. There are few inflexible rules for entrance. Some-times a prospective member undergoes a strict initiation rite where he is beaten by several gang members to prove his toughness, as when Paulie's arm was broken. Nico, however, claimed that he walked into a Lions meeting and just became a member after he quit the Nobles, whom he did not like. He already had a reputation. The initial fight helps to establish a reputation within a gang, but if a potential member already has one established, he may not be required to prove his worth. There are also several ways a youth can leave the gang. Some just drift away, others are beaten if they try to leave, and some buy their way out. Lou was very concerned one day because the gang claimed that inflation had driven the cost of buying his way out from twenty to thirty dollars; Lou was only willing to pay twenty. Finally, he said, they let him go for twenty because he had been a member for so long. Len drifted away by spending less and less time with the other gang members after he married.

There are also financial obligations to the group. Dues are paid with varying regularity but are always expected when asked for. They change according to season, the amount of money the group has, and what is needed. At one point, when the Lions wanted guns, the dues were five dollars a week. Other times, when the majority wished to go to a dance with a three-dollar entrance fee, they would vote to spend their dues at the dance. When one member obtained a pound of marijuana, they all sold it and the profits were put into the gang's kitty, but not until after an argument over whether the profits should go to the individuals or to the gang. Dues were not paid during this period.

Some rules and regulations are considered necessary. Fred of the Red Shirts (an image defender group) said, "You got to keep the dudes in line if you're going to have a good club—Enrique and Gilberto are the only ones who can." It is thought that overly strict rules and regulations might drive the members away.

Friends and Partners: Gang Cohesion

Friendship, although sometimes strained, and mutual support are important factors in group solidarity. Though some studies claim that gangs have few internal cohesive mechanisms such as group goals, membership stability, and role differentiation (Klein, 1971), on 32nd Street members bolster each other and individual friend-

ships are solidified into partners that frequently entail significant
mutual sacrifices.[20]

Examples of the social support given members can be drawn
from the excuses made when a member loses a fight for his personal
reputation: the enemy did not fight fairly, he was much bigger, or he
had a weapon. It is not the fault of the gang member if he seemed to
end up at the bottom or sustained a larger wound. His reputation is
not lowered as much by his loss as his opponent's win is deflated.
There is no zero-sum game in terms of winning or losing a fight: no
one loses completely. It was obvious to everyone that Sam had lost
a fight. (It was not defined as a gang fight.) He had a black eye and
looked terrible, but everyone had an explanation for the situation:
the other man had a bottle, Sam was jumped from behind, the other
man was bigger. Privately several observers, including Lions, told
me that the reason the other had a bottle was that Sam had a knife.
Everyone thought Sam had fought hard and no one wanted him to
feel that his esteem was lowered. His reputation was weakened outside the gang, but no one would admit this within the gang.

Most important, there is always someone around to hang out
with. Meeting day after day in the same location provides a sense of
continuity and social support. Even when the temperature drops
below freezing, several of the Lions can be found at the park. Even
the members who are going out steadily with a particular young
woman usually bring her to the park for a part of the evening. She
usually talks with the other women and he with the Lions. When
several of the Lions joined the Brown Berets and began to spend
less time at the park, the others continually bemoaned their
absence.

Being a partner connotes very close ties with another man, and
these relationships are generally long-standing and public. In fact in
extreme cases a man will to to jail for his partner. Partners always
stand up for each other and can say almost anything to each other.
One of the Lions went to jail for a murder but never revealed the
name of his accomplice (his partner).

There are, however, characteristics of this system of obtaining a
reputation and maintaining honor that make trust and close ties
among gang members difficult. A member's status within the gang
is important in judging whether or not an incident is a collective

insult and in legitimizing the absence of a member from gang action. Status within the gang is based on the evaluation of a member's reputation in the street, and that reputation is precarious. It may shift with each new attempt to assert and defend a claim to precedence. With the sensitivity of gang members to insult and the precarious nature of reputation, there is always a possibility that one gang member will judge another's behavior as not properly deferential. While both Jim and Ham were regular members of the gang, neither was in the small inner circle. Jim was smaller than Ham but probably faster. Ham almost killed Jim one summer evening in the park. Jim called Ham, who is very dark, a "nigger" to his face. Ham interpreted this as an intended insult and started to fight. Several good punches were thrown before Ham's sister was able to separate them and drag her brother home. Because everyone is so sensitive to insult, it is possible for anyone to be perceived as an insulter, with the exception of one's partner.

This type of situation accounts for much of the fighting within the gang. Over an eighteen-month period, however, there were only three fights among the Lions that progressed further than a few teasing shoves or some verbal insults. Each time it looked as though there might be a fight, it was stopped by other members. If a fight had continued, a reordering of status relationships might have been necessary and someone might really have lost. Instead the hierarchy remained fairly loose with attempts to build a strong reputation focused on challenges outside the gang. A successful challenger can improve his reputation without a fellow member actually losing status. Moreover, the extensive and intensive mutual obligation system links members both existentially and symbolically and minimizes internal competition.

The Reputation Hierarchy among the Lions

While friendship is an important aspect of group relationships, it can and does become problematic among individuals who do not all have the same status and must frequently rely on others to support and reaffirm their reputation. If the group were strongly and strictly hierarchical, no friendships would be formed because in any relationship one would be dominant and the other subordinate, an impossible state for any honorable man. For trust to develop, a relationship must be experienced as egalitarian, otherwise the dominant person would always be expecting the subordinate person to attempt to improve his position.[21] While there are some differences in status among the members of the same gang, most of the time the members played down any differences unless the individual did something that the others did not like.

A reputation is based on more than just fighting ability, so those with less skill in combat may build a reputation in other areas. If fighting were the only criterion, then the person who beat up all the others would be leader and there would be a constant struggle within the group. But there are few fights among members of the same gang. Verbal skills, knowledge of the streets, dressing well, and relationships with women, all characteristics difficult to measure, enter into the evaluation of reputation and allow a blurring of the status hierarchy because of the difficulty of actually ranking members according to all those characteristics and skills. The Little and Junior Lions provide several examples of developing a reputation.

At nineteen, Gilberto's reputation was the biggest and most extensively known among the Lions. The many elements on which it was built illustrate the diversity of criteria available. Gilberto's name was known throughout the community. He was not the best fighter in the group, nor the best negotiator, but he was probably the most successful with women and had several children to prove it. He married but set up a separate apartment where he could "have his fun." Moreover, he had been in the juvenile detention center twice—once on manslaughter charges and once on several counts of aggravated assault and battery—both worth doing time for. Gilberto was never scared of fighting at the right time. One of the Lions explained: "He's a good leader. He knows what fights to get us into and he takes care of his own personal business without getting the dudes involved. He keeps his own shit where he can handle it."[22] He was shot and killed in front of his house by a rival gang member at the age of twenty-six.

High, frequently confirmed status permits some deviations from group expectations. Nico was part of the inner circle along with Gilberto. He was a skilled and established fighter who had won many battles, knew when to fight and when not to, was a skilled negotiator, and had several girlfriends. His skills as an image promoter were so well established that he was accepted as a member without any question. While he fought with the gang a number of times in the beginning to establish his membership, his status was high enough that his absence from a fight did not threaten the group. Besides, it was explained, he already had two bullets lodged in his back. While others were chastised for not finding out about a fight, Nico waved good-bye as the others pursued the enemy. He was also a success with women. Before he married he always had an attractive steady girlfriend and saw someone else on the side. His work skills were praised because, though he held a steady job, he always spent time with the gang before he went to work on the midnight shift. When crucial decisions were made, whether or not he was involved in the outcome, he held a central position in the process. He was made captain of the softball team. Though he was not the best player, Nico was the only one who could assign positions and organize the practice sessions without problems from a number of the players. His reputation came from a variety of sources: fighting skill, verbal skills, and success with females.

While fighting is important to be part of the inner circle, a person must also know when to fight. Sam had only minimal influence in the inner circle though he was a long-time gang member and could be counted on to be at the regular bench and to engage in gang fights. His reputation was based upon a few good fights and his very attractive Anglo girlfriend, who pursued him constantly and whom he properly ignored while he flirted with other women. His reputation was limited by his occasional inability to distance himself from a situation to make a rational judgment. He frequently wanted to fly into action. Once he wanted to go after the Nobles when no one could find the guns. Enrique and Nico stopped him and sent out two scouts to find out what the Nobles were up to first. When he was carrying a gun at the park and failed to hide it before the police stopped at their bench, the others thought he deserved to be arrested.

Being outside the inner circle has its disadvantages. When Amos's parents gave him permission to decorate and use their basement, Sam was excluded from the regular group allowed to use it.

The entire group was invited only for parties; otherwise only Gilberto, Nico, Enrique, Rico (because he was Enrique's brother), and Len (because his girlfriend was a friend of Enrique's and Rico's girlfriends) could enter without permission. Occasionally others were invited. Though Rat Man had a poor reputation he was invited sometimes because he had built the bar and stolen the lights. Sam resented his exclusion, particularly one freezing Saturday night in January when he and Sal were the only ones who showed up at the park. They spent the evening running around the neighborhood looking for the others but found no one and by nine left to go home. I bumped into Len with his girlfriend after I left Sam and Sal and he invited me to join the others in the basement clubhouse.

Even a tough fighter can have a poor overall reputation. Rat Man, though a good fighter, was considered a loser by the Lions and by most people in the community who knew him. He got into trouble too frequently. By his own account, at seventeen, he had been in jail twenty-seven times and had dropped out of the seventh grade. According to other Lions, that left him with little chance for the future. He was unable to make rational choices. Going to jail for a serious charge is acceptable but too many arrests limit future choices. Rat Man had also become involved in a fairly profitable burglary ring outside the gang. He gained little status from this role but was respected for his daring in fights, his ability to survive a large gaping wound, and his ability to find a weapon when none seemed near.

Because of his low status, the Lions did not seem able to get bail together for Rat Man as they did for others. One said he hesitated because he thought that Rat Man might jump bond. His mother wanted nothing to do with him, so his girlfriend at the time, Ivy, got the money together. Less than half of the $100 came from the gang.

Though he is considered a loser by almost everyone, Rat Man did not admit that his life did not fit into conventional patterns. One night the Lions were joking about women and I asked Rat Man how many mistresses he was going to have after he married. He was genuinely hurt by the suggestion that he was not capable of settling down; furthermore, he replied that he would not marry a woman unless he really loved her. He was going to do all his fooling around now (he was doing a lot of it). He left the state in 1973 after jumping bail on another charge.

No matter how much bravery a member demonstrates, he must know when it makes sense to fight. Sal is unable to make a sensible decision about when to fight. His reputation extends beyond the Lions as a crazy person. Once he wanted to rob a corner grocery store a few blocks from the park. He had no plan for entrance or escape. Rico and Ronny told him he was stupid and they would not go along with the job. The idea collapsed because he could gain no support. Another time all the Lions were standing next to the pool on an evening when the police were playing basketball in the gym. Sal proposed that they break into the policemen's lockers and steal their guns. Enrique explained very carefully that the police were not likely to have left their guns in their lockers because they were easily broken into. Sal then proposed to break into the police car trunks to find some weapons. Enrique repeated that the police knew the Lions were in the park and would not leave their guns where they could be stolen. Even if they succeeded, Enrique stated, the police would know immediately who had done it. Sal received little esteem from the group as no one paid him deference. Not even acts that might have been considered honorable if others had performed them were evaluated as such. His identity as a crazy person was used to interpret all his actions. He was, however, allowed to remain in the gang because he was able to hold his own in collective fights.

The Fragility or Permanence of a Reputation

While identity and status must be continuously reaffirmed in inter-action with peers, a reputation can, after a number of years, exist without the supporting behavior. Like the identities constructed by the men of Jelly's Bar (Anderson, 1978), the identities and reputations of these young men are constructed in interaction with peers and, for this group, through explicit and sometimes deadly competition with them. Identity and status are thus precarious and continuously reevaluated. Once one has obtained a solid reputation, either as one to whom deference is owed by many or as one to whom little deference is paid, the outcome of each triggering situation becomes less crucial. Enrique, Nico, and Gilberto could by the time they turned twenty-one ignore attempts not to give them proper deference. Once a reputation is established, it allows an individual to deviate from that pattern without hurting his reputation. It also makes it difficult for a person to change that identity. The same is true of the collective identities of the gangs as their members mature.

Self-Image Defenders

A few groups and many individuals are not image promoters but are sensitive to intended insult and manage to place themselves in situations where they feel they must fight in order to maintain the respect of others. They rarely go out and promote their claim to precedence; that is, they do not intentionally create potential triggering situations. But they expect others to respect their personal space. Some have been in gangs and dropped out, others regularly congregate on certain corners with their friends, sometimes getting into fights but more often just sitting, talking, and drinking. Their life-styles vary except that they are all to some extent sensitive to aspersions cast upon their honor. They are concerned with verbal skills, being "cool", and dressing well. The Red Shirts are the only young *named* group, but there are smaller groups that always congregate in the same place and can readily be identified by that location. Other groups share interests such as sports and spend time together practicing.

The Red Shirts were a social club; its members never fought in the name of the group. While few of the Red Shirts directly provoked incidents, some members of the group made alliances with a gang if trouble were expected at a public event. They had never been challenged as a group. Several of the older members had belonged to a very tough gang before they joined the army and went to Vietnam. They shifted from image promoters to defenders when they returned to relatively decent jobs. Several went to college. They rarely fought but smoked marijuana and a number sold small quantities of drugs.

The Red Shirts acquired a basement in a house near the park, which they fixed up with old furniture, psychedelic lights, posters, and a beautiful bar. Their frequent parties were huge events attended by several groups and gangs. The basement parties were frequently so dark that it took several minutes until a new guest could see the others. Many were so crowded that there was barely room to dance to the music that poured out into the streets along with the smell of marijuana. During one party a rumor started that the Aces were coming after the Lions. Many of the younger Red Shirts pledged to support the Lions if they came. The Red Shirts did not own guns because they spent their money from dues on parties, drugs (acid and marijuana), and liquor, but that night they had knives and broken bottles to fight with and were as enthusiastic as the Lions. A watch was placed outside and people kept running in and out. There were two false alarms but by 1 A.M. the excitement peaked and people started leaving for home. By 2 A.M. almost everyone had left.

Fred, a nineteen-year-old member of the Red Shirts, frequently interpreted actions as insufficiently deferential and reacted violently, though he felt that the Lions went to extremes, that they were slightly crazy. But he liked and respected the Lions, spent time with them at the park, and always invited them to the Red Shirts' parties. He could be provoked to defend his honor. On one occasion he claimed that several of the Senior Greeks were attempting to test his claim to precedence and he started carrying a knife. One day he crossed the street and was going to take a swing at a Greek but thought better of it and backed off. The following week, Fred said, a man walked up to him and told him he could not fight, so Fred punched him. Fred came to the park the following day with a black eye, telling everyone he leveled the man. Fred is often criticized because he swears and boasts in front of women, but according to one of the Lions, he knows when to fight. While he rarely seeks actively to demean others, he is usually ready to fight if he appraises a situation as demeaning to him and he is respected by the Lions for it.

While Fred's reputation as a tough fighter is frequently challenged, many of the image defenders have weak reputations as tough men and consequently are infrequently given less deference than they expect. It is hardly worth the effort for someone with an extensive reputation to place someone without a big reputation in a demeaning situation to which the latter would have to respond violently. The former would gain little even if he killed the other. The fight would be unfair. Contests of honor occur only between equals. On one occasion, Tiny, a gang member whose name reflected his size but not his fighting ability, beat up someone his size but with no reputation at all. His fellow gang members laughed at his rumpled shirt and disparaged him, calling him a "punk."

While Fred and many other image defenders are not as concerned as are image promoters about establishing a reputation based on fighting skills, they often are friends with promoters and associate with them. This involves some risk for an image defender, particularly one who is a good fighter. An image promoter may challenge him to enhance his reputation or may try to get him to join a gang. A gang sometimes assumes that an image defender wishes to join because he spends so much time with them. They may challenge him to a fight or, as many of the defenders are good fighters, an image promoter may intentionally insult a defender in order to enhance his own reputation. The Lions mistakenly thought that Monk wished to be a member of their group. Monk described the situation:

> The Lions surrounded me the other day by the park and
> Amos told me I was a member of the Lions 'cause I was at
> one of their meetings a couple of weeks ago but didn't show
> after that and he was going to beat me now. I told him I
> wasn't a member but just was around at a meeting. He
> stepped in front of me but I hit him hard in the face and
> ran. I guess he really thought I wanted to be a member
> because I dress like them and hang in the park.

While he is a good fighter and he liked several of the Lions as friends, Monk had little desire to challenge another's claim to deference. His refusal to join demonstrated his lack of respect for membership so that the Lions had to make a public effort to reassert their claim to precedence. Nevertheless, despite the threats, there was no confrontation. During a short tension-filled period Monk carried a gun and stayed away from the park. Several months later he began to associate with the Lions again as though nothing had happened. He joined the Army several weeks later.

Many of the image defenders rarely fight and some have never been in a gang. Rarely do they define situations of normative ambiguity as questioning fundamental properties of self. Since they do not interpret events within the framework of honor, they fight infrequently. That does not mean they necessarily have a poor reputation. Felipe was more interested in women and clothes than in reputation. He had never been in a gang but joined a group of friends on a street corner after school and work. He had success with women (several called him every evening), and his friends and classmates respected him for this. He was also able to dress well because he worked after school. His new coat was so nice that it was stolen twice from his locker in school. After the first time, he saw it on another student and got some of his friends to get it back. The second time it was gone for good. His reputation, however, did not extend beyond a small group of peers. According to his sister some other youths felt he was conceited and acted superior so they intentionally insulted him and he had to fight. He received a black eye and scratches. While he was still an adherent to the code of honor, his status was not dependent upon the result of his fights.

Ernesto dropped out of the public high school in his junior year because he frequently fought in response to situations he defined in terms of the honor code. (He then worked his way through a private school from which he graduated.) He claimed he was involved in at least one fight a week in public school and was also involved in incidents out of school. When his brother came home from the army and some young men made comments about his uniform, Ernesto and his brother got out some bats and chains and went looking for the offenders. When they found them, Ernesto and his brother smashed the offenders' faces so hard that they fell down the stairs and did not get up. Ernesto told this story with relish but did not fight after he left Tudor High. While unlikely to provoke a fight, he saw others as challenging him and, because he was a good fighter, many saw the possibility of beating him as a way of enhancing their reputations.

Carlos, on the other hand, had been a member of the Lions at fourteen but found membership of little interest. At eighteen he still

got into fights over challenges to his honor, about which he sometimes felt silly afterward. One night he was walking home along
32nd Street, having had quite a bit to drink, when he saw a Lion
who could barely walk. He leaned over to see if he could help. The
Lion must have interpreted his move as threatening and hit him in
the face. Carlos would not tolerate that insult and proceeded to fight
the Lion. Carlos's reputation was enhanced by his ability to negotiate with groups. He became a worker for a community organization and was active in the Chicano movement. He generally spent
time with those interested in politics but maintained the respect of
gang members and frequently associated with them.

Benny's reputation was that of a loser who tried hard but would
never succeed in anything. He and a few of his friends even tried to
form a gang. They appeared to be waiting for someone to challenge
them as they tried to look tough lounging on Benny's front stairs.
No one paid any attention to them and Benny and his friends quit
calling themselves the Sharks after several months. At fifteen
Benny liked to think that females found him attractive but none
would go near him. While he said that he would have defended his
honor if someone had breached a rule of interpersonal etiquette,
everyone ignored him even when he acted tough. When they mentioned him, it was with pity or laughter. He was a social zero who
could offend no one by his actions.

Most image defenders are not feared by others because they do
not actively provoke fights, but if they appraise a situation as
placing them in a demeaning light, they will fight. Image promoters
may prey upon the tougher of these youths because they can increase
their reputations by beating image defenders. The image promoters,
however, need not fear image defenders, because defenders do not
actively try to demean promoters. It is to the image defender's
advantage to avoid confrontation with the image promoter. As
many of the image defenders have good reputations, they are
respected by the image promoters and their orientation is considered legitimate.

The Rep Avoiders: Protecting the Honor of Females

Some youths rarely fight, but there is scarcely an individual who has not been in at least on fight or feels that he would never need to protect his honor or that of a female relative. Their concern is largely for virtue, the reputation of their family, not honor as a claim to precedence. These youths assiduously avoid defining situations as demeaning and excuse others' actions as poor taste. One spring there were many robberies at gunpoint at Tudor High. Pablo, a senior, declared that on principle he would not let anyone take his money without a good fight. He vehemently stated that it would be cowardly (unmanly, therefore, dishonorable) not to fight, even though he never carried more than five dollars. His sister told him he was crazy. Few of his friends really believed he would fight. His friends rarely congregated on corners but usually got together in front of someone's house. They kept to themselves and did not try to develop reputations so that they were not well known.

Roberto, an Ivy League college sophomore, rarely fought, but when he found out that some of the Nobles were making passes at his sister, he tore off after them. He "regained his senses," as he put it, when his brother grabbed him and pointed out their situation. The Nobles had guns and there were many more of them. "I guess," he said reflecting afterward, "that we all cannot be pushed beyond a certain point. We Chicanos all have hot blood so we explode at one point."

These youths are rarely confronted by potentially violent situations because image promoters seldom see the possibility of enhancing their reputations by challenging them. Most rep avoiders try to avoid such situations and are generally ignored by the others. They are infrequently challenged because they have no or little reputation and others would have little to gain. There is always a risk, however. Very few youths are never provoked to fight. For most, some situation—whether an insult to their manhood or the protection of a sister—makes them feel they must use other than verbal responses. Escaping violence entirely is not a real possibility for a majority of these males.

Not all members of one family fall into the same category or are even members of the same gang. It is not unusual to discover a tough image promoter whose brother has little to do with the streets. It is more than family background that establishes identity orientation. Moreover, strict orientation implies little about school or job performance. A youth's membership in a gang does not necessarily imply anything about his orientation in other settings.

One can be well respected either as an image promoter or as an image defender. Image promoters or defenders have little overt respect for rep avoiders and typically ignore them. Moreover, most rep avoiders are largely unconcerned about what those outside their small peer groups think.

There are few efforts to develop and maintain overt indicators of distinctions among groups like those Anderson (1978) found among the groups in and around Jelly's Bar. Nor are youths generally forced to join gangs. The youths here are using their scant resources to play out variations on how to be honorable. It is the common theme, honor, that runs through all the groups and links youths to older generations, and it is this code of personal honor, not social disability, as Short and Strodtbeck (1965) argue is the case among black and Anglo gangs, that sustains the traditions of violence. Self-esteem is an important factor in precipitating violent incidents. The self-esteem of the 32nd Street youths, unlike that of many other gangs studied, not only is based in a concern for peer group status but is defined in terms of a code of personal honor that finds grounds for a violent response in breaches of interpersonal etiquette and violation of a female relative's sexual purity. The meaning of violence, however, varies. The use of honor-bound definitions of situations to create a reputation among peers deviates from the expectations of most of the older generation. While parents understand why young men fight, they do not necessarily approve of their sons developing identities as "tough warriors" by gaining status from their fighting skills. Most of the time parents can ignore that identity because the youths respect their parents in their homes. This identity as a "tough warrior" makes it difficult at times for a youth to avoid a fight in school and for a gang member to give up gang status when he has achieved adulthood.

The gang provides a culturally acceptable peer group in which an individual can act as a member of a collectivity in the otherwise individualistic, competitive world of the streets. A youth can be a "tough warrior" and experience the solidarity of a collectivity. Membership is one way of mediating the tension between the basically competitive experience of getting a reputation and succeeding in school and the solidarity experienced within the family unit. There the collectivity is considered more important than the individual member.

6

Femininity and Womanhood:
Virginity, Unwed Motherhood, and Violence

One warm Saturday evening in late September, more than sixty people were drinking, talking, and listening to the latest soul music and love songs on their portable radios. The Lions were gathered around their bench and the Senior Greeks around theirs. Sally and her friends, like many others, ambled from bench to bench. It was peaceful; there were no rumors of enemy gangs and the only disagreements concerned who would go buy the wine and beer.

At 10:30, Sally and several of her friends headed out of the park to see if they could find someone to buy more pineapple wine. As they passed a bench where several of the Primroses (a female gang from the western side of 32nd Street) were drinking, Sally tripped over a member's foot and a violent struggle ensued. A circle immediately formed around the two young women, and when some young men attempted to separate them, the combatants clawed the men. Several other young women attempted to join the fray but were held back by their boyfriends. One young woman was so drunk and excited that friends dunked her head in the water fountain to calm her down.

Blood flowed as they struggled, pulled each other's hair, scratched, punched, bit, and ripped each other's blouses. The crowd was enjoying the scene and began to cheer them on. The women were separated for a few minutes, just enough time to wash their faces and to be encouraged by their friends. One of them grabbed a quart beer bottle and swung it at the other, but the bottle did not break. The fight continued for about another half hour until they were separated. Each side declared a victory and swore that a return engagement was necessary.

After the fight, four of the young men stood around recounting the highlights of the fight and laughing as they imitated the combatants. "Hey, why don't we ask Sally if she wants to join our club?" one of them joked. "Yeah," replied one of the others, "she probably could beat up dudes too—sure wouldn't take her out, she might beat me up."

Sally was punished by her mother and had to return home by six o'clock for three weeks, but she swore revenge on the young woman who had come to Sally's park and had "intentionally" tripped her, an act that demonstrated her disdain of Sally and her friends. The men's comments show that fighting enters into the evaluation of a woman's character, as do appraisals of her sexual activities.

Lydia and Fredo had been going out for nearly two years when she became pregnant. By her account she had fallen in love with Fredo when, at age fourteen, she first saw him at a party. He was the one man in the world for her, she said. Fredo fell in love with her several weeks later after she managed to see him several times. She claimed she could not resist his advances and they began having sexual relations several weeks later. Fredo was a Lion and spent much of his free time in the park with the gang. He worked and also made the honor roll at a Catholic high school. She would wait for him at her parents' home and they would come to the park together. When she quit school in the eleventh grade, Lydia began to spend more time with Fredo at his parents' home, where he shared the attic room with his brothers. Lydia felt very uncomfortable with his parents so they frequently went straight up to his room.

During her sixth month of pregnancy, she fell in a bathtub and lost the baby. She and all her girlfriends were very upset. Her mother cried, though originally she had not been happy to learn that Lydia was pregnant. Soon afterward, Fredo was arrested for assaulting an officer and sentenced to jail for six months. Lydia remained faithful, visiting him often.

She became pregnant a second time. Fredo procrastinated but finally decided that they would marry, claiming that Lydia had stood by him and he was sure it was his child. They married just before the baby was born. Lydia stayed home with her daughter for about a year before taking a job. Three years after the birth of her daughter she began to think about having another baby but was not sure she was ready.

These examples express elements of what a young woman *should* and *should not* do if she wants her identity to be evaluated positively. We have already demonstrated the symbolic importance for women of the values of virginity, motherhood, and submission to men. If young women were governed by the rules that follow from these cultural symbols, they would remain demure virgins until marriage and then would become submissive, loyal wives and mothers. However, the behavior of many young women is not in accord with these expectations. In fact, community residents have estimated that as high as 70 percent of young women lose their virginity before marriage. Many become pregnant before marriage, and some do not marry the fathers of their children. If the traditional expectations concerning a woman's sexuality were followed, these young women would be evaluated as having failed to develop an approved sexual identity. Others, like Sally, fight. This behavior violates traditional expectations concerning femininity, submissiveness, and passivity. Aggressiveness is uniquely embedded in the masculine identity of independence and domination. Traditionally, a young woman who engaged in sexual activities before marriage or who behaved aggressively would be evaluated as dishonorable or shameless.

A young woman today on 32nd Street can restrict her sexuality in the eyes of her audience, that is, remain chaste from their perspective while engaging in sexual intercourse and becoming a mother prior to marriage. But only a few young women appraise positively an encroachment into the male province of aggressive behavior. Why the dilemma between passion and virginity can be successfully resolved and the dilemma between aggressiveness and femininity cannot is closely linked to traditional notions of womanhood and femininity. The manner in which a young woman resolves these dilemmas becomes a salient aspect of her identity.

Freedom and the Male Advantage

Freedom from direct supervision is perceived as threatening to a young woman's chastity. It is the moral duty of the men in her family to protect the family honor by guarding her sexual purity. Since the men cannot live up to the responsibility, women inevitably must fail if they are not careful to avoid situations that might be tempting or appraised as tempting. Most young women have some freedom from parental supervision, whether that freedom is granted or taken surreptiously. In addition to school, there are parties, dances, weddings, and *tardeadas* (late afternoon dances that are generally well chaperoned) where young women can meet young men. There is always somewhere to go and usually some way to get there. A young woman may have to skip school or say she is going to a girlfriend's home, but freedom is possible. For privacy, an unsupervised apartment is frequently available. If not, the truck yards behind the park can be used.

When chaperones supervised all behavior, young women had few options. Now, with little supervision, she has the freedom to make her own decisions, constrained only by social expectations. While dances and parties are considered good places to meet young men, attendance at these affairs does little to maintain a young woman's identity as a virgin. All dress up in the latest outfits, do their hair, and apply just enough makeup so that people nearby can tell that their faces are made up, but no one can tell from a distance.[1] While there are frequently parents or relatives at weddings and cotillions, there are few at the dances, where rock bands play in dimly lit rooms (often the basements of local churches) and alcoholic beverages are sold to anyone. These are not affairs most parents willingly allow their daughters to attend, especially if parents are aware of all that goes on. It is extremely difficult for a young woman to maintain her identity as a virgin even if she does not engage in sexual intercourse.

According to traditional values, when two unmarried people engage in sexual intercourse, a man's gain is a young woman's loss. His status goes up as a man who can successfully seduce women and hers goes down as an unmarried nonvirgin. She is dishonored and her value is decreased in the eyes of the young men. Any man who marries her becomes a retroactive cuckold.[2] For example, Gilberto received much of his status from his skill with young women. The following is a brief description of his amorous affairs, which I validated from a variety of sources (male and female) or saw myself. He started seducing girls successfully when he was fourteen, and though he flaunted his affairs, they all stayed. He started seeing Alicia when he was fifteen and she was fourteen. They engaged in sexual intercourse within a few months, while he was still seeing several others. According to Gilberto, she was nowhere near the top of his list. Alicia, however, was in love with him and thought she was his special girlfriend. Within nine months she was pregnant. Gilberto was incarcerated about the time of his son's birth. When he failed to pay attention to her after he was released, Alicia blamed her infidelity during his jail term. All his friends thought his success at not being caught (marriage) was to be commended. The seventeen-year-old man Alicia married when she was twenty-four is both pitied and ridiculed. Only someone who was naive would marry her, it was claimed.

Gilberto continued to see many young women and it was rumored that he fathered another child. A year later he got a sixteen year old pregnant and married her. "She was pretty and I was the first one she had," he told people. Two years later he had already found a second apartment for his extramarital activities. I saw him when he was twenty-one flirting with a thirteen year old and asked him whether she was too young for him. He replied, "I'm just training her now—getting ready for the future." The other Lions listening to the conversation cheered.

Today young men need not fear drastic reprisals by the young woman's family. In the past they might have suffered grave injury when the family sought revenge to uphold its honor.[3] Today, unless she becomes pregnant, her family may know little of her behavior, except if she has a relative about her age who finds out through the rumor network. If she does become pregnant, then her parents probably will try to arrange a marriage. Most fathers will not risk a jail sentence by assaulting a daughter's lover. Because unmarried women have some freedom, and because the norms for them require virginity while the norms for men encourage seduction, the situation is problematic for women.

Maintaining an Identity as a Virgin

Without the institution of chaperonage, it is difficult for a young
woman to maintain her public identity as a virgin. The sexual attributes of a young woman's identity are continually questioned.
Adults and her peers attempt to check her biography[4] to determine
whether she is what she appears to be and what her motives are.
Even a young woman who rarely goes out must be exceedingly careful in her dealings with men in order to maintain her identity as a
virgin because there are always people who may try to discredit her
sexual identity. Some young women remain "pure" or are able to
maintain that image by rarely being seen in public and by spending
most of their time outside school or work at home. For example,
Linda rarely was allowed to attend a dance, and then only with her
parents. One semester she had hoped that her straight "A's" would
be enough incentive for her parents to allow her to attend a party for
the opening of the new community center. It was not. Rarely was
she permitted to visit her girlfriends' homes. Linda and young
women in her situation invite no suspicion about their virginity and
few rumors circulate about it.

Other young women take greater risks by being seen alone with
young men. This behavior itself *may* be enough for rumors to start
about their virginal status. Some young women are able to avoid
public scandal while going out because others appraise their public
actions as "not too obvious." For example, Sylvia maintained both
her virginity and her identity as a virgin though she went out
frequently and at twenty bought a car and was working. She and
several friends frequented some of the local lounges with Mexican
dance bands, but she was never seen going home with anyone and
never danced with any one partner for two consecutive songs. Even
two years later, when she dated one man steadily and finally slept
with him, she never flaunted her behavior. It was several months
before others were aware of what was going on. A woman's identity
rests not only on her own behavior but on her partner's actions and
others' appraisals and evaluations of her actions.

The risk of losing an identity as a virgin is increased by the fact
that young men gain status from revealing their sexual exploits to
their peers. Thus a young woman's loss of virginity may become

public even if she behaves "properly" in public. Annie thought she was safe; she had been going out with Humberto for several months and was in love with him. She went with him to his aunt's apartment one afternoon when the aunt was not at home and there they engaged in sexual intercourse. Three days later I heard about it from two different sources. Two days later, when I saw Annie, she had just discovered that everyone knew and she was very upset. Though maintaining one's virginity until marriage, particularly one's identity as a virgin, is the ideal state and has some real advantages, it is a reality for a minority on 32nd Street.[5]

Virginity at Marriage

Virginity at marriage generally ensures a church wedding; otherwise, the religious ceremony may be postponed or eliminated. It is argued that this makes divorce possible later if the marriage does not work out. While some couples do divorce, others marry in the church after a few successful years of marriage. Marriage in the Catholic church gives a woman greater assurance that her husband will continue to support her.

If a young woman was a virgin at marriage, her public character is evaluated positively and it is generally believed that she will remain faithful to her husband. The husband then demonstrates his respect for her by spending time at home and taking her out. If she was not a virgin at marriage, particularly if she is thought to have had sexual relations with men other than her husband, he may have less respect for her and is more likely to spend time away from home. Lena became pregnant at fifteen by her first real boyfriend. They maried but did not have a church ceremony. Her mother explained, "They're young and later if it works out they'll get married in a church, but we got to wait and see after the baby's born." They married in a church a year after the child was born, and while Lena's husband frequently went out "with the boys" on the weekends, he also stayed home regularly and took her out to dinner often.

This was unlike the situation that occurred after Rita gave birth to a son and married Dave, the father. Dave told several people that he knew he was not her only lover and several of their friends suspected that he was not the father of the child. Several people said that he was a retroactive cuckold. Her behavior after marriage confirmed this view of Rita in the eyes of his friends. She was constantly at the park with her baby and her friends. The baby was poorly dressed and his diapers were rarely changed. Dave came home infrequently and gave Rita little money for food. Only by seeing several other women could he reaffirm his masculinity, that is, demonstrate his independence and domination in the relationship in the eyes of his peers. A cuckold is not viewed as in control of the relationship. The loyalty of a husband is commanded not only by a wife's virginity at marriage but by the boundedness of her sexuality both before and after marriage as evaluated by her husband and other community members.

Normative Conflict: Chastity and Submission

Managing the appearance of virginity becomes markedly more difficult once a young woman has fallen in love and is seen by others as having done so. Not only does she experience the tensions between remaining a virgin and submitting to the sexual demands of her boyfriend, but others view submission to his demands as almost inevitable. They evaluate her actions within that framework. Each stage in the development of a relationship brings her closer to the crucial decision of whether or not to maintain her virginity and the time when others begin to question that virginity.

The process of falling in love passes through socially defined stages. At each stage people are more likely to view her as having engaged in sexual intercourse. The first step is defined by both men and women as "very loose" with "a lot of looking and a little casual conversation." One thirteen year old explained the procedures in building a relationship with young men:

> At first you just look at them a little more than the other dudes. Then you might say hello or go to a place where you know they hang out with their friends and kind of keep walking by and maybe talk to some of his friends that you knew before. Or maybe you know his sister. You kind of let the word out that you're interested. Then if the dude is

interested, he may come over to rap to you and you might decide to meet him someplace. Then maybe you can agree to see each other.

The second or "seeing" stage is usually reached when the two agree to meet or see each other in the usual hangout, but few obligations exist on either side. Any young man or woman can see more than one person at a time. A woman should not be blatant about how many men she is seeing, as others might question her virginity, though at this stage the risk that she will give in to his demands is appraised as small. Elena, a well-dressed and attractive fifteen year old, explained:

> If you're seeing someone, you can't blame him if he has some hickies [love bites] 'cause he can see anyone he likes but it really hurts if you start to really dig him. You can have hickies too, but some dudes get real mad. They think they own you when you are seeing them. Sometimes a dude will ask you right away to go out with him. That's your downfall. Both of you are tied then—no more hickies except from him. If a dude comes with hickies, you got to let him know you know he is not supposed to be seeing other chicks.

The third stage, "going out," is accepted by young women when they begin to fall in love. Going out with someone, as Elena stated, is appraised as their potential downfall. It becomes the triggering situation in which a young woman must decide whether to submit to the demands of her boyfriend, give in to her passion, and engage in sexual relations, or whether to deny his wishes and remain a virgin. Acting according to one norm precludes following the other. If chaperonage existed, this situation could not occur. Without it, each young woman must decide for herself and her decision, when suspected or known, has consequences for her identity. For example, Laura's behavior changed radically in a rather short period of time. She started seeing Tim just before her sixteenth birthday and frequently boasted about her flirtations with other men in front of a large audience. Frequently, when she and Tim agreed to meet, she failed to show up or arrived an hour late. While she was talking to him, she would break off the conversation to yell a greeting to another male. After two months there was an abrupt change in the relationship; she no longer looked at or talked to another male and would not come to the park until Tim arrived. He had asked her to go out with him and had told her not to go to the park unless he was there. Until that point, she rarely missed a day of school, but later, in order to please him, she attended several daytime parties with him and stayed out late, incurring her parents' anger. Five months later she came to me worried that she was pregnant. She was not then, but she became pregnant several months later. She explained that when a young woman is in love she ought to give in to her boyfriend's demands.

By giving priority to male domination over her virginity, a woman may diminish her standing in others' eyes. The dilemma is acute: either choice will satisfy one value and negate the other. If the young woman submits to his demands, releasing her passion, she heightens the risk of discrediting her identity as sexually bounded. If she refuses to submit she may be seen as too independent. Because others perceive her as being in love, they may suspect that she is engaging in sexual intercourse. Then, if she does not become pregnant, others may think that in anticipation of sexual activity she has used birth control.

Birth Control

A young woman who wishes to engage in sexual relations and not get pregnant can use some form of birth control. Several of the more practical local priests even condone its use. Birth control pills are readily available from local doctors and most young women have enough money to obtain them. Community residents also frequent a Planned Parenthood office in a nearby area. Young women are aware that birth control devices and information are available, yet few take advantage of this knowledge.[6]

Ignorance, lack of availability, or Catholic condemnation of the practice cannot account for the failure of the young women of 32nd Street to use birth control. Most young women are aware of birth control techniques from Planned Parenthood discussions in the school, from talks with older married sisters, from discussions among themselves, and from the media. One young woman told me that Planned Parenthood had given a lecture in her ninth grade class and that the students had spent several weeks afterward discussing the new information. Alicia, who was unmarried, and I had a long discussion one night about the pros and cons of various birth control techniques, their availability, and the chances of becoming pregnant with each. She could have given a comprehensive lecture on birth control and acknowledged that she had learned much about it from her married sister, who had two children and was taking birth control pills. Two months later, Alicia became pregnant with her second child.

While not an especially frequent topic of conversation, birth control is discussed among many groups of young women. Ivy acknowledged that her doctor had given her pills after the birth of her first child but she had thrown them all away (she did not marry her son's father). Several other young women who had already had children acknowledged having done the same thing. It emerged in this conversation that several of them also had married sisters who were using the pill after they had had two or three children.

A few parents even encouraged the use of birth control. One young woman, who at fifteen was staying out all night, refused to go to Planned Parenthood though her mother encouraged her to do so and her sixteen-year-old sister was pregnant, very uncomfortable, and unmarried. Though not all mothers would have approved of this woman's efforts to get her daughter to use the pill, many of the older women with large families of their own explained that they were tired of taking care of their daughters' or sons' babies. They saw the advantage, if their daughters were out of control, in encouraging the use of the pill. This is not the community norm.

The pill was not seen as inappropriate in all situations. In fact many of the young women who did not use birth control before becoming pregnant and marrying in 1974 were using it when I returned in 1977. After marriage they had decided to delay having more children. Ramona, who had given birth to a child before marriage, said that she and Enrique needed the money from her job so she did not want to have a second child. When their son was almost three, she began thinking of having another child, as did her sister, who had borne a child and married at the same time. I had similar discussions with several other young women who had refused to use birth control before marriage but used it afterward. Young women know about birth control and where to obtain birth control devices, and they do not make a blanket judgment about its use. Most young women, however, do not use it before marriage. The reason is linked directly to the local conceptions of virginity, passion, and motherhood.

Managing an Identity as a Nonvirgin

Though some women marry before they lose their virginity, many young women do engage in premarital sex, usually without birth control. Their identities are evaluated not just on the act of premarital intercourse but on how they handle their lack of virginity when it becomes known or suspected. Two factors are frequently salient in imputing meaning to a woman's actions: the type of account she uses to explain her loss of virginity[7] and her public behavior with men and toward motherhood. If she meets the criteria set by her peers, her sexuality is approved as "bounded" (restricted) whether or not she engages in premarital sex and becomes pregnant. There is no public scandal and she retains her high evaluation as chaste. If she fails to be appraised as meeting the criteria developed by her peers, if she is seen as giving in to her passion, her sexuality is viewed as "unbounded" and their evaluation of her falls.

Bounding Sexuality: Respect for Virginity

The estimation of a young woman's intention to engage in premarital sex forms the basis for evaluating the sexual attributes of her identity. Demonstrating her lack of intention to engage in premarital sex can bound her sexuality in the eyes of her audience of peers. To do so, she must account for her actions in terms of being in love and having given in to the sexual demands of her boyfriend in a moment of passion. Since she can be seen as having no control over her passion, the spontaneity of the situation and the need to submit to her boyfriend's domination can account for her actions. Others can perceive that she continues to respect virginity, that only under the conditions of being in love did she submit to the desires of her boyfriend. Her actions remain largely consistent with the values of virginity and male domination. Her sexuality thus remains relatively bounded in the eyes of peers.

Much careful work goes into trying to give the impression of bounded sexuality. Women develop very complicated maneuvers to avoid being appraised as overly forward or aggressive. Women usually refuse to telephone a man, because it might be interpreted as pursuing him. Several techniques of pursuit are employed: a group of female friends may casually pass by the place where the young men they like spend time, or a woman may mention to a friend of the boyfriend something she wants the boyfriend to hear. The car I bought during my third year of research became an excellent vehicle for casually cruising the community to look for the young men who interested the young women. Three or sometimes four females would climb into the car and would laugh and discuss the males as we drove by their usual hangouts. Every time they saw someone they knew, they would yell out the window, and if it were someone of particular interest, they would ask me to pull over. If they saw a young man one of them really wanted to see, they would frequently quiet down and ask me to drive around the block several times until he noticed. When no car was available, which was more often the case, several young women would get together and walk around the community. They would never go alone. Rarely does a young woman go anywhere by herself, even to the rest room at dances. Precautions are always taken to avoid being regarded as forward or independent.

An independent or aggressive appearance is avoided through rigorous standards of dress. Young women attempt to appear sexy by revealing very little. One young woman pinned the front of her blouse closed because the "V" was too low. When another young woman showed up at the park with jeans that had a zipper reaching from each cuff to her waist, she was criticized by many for her suggestive attire.

A woman's sexual identity is bounded not only by her premarital sexual activities but also by how her activities are interpreted by others. For example, Ramona had been going out with Enrique for more than two years when she became pregnant. Her sexual identity before marriage remained bounded because she demonstrated no intent to engage in sexual intercourse, expressed her love for him, and followed his wishes. Moreover, she did not publicly express her sexuality, refraining from seeing him much in public without others around and not talking with other men. Most who knew her believed she had been loyal to Enrique during that period, they were in love, and she had acted according to Enrique's wishes when she succumbed to his advances. Enrique perceived her as faithful to him, unlike his previous girlfriend, who had been seen with several men while she was supposed to be going out with him. In fact it was "proven," in Enrique's eyes, that she had been sleeping with another man. Ramona, to his knowledge and that of his friends, neither chased him openly nor saw anyone else during their relationship. Her sexuality was perceived by others as remaining bounded and Enrique married her as soon as she told him of her pregnancy. Three years later they were still married and had married in church before baptizing their child.

Unbounding Sexuality:
The Public Expression of Passion

Some young women do not interact with young men in a manner that might establish their sexuality as bounded. Because of what is seen as their public pursuit of men, they begin to be perceived as "loose women" and to obtain identities as women who openly display their passion (unbounded sexuality). For example, Alicia frequently acted in what seemed to be a bashful manner with men. She claimed that she was not going to get involved again and that she wished Gilberto (the father of her son) would leave her alone. Sometimes Gilberto would grab her and strike her, while she just gritted her teeth. However, her interactions with him at a party were perceived as flirtations. Many of her peers unsympathetically described Alicia as a "flirtatious bitch" who caused most of her own problems. They thought she threw herself on men and tried to "capture" (their word) a man. Some viewed her with disgust while others saw her as pathetic. One of the members of a male gang remarked, "She's OK, she helps us carry the heats, sneaks them into dances, and she'll take them off you if the cops are coming. Remember the times she hid that .45 in her kid's carriage with him asleep?"

Pierre, a member of the Lions gang, fathered her second child. She had tried very hard to develop a good relationship with him, but she complained publicly if she could not find him and constantly followed him around. He began to ignore her; yet she continued to come to the park, to discuss their relationship, and to ask for him. Finally she broke up with him, but she was already two months pregnant. Alicia could have gotten married only by not pursuing Pierre, as the pursuit was interpreted as a public expression of her passion and, therefore, her sexuality was unbounded.

Christina had a similar problem. A sixteen year old who was aware of how attractive others thought her, she constantly flirted with young men. While they loved her behavior, they inevitably made nasty remarks about her, and when she became pregnant after going out with the father of her child for over a year, he refused to marry her. Instead of staying home, she continued to flirt openly with a number of young men. The talk about her became more extensive and increasingly negative. Once her child was born, Christina came to the park every night, leaving the new baby with her mother or dragging her daughter along with a dirty face and wet diapers. Several of the young men claimed to be sleeping with her and the talk about her continued. At twenty-three she still had not found a husband but had borne a second child. Even the young women who used to be her friends did not associate with her anymore.

Men evaluate a woman's worth as a wife in terms of the boundedness of her sexuality. Open pursuit of a man illustrates unbounded sexuality. By overtly and aggressively attempting to lead a man into marriage, a woman alters the meaning of her sexual activity for her audience and reduces her worth in their eyes. Only exceedingly veiled and subtle pursuit of a man permits sexuality to be seen as bounded and her value as a mate to remain high.

The use of birth control by a single woman is an explicit indication of her intention to engage in sexual intercourse. She cannot explain such action as a moment of passion, the culturally acceptable account. Moreover, birth control is perceived as allowing a woman to engage in sex whenever and with whomever she pleases, the archetypal instance of unbounded sexuality. Her passion need not be controlled. She is also explicitly negating the importance of motherhood. Thus, the use of birth control is thought to provide consummate evidence of an unmarried woman's impurity.

There are young women on 32nd Street who choose this path and attempt to justify their behavior.[8] They declare that sex is fun and there is nothing wrong with enjoying themselves and avoiding pregnancy. They still live within the community, however, and experience the dilemma of their stance when they think about marrying and settling down. For example, Sally, June, Allison, Peony, and several other young women expressed a desire to enjoy themselves and did not worry excessively about the morals of most of the community members. Yet they were not completely immune to gossip about their moral reputations and were upset to find that a gang with whom they had spent a summer had spread rumors about them throughout the community. For their social life they went to another community where their sexual identities from 32nd Street were unknown. Sally declared:

> The dudes from the north side are finer anyhow. We go up
> Fridays and Saturdays and look for some fine-looking
> dudes. We're tired of the dudes from 32nd Street, know
> them all already and they don't dance. On the north
> side they got some fine dancers and they always ask you to
> dance. We want to have fun.

They know they would not be viewed as good wives and are aware of community evaluations of them. Willing to risk being seen as undesirable marriage partners, they are not fully convinced that the benefits of being sexually liberated outweigh the risks of failing to find a husband.

One of Sally's friends, Eugenia, married a young man from another neighborhood who, Allison explained, knew nothing of their reputations on 32nd Street. Discussing Eugenia's marriage and how she got the man to marry her, they wondered aloud whether they would be as successful. They were bitter about their reputations on 32nd Street and hoped they would not become like the women of the Senior Greeks, whose homes were always open to the men and who seemed to engender no more respect than a piece of property. If a Greek wanted to have a few of his buddies over for beer, these young women were expected to open their apartments and to make the men comfortable. In return they received some money, companionship, and the feeling of being important through their attachment to men with big reputations. However, these women garnered little respect from anyone, even the Greeks, most of whom had wives and children.

The public evaluation of unbounded sexuality allows a woman few options for marriage within the community. Unlike the women who are perceived as attempting to bound their sexuality, these women, viewed as making no such attempt, are seen as deviants. They have in part accepted the evaluations of their identities within the context of the local cultural system, yet they wish it were otherwise.

Motherhood: The Potential for Transforming Identity

For many young women, unwed motherhood becomes an important aspect of their identity.[9] Becoming an unwed mother still leaves open the question of the boundedness of a young woman's sexuality.[10] Motherhood allows her an opportunity to continue to negotiate an identity of bounded sexuality. Unwed motherhood is not the culturally approved route to becoming a mother—a young woman is expected to remain a virgin before marriage—but motherhood itself is a valid and esteemed role. In other words, motherhood can resolve both symbolically and existentially the dilemma between passion (unbounded sexuality) and virginity (bounded sexuality), where virginity, submission to men, and motherhood are all held to be important symbols of femininity.

By not pursuing men and by accounting for her lack of virginity in a culturally approved manner, a young woman may begin to transform her identity from a potentially "loose woman" to a good mother. Becoming a mother certifies that she has not used birth control and has achieved a desirable role. Transformation of identity describes the "destruction of one social object and the constitution of another" (Garfinkel, 1956: 421). It is more than the addition of new attributes to the former identity; others see the individual as a different person. Past interpretations of activities and motives are replaced by new ones.

To completely transform her identity to one of bounded sexuality in the eyes of the community, a woman must concentrate her activities around the role of mother, not openly pursue men, and explain her nonvirginity in terms of being in love and succumbing in a moment of passion. Her sexuality may then be seen as bounded, limited to and by the role of mother. Her past actions are reinterpreted in light of her new status as a mother. She can claim the symbol of motherhood.

This is more than an individual's rationalization of a deviant act. It is a cultural reinterpretation of her identity. The meaning of her experience is discussed and agreed upon by others and there is a collective reinterpretation of her essential nature. The act of becoming a mother does not, of itself, alter a woman's identity. Motherhood does not bound her sexuality if she attempts to blame her pregnancy on a lack of knowledge and if she is perceived as failing to take an active role in mothering. Continuing an active sex life effectively destroys any claims to the positive meaning of motherhood.

Laura became pregnant at seventeen but did not marry the father of her child. She stopped going to the park when her pregnancy became obvious. Six months after the birth of her baby, she started to work and left the baby with her mother during the day. Once or twice a week after work she took the baby to the park for an hour and talked to her female friends but to none of the young men. She rarely went to dances and never flirted openly with males. Whenever anyone mentioned her name, she was referred to as a good mother. Ivy, on the other hand, played a dangerous game. Several young men claimed that she was flirting too much in public. They agreed with one who said, "She's already got one kid now and she'll probably have another if she doesn't get married soon or stay inside. She's been fooling around a lot and people are beginning to talk." She was viewed as a borderline case because she did bring her child with her when she came to the park. Several of the Lions thought that it was wise of her new boyfriend (not the father of her child) to prohibit her from going to the park once they started going out. He married her a year later and she stopped going to the park altogether. Her sexuality remained bounded.

Margarita, at seventeen, was also able to maintain the bound-

edness of her sexuality when she became pregnant and did not
marry the father of her child. There had been rumors that she may
have used birth control. She had been going out with the same
young man for almost three years and had not become pregnant,
though everyone suspected she no longer was a virgin. She and her
boyfriend would wander away from crowds and disappear for a few
hours. After the child was born and she decided not to marry his
father, she stayed at home most of the time or stood in front of her
parents' house with her baby and talked with girlfriends. When her
name was mentioned, she was called a good mother and most people
approved of her not marrying her old boyfriend. It was frequently
predicted that some man would soon marry her.

When others view a young unmarried mother as not demonstrating responsibility and devotion toward the child, her salient
identity as a mother is disallowed. Elena, like Alicia, failed to
demonstrate publicly her dedication to motherhood. When she
brought her daughter to the park, Elena would frequently leave the
child with others and go off to sniff glue with friends. The Lions,
who liked Elena's company, claimed behind her back that she was
not a responsible mother and might hurt her daughter by her
foolhardy behavior. Failure to be appraised as a good mother
further denies the importance of motherhood, which makes it increasingly difficult to find a husband. Only marriage could bound
their sexuality, but few men in this community want wives whose
sexuality is evaluated as unbounded. If their sexuality has been
viewed as unbounded in the past, they remain suspect even when
they marry.

Insult and Violence

A young woman's identity is linked not only to her sexuality but to
her feminine behavior—forgiving, submissive, and not aggressive.
Aggressive behavior is masculine behavior and is expected only of
men.[11] Nonetheless violence is not unknown among young women.
Its acceptability, however, is limited. While weapons, except for an
occasional beer bottle, as in Sally's fight, are rarely used, some
fights become very violent. Gangs made up of young women fight

over men.[12] Some groups are affiliated with male gangs while others are independent, but they are in many ways different from male groups. While some have sweaters, their membership is much smaller and in general the groups are much shorter lived. Few are divided into age groups. Most do not have widespread reputations and none of the gangs congregate in large numbers on specific corners or park benches. Most of their time is spent planning and giving parties and baby showers for members. Some of the parties are attended by nearly fifty young women, and they all talk and dance. Most members drop out with marriage, unlike the young men. Many of the fights among women are not gang related.

For males decreased self-esteem is crucial in precipitating violent incidents. For them, self-esteem is embedded in a code of personal honor that includes all breaches of interpersonal etiquette. While young women also claim respect from their peers and are sensitive to aspersions cast upon their honor, they have no culturally acceptable response if their respectability is questioned.

Within this social context violence by women is typically viewed as unfeminine behavior. Some women, however, feel that fighting is a valid means to defend their honor. While many men enjoy watching women fight, they evaluate violence as unfit conduct for their girlfriends. Most young men do not want their girlfriends to be seen as out of their control, so they stop them from fighting. Ramona and Raquel, who were members of the Blue Dolphins, were asked to join a fight by members of another gang with whom they were friendly. Just as they were about to leave the park, Enrique and Rico grabbed the two and told them to stay where they were. Both were upset by their boyfriends' actions but followed their orders. A woman's fighting reflects not only upon her boyfriend's or her family's inability to control her but upon her lack of submissiveness, her lack of femininity.

While some women approve of violence as a response to an insult by a female, few would approve of a woman fighting a man. Such behavior would be unfeminine and would challenge someone who is superior, who has a "right" to domination. One summer afternoon the Lions were sitting quietly on their usual bench and the Lady Lions (not directly affiliated with the Lions) were running back and forth excitedly, waiting for the women with whom they had fought the previous day. The Lady Lions were proud of Esther, who had won her first fight. The Lions made sarcastic jokes about them and their "toughness." Four very tough-looking young women (seventeen or eighteen years old and not Chicanas) from another neighborhood arrived at the park at 6:30 announcing their willingness to fight on behalf of the Lady Lions. After an initial exchange of teasing remarks between the Lions and these new arrivals, Gilberto angered one of them enough that she called him several very insulting names. He returned the insults and she pulled a knife on him. Gilberto jumped off the bench and started prancing around in front of her waving his arms furiously and laughing. She lunged at him and he pulled further away and began to walk backward around the park. The other Lions cheered wildly but the Lady Lions seemed shocked at her aggressive behavior. When the outsider took a second lunge at Gilberto, he stopped interpreting this situation as a game. He grabbed her arm and took the knife away, punching her several times until she fell down. Coming back to the bench he stated, "I don't like it when girls try to act like men. If they do, you got to treat them like men."

Ironically threats or rumors of fights and actual fights at dances are just as likely to occur among the young women as among the young men. There are frequent rumors of female groups coming in from another community and frequent threats of violence. At one dance in a church basement, there were three fist and scratching fights under way simultaneously between women from 32nd Street and others from an area farther north. While no one was seriously injured, one young woman had a scratch across her face that may have needed stitches. After about fifteen minutes, with many of the males and some of the females holding others back, several young men broke up the fight. One young woman gave one of the peacemakers a black eye. Sometimes the scene of the threats and fights is the women's room. These fights are usually over attempts to steal a boyfriend, thus indicating a lack of expected deference.

Since there is no acceptable cultural resolution for this type of situation, there is some conflict about the evaluation of women who use violence. A minority of young women evaluate violence as justifiable under specific conditions, while most see it as unfeminine behavior. The men are amused by a fight among women but hold little respect for those who fight because aggressiveness reflects masculine behavior: physical expression of self is a masculine trait. Given the symbols of femininity, there is no way within the culture to resolve this dilemma without a complete revision of sex role expectations.

This chapter has explored the relationship between private actions and public knowledge concerning young women's sexual identities. By attempting to resolve the dilemma between the expression of passion and the maintenance of virginity, the young women have adapted the traditional values to meet the needs of a new situation. They have adjusted the values of virginity, submission to men, and motherhood. Moral order has changed. Each young woman in love must choose whether to remain a virgin or whether to submit to her passion in accordance with the demands of her boyfriend. Either choice can be highly esteemed. Submitting to her boy friend is much more risky, yet if she follows the expectations of her peers by accounting for her behavior in terms of a moment of passion, by not pursuing men, and by becoming a good mother, she maintains the boundedness of her sexuality. Becoming an unwed mother can be explained only in terms of the legitimizing values associated with femininity and womanhood, not in terms of ignornace or lack of birth control.

A woman's role expectations remain firmly embedded in the traditional symbols of femininity and womanhood and are kept separate from the male province. When actions cross sexual boundaries, as in the open expression of passion or the use of violence, there is resistance to cultural change. A scandal is created when a woman's participation in such activities, for example, the use of birth control and violence, becomes public knowledge. The use of birth control places a stigma upon a young woman and alters her identity, not because of moral convictions against birth control but because its use reflects unbounded sexuality, the open expression of passion, which is legitimate only for men. Moreover, birth control denies the importance of motherhood. Using birth control can be regarded as irrational within this cultural context, which views such behavior as deviant.

A woman's public expression of aggression, particularly

violence, is negatively evaluated. Violence is a male prerogative and is justified to maintain male honor, but a woman must uphold her honor by controlling her passion, either by remaining a virgin in the public's eye or becoming a good mother. Violence is the antithesis of femininity. Most of what is considered masculine—violence, aggressiveness, domination, and the uncontrolled expression of passion—is the opposite of femininity—submissiveness and controlled passion (bounded sexuality).

With those cultural constraints on the woman's role, the public does not readily accept young women who attempt to succeed in the individualistic, competitive worlds of education and employment. Remaining submissive and dependent and succeeding in the world outside the family and the local peer group are difficult. Some young women retreat from school or economic success and concentrate on family and peer relationships. Others balance the worlds of family and school or work. Others break with the traditional expectations of womanhood and femininity and attempt to succeed in the competitive spheres of higher education and work, frequently causing public scandals in their pursuit of the American dream.

7

Education and School Authority

Wearing their caps and gowns, the more than four hundred eighth grade graduates arrived in yellow school buses at the new downtown auditorium. Confusion and enthusiasm spread among the graduates and more than one thousand guests, who wandered around taking pictures. All were dressed for the occasions, the graduates in new dresses or suits, the family members in their best clothes. Many of the parents took the day off from work.

For more than fifty minutes the graduates marched single file into the hall. After the speeches and award announcements each student's name was called as everyone clapped. The loudest and the most prolonged cheers were for each of the graduating Lions. Fifteen of the Lions attended the graduation wearing their gang sweaters. That evening they had a celebration in the park.

Though eighth grade graduation was obviously an important event for the Lions, this does not mean they were careful about attending school regularly. Most of the Lions in the audience were high school dropouts, and those who were still in school had attended the Red Shirts' midweek party, where more than two hundred guests had been entertained in the course of the day. While this party was more extravagant than the usual daytime parties, it was not uncommon for youths to skip school to attend small parties or go downtown to the early movies. Moreover, threats or violent incidents were not uncommon in school. One gang member dropped out of high school after he had a gun stuck in his back twice in one week. One young woman who was not a gang member was surrounded by five female students and physically threatened. She was saved when several of her friends arrived and threatened her attackers.

137

These events exemplify some of the experiences in and attitudes toward education and the schools. On the one hand, those who achieve in the educational sphere are supported in their endeavors. On the other hand, many of the students in the Marsh Upper Grades Center and the high schools spend very little time in school. The majority never graduate. Why do youths drop out when they value education and receive some peer support for pursuing it? Why is there so much violence in the schools when students know how to act according to school rules and do so most of the time? This chapter explores some aspects of the disparity between the positive evaluation of education and the negative expectations that encourage students to disrupt school and drop out.

Education and the American Dream

Few youths criticize anyone for doing well in school or fail to acknowledge an individual who performs unusually well there. When Ronny, a Lion, graduated from parochial high school at sixteen, there was a celebration at the park. Some youths are criticized by their peers if they drop out just before graduation. The Lions do not have a very good educational attainment record, yet they were critical of Nico, who had been on the honor roll, for dropping out of parochial high school before graduation. The others claimed that they would not have dropped out at sixteen had they been doing so well and been so close to finishing. While most gang members do not go further than the ninth or tenth grade, they support the value and goals of education.

Other nongang youths in the community also support the idea of education, yet few of them are able to graduate either. People throughout the community say that education is good and that one should finish school. Promises by dropouts to obtain a general education diploma (GED) are often fulfilled. Young people encourage one another to pursue education and sometimes tell one another that education is necessary to get ahead. General approval of education, however, is not sufficient motivation to persuade most students to finish high school.

Explanations of Failure

Many studies have examined the failure of the poor in the inner-city educational system: some blame the nature of lower-class culture,[1] others blame socialization,[2] while still others blame the structure of the educational system at the district, the school, or the classroom level.[3] The problems of educating children whose parents are un-educated[4] and who attend inner-city schools[5] are well documented, as are the special problems of the Spanish speaking in English language schools.

Within the school, it is argued that tracking is independently related to achievement and delinquency whether measured in terms of college applications and admissions (Alexander, Cook, and McDill, 1978) or intelligence quotient (IQ) (Rosenbaum, 1975).[6] According to Alexander, Cook, and McDill (1978), curriculum content, pace of learning, students' belief or lack of belief that they will achieve, and the degree of encouragement by peers, teachers, and counselors vary across tracks and are responsible for different educational aspirations,[7] though there is little data on how the aspects of tracking actually affect educational outcomes. Studies of classroom interactions of students and teachers have found that teachers' perceptions of ability shape treatment of the youths in such a way as to fulfill those perceptions.[8] In other words, those who are defined and treated as less intelligent do worse than those who are defined and treated as intelligent, no matter what the measured intelligence level. In general, the specific context of schooling seems to be instrumental both to individual and to group achievement.

To clarify the relationship between the school, the lack of achievement, and the violence on 32nd Street, it is necessary to understand the legitimacy of a school's authority to different groups of students, that is, how students interpret and evaluate school attendance. Authority here refers to asymmetrical relations in which superordinates command subordinates;[9] legitimacy (authority worthy of support) is imbedded in the cultural context of the meaning of authority and justice.[10] For authority to be seen as legitimate, the values embodied by the system of authority must be seen as worthy of endorsement, that is, deemed rational (good means to a valued goal) and reasonable (making sense in terms of individuals' perceptions of themselves and their goals). Therefore, for a positive, or at least nonantagonistic, evaluation of school authority to exist, the authority of the school must be viewed as both rational and reasonable.

Approximately 30 percent of the 32nd Street youths are graduated from high school. Many of them do not attend the local comprehensive public high school, Tudor. Though education is highly evaluated both by parents and by students on 32nd Street, students do not find the local public schools either rational or reasonable. Moreover, peer group expectations encourage skipping classes, dropping out, and violence within the school.

The Context of Authority Relations

Students are typically in a subordinate position in school. The school personnel make the rules, set out what they are to learn, decide their grades, and determine whether they may remain in school. In the Marsh school, Tudor High, and Tudor's ninth grade extension school, the 32nd Street students are subordinate not only to staff but to other students as well: they are placed in the lowest tracks and are consistently given poor grades. Only 10 percent of Tudor High students were in regular or honors tracks; the rest were in special classes for slower learners, the poorly adjusted, and the educationally handicapped. Few students in any track receive much above a "C" average.[11] Education is not only an abstract goal for success in the American dream, it is an experience formed by a particular school system, school, set of classrooms, teachers, other school personnel, and peers. It is the authority of a particular school and its personnel that is deemed legitimate or not, not education as a valued means to economic and social success.

Judging Rationality

Remaining in school is generally viewed by the wider society as the means to a variety of goals: certification for a job, survival skills for a complex modern society, and education for good citizenship. For most 32nd Street youths, the few payoffs for remaining in school often do not seem worth the investments required: few graduates obtain good jobs, few meet their future mates or make new friends in school, and few learn much in their last years in school.[12] It is not viewed, however, as totally irrational to stay; there is not much to do for a student who drops out.

People used to think that a high school graduate could get a job not available to a nongraduate, but from what these youths can see, graduation assures them little. Moreover, in Tudor, few courses train students for the highly technical jobs of today. The youths of 32nd Street see their friends who graduate employed in the same un-skilled or semiskilled jobs as the nongraduates. It is common to hear stories of those who graduate and work for less money than those who dropped out. The Lions frequently cited the case of Ronny, who graduated from high school and got a job loading trucks at minimum wage and Len, who did not finish the tenth grade, got a similar job for more money. Acceptance into skilled unions with well-paid jobs is infrequent even with a diploma. The relationship between finding a well-paying job and high school graduation is ambiguous to most youths.[13]

Moreover, there is little counseling by school personnel about staying in school, careers, or further education. The ratio of four hundred students to each counselor is overwhelming to the counselors. The students are often not informed about available options, and the counselors often do not communicate well with them. One of the counselors claimed:

> We don't have time to deal with the kids. They tell me
> they're bored . . . what can I do about it? I tell 'um they
> can't be bored and school is interesting. What can I do with
> four hundred students? I don't understand their problem.
> We got problems here with gangs and kids busting up the
> place. That's the worst problem here.

Most of the staff worry more about violence than about education and few help students make academic or career decisions.

The counselors at Tudor High are aware also that the teachers and counselors at the Marsh school have already advised many of the most promising students to attend either parochial schools or the better vocational training schools. All eighth grade students in the city receive information on vocational schools and their entrance requirements, but only a few of the students, those whom the teachers evaluate as successful, are actively encouraged to go. Some of the students are already so far behind in reading and math that they do not meet the minimum requirements for vocational schools. One teacher started a scholarship program to send students to expensive parochial schools. If students wish an alternative to Tudor, they and their parents, who have little experience with education or the Chicago bureaucratic school system, must pursue alternatives without assistance. Only a few do.

The young women find it no more rational to stay in school than do the men. The majority have few career aspirations. It is not that they are oriented toward the present, but motherhood, not work, is perceived as salient in their future. If the economic situation of the males does not change, however, many of these women will probably have to work. The only reason to stay in school, some young women believe, is to find a husband, but the payoff is limited. Most of the young men drop out and few social events revolve around the school. The place to meet young men is at local community events. Youths who socialize in school and eat lunch together are those who meet and are together outside. Rarely did youths say that they met nice people in school. Friendships may develop in the Marsh Upper Grades Center but generally not in high school.

The organization of the typical class—the teacher lecturing and asking questions and the students responding—encourages and rewards public competition rather than cooperation and private accomplishment.[14] This makes many female students hesitate to respond. Public identification as a "brain" can cause problems for a female in her relationships with her male classmates. Rosana, an attractive and intelligent eighth grader, found no one to take her to the class prom. During one discussion of whether to wear long or short dresses, she broke down in tears. Her friends explained to her that she should try not to act too smart in front of the male students. One of her friends then asked her brother to take Rosana, but he said she was too smart for him and all his friends would laugh. Being perceived as academically superior to others does little to enhance a female's relationship with males.

The payoff in terms of increased intellectual skills for each additional year of schooling is minimal for most of the youths. The reading scores decrease relative to national standards with each additional year of schooling. Many experience their classroom time as time wasted. An example of such an experience comes from one eleventh grade regular level English class. The teacher read Chaucer aloud to the class for the entire period while many slept. He did not require them to read or write anything until the second semester, when he asked for a term paper. Most lower level English classes require less. The students do not seem to learn much by staying in school and most students are aware of this. As one student told me, "We just stay in school because we have nothing better to do. It gets boring to stay home all the time and where can we get a job at sixteen?" Many others echoed this young woman's words.

Many teachers are appraised as not trying to teach anything and being poor at explaining things. Some evidence bears out this appraisal. Several ninth graders failed algebra the first semester. After being tutored for several weeks, they all passed the next semester. Moreover, the students think the teachers are not interested in teaching. One student explained, "Most of the teachers are here to collect their pay and go home. They don't like teaching us. One teacher told us, 'I get paid to sit here. I don't care what you do in class.' Man, she didn't even want to try to teach us." One junior said, "Most teachers don't give any homework 'cause it means they would have to correct papers." It is easy money for them, a third student claimed.

Those teachers who do not maintain discipline, whether through lack of skill or effort, are seen as not caring what goes on. The following points came out in a discussion with a ninth and two eighth graders who frequently skip classes. They talked about who the good teachers were and what was good about them. A bad teacher loses control of the class and teaches little. One of the eighth graders explained, "I hate Mr. Saxon's class 'cause all we do is throw paper and talk. He threatens us all the time but it doesn't do any good. There's nothing he can do to us and we can't learn anything." Some teachers are perceived as being drunk or on drugs and unable to say anything that makes sense to the students.

There are some good teachers who are strict but fair, teach

something, and try not to disparage students. One teacher who was considered good was also seen as very strict by many students. The teacher clearly indicated what work was expected and the consequences if the work was not completed. She then followed through. Independently, several students claimed that they had really learned something from her.

Their lack of basic skills confronts the students daily. For example, Ronny brought a crossword puzzle to the park and was reading the questions aloud while Nico helped. Several other Lions gathered around but could not get any of the answers. Enrique, who had gotten as far in Tudor as Nico had in parochial school, became very frustrated when he could not answer any of the questions. It was not that he did not want to learn or could not. He was very articulate and several weeks after this discussion he started classes and got his GED.

These are the experiences not of isolated individuals but of youths who continually communicate. Discussions concerning individual experiences become collective definitions and expectations. The lack of benefits from attending class is widely recognized and discourages any commitment to attend class and finish school. With the extensive cutting and dropping out, much of the youths' lives occurs outside school. Cutting classes and dropping out of school to be with friends become generally acceptable. This acceptance helps to create a social world where it is difficult not to cut or drop out. Individuals who spend so much of their time in an age-graded universe find it hard to ignore the expectations that regulate social relationships within it. For example, Anita found it very difficult to stay in school when her boyfriend dropped out. Not only did he like to go to the movies or attend parties during the day, but he kept teasing her about her "brains" and asking her whether she was going to stay in school forever. Her dilemma was resolved when she became pregnant in her senior year; her boyfriend married her and she dropped out.

As the possibility of academic success appears to diminish, youths increasingly turn to their peers for confirmation of their self-worth. Because social life goes on outside the school, a youth must cut school to be with friends and be accepted in peer groups. Celia, a high school freshman, explained, "We went downtown this afternoon and to the northside. They got real nice shops there and me and my friends only cut sixth, seventh, and eighth periods. That isn't too bad. My mom doesn't let us go after school." Then Linda, her younger sister, claimed:

> Me and my friends cut out from Marsh school to go to
> Fasties for lunch. We buy each other burgers when we got
> money. You know this new dude came with us yesterday. I
> only had a coke but the others had burgers and he paid for
> everything! It's fun over there then we don't go back [to
> school] sometimes. I really was going to stay in school today
> but some of my friends came by my locker and asked me if I
> wanted to see this movie this afternoon.

Letty, a seventh grader who received all "U's" (unsatisfactory) on her report card except in two classes, said, " 'Cause my friends are not in them. We talk all the time and fool around in class." Letty, too, is always cutting classes.

The result of excessive unexcused absences is automatic failure. To repeat is to take the same classes that were boring the first time. Cutting and dropping out become accepted, encouraging similar actions in others and thus perpetuating the phenomena. The students have small commitment to an institution that seems to give them little in return for their efforts.

Judging Reasonableness

The inconsistency between their self-perceptions and the way youths are viewed by school personnel is great. Both individually and collectively the students have a much more positive image of themselves from activities and interactions outside the school than they have of themselves inside the school. This gap is experienced frequently in interaction with the school personnel. Moreover, school authorities do not try to encourage attachments to the school through activities such as sports, student council, clubs, or dances. The only school activity by which students may judge themselves is academic achievement. In view of the limited alternatives and failure, it is not surprising that situations of normative ambiguity arise in which a youth must decide whether to define an interaction as insulting and demonstrating lack of respect for him, an offense to his honor, or whether to ignore the incident in the context of getting ahead. It is difficult for most youths to say, "I'm smart and what you have said is dumb, so I can ignore it" given the generally poor achievement. It is much easier to take offense and either hit the offender (an honor-bound response) or drop out (an adaptation to the poor educational situation).

Many of the youths believe that teachers "have an attitude" toward them (look down on them). This belief is supported by many statements teachers make about students. One male Marsh school teacher explained to me that all his students were "potential killers." Another teacher, a member of an extreme right wing group, explained that she had to "tame the natives" by eradicating their culture and instilling in them their duty to the American flag. Propaganda leaflets that she gave out as class prizes explicitly claimed that the white race was supreme. While these are extreme examples, other teachers' actions reflect similar feelings. Rosita explained how she reacts without explicitly violating any rule when a teacher demeans her publicly in class. "When a teacher tells you to sit, you do, no matter where you are—on a desk, the floor, or a dude's lap. When she says take your gum out of your mouth and throw it away—take it out with your fingers and throw—particularly at someone you know will scream." Teachers appear continually to question the moral character and intelligence of their students.

For example, at fifteen Felipe failed his sophomore year because of too many unexcused absences and was scheduled to repeat the same classes. The counselor added a course in shop, but Felipe wanted an art class. He was informed that it was impossible. He told his counselor about his interest in art and was told that it did not matter. He dropped shop and expressed pessimism about whether he would actually stay in school much longer. A few months later he quit.

Students also notice the rapid exit from the community of school personnel at the end of the school day and their lack of attendance at major local events. This indicates to the youths that their teachers think the neighborhood is not worth spending much time in and that the residents are not interesting or worthwhile people. By contrast, a teacher who spends time after school and on weekends visiting his students is very popular.

The students know that many of the teachers and administrators are completely unaware of their lives outside school or outside the classroom while in school. Frequently teachers cannot identify gang members and do not understand what it means to be a member. Many gang members use their good manners in class most of the time. Harry, a Lion, graduated from Marsh with the title of "best-dressed male." When the award was bestowed upon him at the prom, few teachers knew that he was a Lion or that he was out back drinking wine, so that he never received the award.

Teachers are also unaware of how students may interpret their behavior. When a teacher encourages a student in front of others, they may feel the teacher is placing the encouraged student in the same category as the teacher, above the other students. Students who are rewarded publicly and who do not compensate by trying to act exactly like their peers often have trouble with classmates. Amelia's teacher had been paying too much attention to her. When she left her books on the desk and went out of the room, her books were ripped to pieces. No one volunteered the names of the students who had done it. Making a student look better than other classmates is appraised as demeaning to the others.

Even teachers who try very hard at their jobs suffer from the atmosphere generated by poor student-teacher relationships. One senior sympathizer with some of the teachers who try but are defeated by the apathetic and sometime violent atmosphere in the school:

> They got a few good teachers here who try to care but some-
> times we make it hard by not trying. Most of the time the
> teachers don't care what we do as long as we are quiet. Lots
> fall asleep. The teachers don't care 'cause there is less
> chance that someone will start a fire in the classroom . . .
> you know that lots of classrooms have been burned. That
> school is waiting to be burned down.

Tracking also tells youths that they are not very smart. One very articulate young man in his early twenties analyzed his educational experiences. An excellent drug counselor, he had an extensive vocabulary of psychological terms but had never finished the seventh grade. He explained that he had always had counseling skills but had been a bully and gang member. While he knew that schooling was the rational means to obtain his goals, his school experiences were so demeaning to his self-respect that even now he finds conventional learning too frustrating. In seventh grade, when he was moved from the lowest level academic classes to the social adjustment class composed of students no one else could handle or wanted, he started acting tougher. "Well you had to be someone. I did not want to be known as a dumb loser," he explained. Bright as he is, he is unable to overcome those early school experiences. After working at a community counseling job and doing very well in the counseling training program, he quit, in part because of the reports he had to write and the difficulty of some of the books he was supposed to be reading. He ended up back on the streets without a regular job. For him the demands of the school were unreasonable, though he thoroughly believed in their rationality. Even when the rationality became salient, the unreasonableness of school left him so scarred that he failed again. Placement in the lowest tracks directly confronts the issue of academic ability, but placement in the social adjustment class also questions moral character.

It is not uncommon in this country for extracurricular activities, to take precedence over academic ones.[15] These activities, whether athletic teams, drama, student council, or fraternities and sororities, have a strong expressive element; membership says something about who a person claims to be (Schwartz and Merten, 1968).

Not only do their academic experiences consistently tell 32nd Street students that they are unintelligent, but there are few other school activities on which to evaluate themselves. At Tudor High sports are not emphasized and there are few clubs, pep rallies, or dances. The only group that receives any support or is validated as a select group is the chorus. Even school dances are afternoon events exclusively for registered Tudor students. There is little expressive activity to link the youths to school.

Students, tired of the lack of school enthusiasm, proposed to paint an ethnic history mural on the shabby Tudor High walls, but the administration denied them permission. Instead, the students had to be content with the dull, dirty walls, broken windows, and broken overhead lights, which gave the school the look of an old factory.

Normative Ambiguity and Violence

Many youths evaluate school attendance as barely rational. This means that many of them lack a strong commitment to do the things they must in order to graduate. Moreover, the school experience is deemed largely unreasonable because school personnel question the moral character and intelligence of the students. In this context students are particularly sensitive to the actions of others that appear not to demonstrate the respect they think they deserve. A situation of normative ambiguity exists. While students often do excuse the behavior of others as merely unintentional and awkward, on other occasions they are likely to see actions as intentional slights whether the antagonist is another student or a school employee. In the abstract, students do not evaluate fighting in school highly. But because there is little commitment to finishing school, and because most students find it difficult to dismiss the actions of others as merely ignorant, violence is often their response. When their honor has been impugned, being suspended appears relatively unimportant. Enrique claims:

> I did real well the year I was in Texas in school. . . . But at Tudor it's different. There's too many other things happening. You got to protect yourself. I just couldn't handle that last year and tried to transfer to another district but they wouldn't let me.

He dropped at the end of his junior year after getting into several fights. Ham, also a Lion, dropped out his junior year claiming:

> Shit, I nearly was blown away [shot] in school yesterday. This dude pulls out a .45 and sticks it in my stomach. You know you can't trust them chicks. They pack the heats [carry the guns] for the dudes. That chick [who handed the young man the gun] was supposed to be going out with a friend of ours.

Women, too, defend their honor in school. Ramona was suspended in the seventh grade for fighting. "All these girls kept hassling me and I let them have it. Me and my girls were pretty tough. I guess we started a lot of fights." She never finished the eighth grade.

A tense atmosphere pervades the school. Even those who wish to avoid confrontations are frequently unable to do so. Siegfried, an intelligent and strong Anglo, was driven out of Tudor by the violence. "It was scary for me 'cause dudes would try to jump me all the time. Once I got beat up by two dudes. I never had anyone to back me so I quit." He went to a private high school and did very well. One time he asked me what it meant to have an IQ score of 134.

The behavior of staff members is subject to similar interpretation. When a staff member suggests that a student is stupid or childish, the student may hit the staff member, risking suspension. The following history illustrates this situation. Jesús had been in the honors section at the Marsh school, but for some reason he was placed in lower track courses in the ninth grade and assigned work that he had already completed. When he entered the tenth grade he was placed in basic and essential classes and was so bored that he attended only enough classes to pass everything except English. That summer session he missed more than the permissible number of days and failed basic sophomore English again, but he passed regular junior English the following year. Jesús was expelled from school on his sixteenth birthday by a counselor at Tudor for unexcused absences. He called his mother and told her about his predicament. When the counselor, overhearing the conversation, laughed at him, Jesús punched him.

The counselor had added insult to injury by laughing, which indicated that he did not respect Jesús. Every year the school system told Jesús that he was stupid and a failure.[16] Though he is extremely articulate and could have argued or ignored the incident, defining the counselor as ignorant, Jesús felt that the only way he could regain any dignity was to punch him.

There is little incentive to follow the conventions of proper school deportment. Moreover, because people fail to validate the students as moral and intelligent, academic skills become useless as criteria for evaluating the students' worth. Under these conditions students turn to their peers for confirmation of self-worth, for validation of their identity. It is not surprising then that youths leave school to associate with their peers and to confirm their self-worth. Nor is it surprising that they maintain their honor by defining breaches of etiquette in school as adversarial.

Graduation: Drift and Some Legitimation of Authority

A few are graduated, even from Tudor. Some graduates appraise and evaluate their experiences differently from nongraduates, while others just drift through. The difference in experiences is due to a wide variety of factors: characteristics of the students, teachers' appraisals of the students, types of interactions with school personnel, organizational patterns, chance occurrences, and many others. What concerns us here are some of the situational and organizational factors that allow youths to define their school as rational and/or reasonable and hence school authority as legitimate. In some parochial and vocational schools, collective definitions of legitimacy develop, whereas at Tudor most youths who evaluate school authority as legitimate arrive as such conclusions individually.

Tudor High

Some youths avoid substantial trouble and do just enough work. Others have career goals or a particular spark that is noticed and encouraged by teachers, who pass along the information about them to other teachers.[17] Because so little work is required, it is fairly easy to do enough to graduate. A student need only attend school the minimum number of days, learn something, and stay out of trouble in school.

For those who have had the support of teachers and have developed specific career goals, success is possible. Some youths develop reputations as being very smart from the time they enter school. By the time they enter the fifth grade, their reputations precede them into the classroom. One, so labeled, told me: "I always smiled and I guess I was a cute kid. I was kind of shy, but the teachers always helped me out and encouraged me. I didn't cause any trouble. I was always thinking and asking questions when I was small." He was constantly encouraged by his teachers and by the time he reached the seventh grade he knew he wanted to attend college. Teachers took him and several óf his friends on special weekend trips to museums, movies, local universities, and special events.

Other students may not be directly encouraged by teachers but have developed enough respect for their own academic skills from relationships with professionals outside the school to demand what they need from school. One student had decided during the summer following the ninth grade that she and her best friend would go to college together. This decision was made as a result of working with a preschool teacher in the Neighborhood Youth Corps. Three days before graduation from Tudor she found out that she was failing because of unexcused absences. She graduated as scheduled only because she cajoled her English teacher into passing her.

Involvement in school-related activities gives the participants some sense of self-worth within the school context. The few who become involved in school activities often graduate. Esperanza and her brother were the only two out of eight siblings who graduated though all had won prizes in elementary school. Esperanza and her friends were involved in political activities in school: starting newspapers, leading political movements, and organizing campaigns for student council. Though often suspended (once for organizing a session in school on venereal disease and birth control, other times for tardiness, too many absences, and cutting classes), she did enough work to pass most of her regular classes and was interested enough in her nonacademic school activities to view school as both rational and reasonable. Moreover, her friendship group was based in school and the confirmation of her self-worth complemented her school performance.

Many students drift through, managing to pick up some skills and stay out of trouble. Caesar graduated from Tudor in four years. He claims he never did any work but because he was able to read and write a little, and because no one else did much work either, he was able to do very well. "Some of my friends were in clubs but they didn't go into the lunchroom or spend time in the hallway [where many of the confrontations took place]. They passed." He also had a specific career goal: he wanted to join the city police. Pablo, a member of one of the toughest gangs, agreed that a student had to "know how to take care of himself" to avoid trouble in school. He had no goal and said he never thought about graduating but did so by chance, as did several of his friends. He was drafted and went to Vietnam.

Some youths are helped to drift through by friends who have collectively evaluated school as legitimate. Lucy graduated after repeating her senior year. She said she was not really interested in school and never got good grades, but she was a very talented artist and was allowed to take an art course in her senior year. She attended one of the city junior colleges. "I didn't dig school much but I kind of had to go. There isn't much else to do and all my friends [including her boyfriend, who received a large scholarship to college] were in school. I knew it was important to finish. I just managed to do it the second time. We cut so much."

Graduation from Tudor does not mean that a student is able to read on a high school level. One of the counselors told a student that her acceptance at a local university was provisional; though she scored among the top students at Tudor, her reading was at the ninth grade level. The student did graduate from college with a respectable grade point.

Catholic Schools

Catholic school attendance is not possible for everyone because of tuition, which reaches $1,200 in some schools. Even if youths work after school, their salaries are often needed for food or rent. Those who attend Catholic schools generally view school not only as more rational (they know they will be able to read and write when they finish) but also as more reasonable, even though the teachers are strict, uniforms are required for females, and behavior codes are specified.[18] While many of the students question some of the Catholic morality that is taught and the strict discipline, the students expect such demands from church personnel. At St. Catherine's Girls' High no obvious ability groupings exist. Nonetheless, the dropout rate of the preselected group in St. Catherine's was estimated by one senior to be about 30 percent in her class.

These students are not different from those who attend Tudor High. They interact in the same context outside the school as the Tudor students. Like other young women they drink, take drugs, and get pregnant.[19] At one women's school seven empty bottles of Seagrams were found in the washroom one afternoon.

In the absence of academic stratification, students with varying academic abilities interact with one another and accept the very smart students. Cliques tend to form around special interests: protest groups, the drama group, and the fashion and marriage groups. Friendships here, unlike Tudor, are made in the school, and several possibilities of gaining and confirming self-worth exist.

School spirit pervades St. Catherine's. During freshman initiation week each senior has her own freshman whom she guides. At the end of the week, which is full of planned activities, gifts, and excitement, there is a lavish initiation ceremony written and produced by the seniors. One year hysterics prevailed while the seniors dressed their freshmen as Raggedy Ann and Andys. The sophomores, juniors, and teachers witnessed the event. After the production many of the seniors took their freshmen out to eat, where they discussed Christmas presents, birthday parties, and future gatherings. This event encourages friendship across age groups. During the year there are also several talent shows and a senior play in which most of the students are involved. A few young men are brought in from other parochial schools for the male roles. One year the females in the audience laughed and shouted when the male lead had to kiss the female lead. The young woman who used to date him was almost hysterical, encouraged along by her teasing classmates. The play was held up for five minutes. Feelings of group solidarity are achieved through these school functions.

The students are often disturbed by the oppressive rules but the restrictions do not hinder the desire to graduate. In fact, the senior requirement of a marriage and family course taught by a nun and a priest serves as a basis for group solidarity. Most of the students say they dislike the class and disagree with the views presented but they have fun by making the nun and priest blush. The nun announced that they were going to talk about sex in the next class. One student shouted, "Are you and Father Tom going to demonstrate?" "Father Tom's ears always turn red when he gets embarrassed. It's really fun to get him like that and not too difficult," one of the seniors explained. Other rules are evaluated as unfathomable and protests are organized. The students were required to wear uniforms to enter the school building. In order to protest, they started changing into their uniforms in the street. That ended that rule.

On occasion, the students have been able through their collective and individual efforts to avoid the consequences of rule infringement. Any student the nuns discover to be pregnant or married is expelled. One young woman managed to stay in school until she was eight and a half months pregnant. She returned two weeks after having the baby. The nuns never knew. She wore sweatshirts under her uniform jacket to hide her pregnancy. All of her peers who knew kept quiet. Though some restrictions are questioned or disliked, the basic legitimacy of the school authority remains intact.

Many of the male schools require an entrance exam. Because St. Mark's did not, many youths who found the gang situation too difficult at Tudor but still wanted to graduate, attended this school. Three Lions graduated with good grades. "Shit, I couldn't go to Tudor High for anything. The Aces would jump me the minute I walked in. You got to be packed [carry a weapon] every day. I want to finish school, not die," Tiny, a gang member, explained. "My old lady really wanted me to finish. She's real proud 'cause I'm the first one in the family to finish and I got five older brothers and sisters," said Ronny on his graduation. "My boyfriend, Rick, got all 'A's' and 'B's.' I hope they let him back to St. Mark's when he gets out of jail because he would graduate in June," Felice told me. Later that year, Rick graduated. Although youths from gangs all over the city, including several Lions and members of other 32nd Street gangs, attend St. Mark's, there are only a few from each gang and few from warring gangs. No gang sweaters are allowed in the school.

The young women tend to find the Catholic schools reasonable and to some extent rational. Many hope to get office jobs and know that they can learn to read and type. The young men worry about

fights, which can largely be avoided in parochial schools. Not only is
school viewed as more rational (one can learn to read) and reasonable, but peer group expectations within the school do not make
graduation more difficult.

Commercial and Vocational Schools

Students who attend vocational or commercial schools also are more
likely to graduate. Classes are often skill oriented, which makes
them rational in the eyes of the youths. Tighter controls on the
students decrease the violence and cutting. None of the vocational
schools for men, however, is close to the neighborhood, and only one
of the women's schools is. Few males attend vocational schools, but
many of the females attend Leslie's Commercial for secretarial, prenursing, or cosmetology training. The better vocational schools
have entrance requirements that few 32nd Street students can
meet.

While the teachers are not viewed as particularly reasonable,
school is thought of as rational, a way to avoid "dirty" jobs. "For a
lot of reasons I don't like Leslie very much 'causes there aren't any
dudes, the building is falling down, the teachers are bitchy, but I
know I wouldn't finish at Tudor. No one does," claimed Rita, who
later married one of the Lions. She graduated with a "B" average.
Many young women feel they may want to work when their family
is older. "I really wanted to graduate even after I had the baby.
They let me back in and I did," Enrique's wife told me. Her sister-in-
law also went back to school after her baby was born. Both returned
to work at a downtown bank several months after they were graduated and continued to work for several years. While these schools
offer the youths little help in developing a positive self-image, they
do less to offend students.

Away from Local Peer Groups

A student can attend and complete public high school outside the
local school district if the student gives the address of a relative who
lives within that district as his own home address. This allows
youths to avoid being drawn immediately into peer group activities.

Jim, a Lion, explains, "My first day at Tudor I got jumped. I said to myself that I would never finish so I went to my aunt's house, got her electric light bill, and told the school I'd moved. I've been doing pretty good and no one knows I'm a club member." Lou, also a Lion, transferred out of the area:

> I had to get out of Tudor 'cause only a few of us ever even got to junior year. Our worst enemies go to Tudor. Here they don't always identify me as a Lion 'cause it's too far away. I still get into some fights in school, but I'm passing everything.

These youths are committed to finishing school and are aware that the local environment would lead them into trouble. Only becoming anonymous during school hours makes graduation possible.

The poor achievement in the schools is related to the organization of and interaction within the local school; however, student expectations perpetuate the failure to achieve and increase the physical dangers to both students and school personnel. The youths, like their parents, are aware of the need for education in order to get ahead in the urban industrial society. Yet most fail within the local school system.

Part of the problem lies in the students' perception that the local school system does not have legitimate authority. Students perceive the schools as lacking rationality (they serve neither to certify nor to enlighten) and reasonableness (both the organization and staff-pupil relationships question student intelligence and moral character). The school is saying they are losers in many spheres: intellectual, economic, and moral. Students do not experience this as isolated individuals; they talk about their experiences, both successes and failures. The school authority's lack of legitimacy becomes collectively understood and affects even those who may not be entirely convinced.

In most communities in the United States, the school is the locus for instilling the individualist's competitive ethic that is so important for success in the business world. While Coleman (1961) and the parents of the mainstream youths he studied were disturbed that these youths were unconcerned with academic competition and achievement, competition and social skills were learned in non-academic school activities, particularly sports (Berger, 1963; Schwartz, 1972). On 32nd Street, this learning of individualistic competition rarely occurs within the school.

While the failure to finish school does place significant limits on job possibilities, it does not mean that youths have given up completely their hopes of achieving the American dream of economic success. Nor does the school system's failure to provide the mechanisms to develop the competitive ethic mean that youths do not mature into competent and steady workers. The problem that many youths face is the constant gap between their desire to do well and the lack of opportunities. Some confront this problem, while others continue to hedge their bets.

8

Earning a Living

Nico attended parochial school and did well but never even started his senior year. At eighteen, while a leading member of the Lions, he started and completed a job training program as a computer operator for a large bank. First in his class, he was hired immediately on the night shift. After two years he was still on the night shift and saw no hope of changing to the day shift, so he quit. After two weeks he went back, telling his friends he could not get a better job. A year later he quit again to spend time with his friends. Several months later, after he married the mother of his child, he started working at a government job, but he quit after two years because he had to work Saturdays, which disrupted his softball season with the Lions' team. He sold some drugs on the side and got some friends and family to help support his wife and son over the summer months.

Nico's ability to find relatively well paying jobs was better than that of most of his peers but his work patterns were similar to theirs. Albert's problems with finding a good job more closely resemble the experience of his peers. He was never a gang member or a troublemaker. In the eleventh grade he dropped out of school but continued to work loading trucks, as he had since he was fourteen. Married and with a child at seventeen, he frequently brought home an odd case of whatever he was loading to supplement his low wages. His hours were often curtailed when business was bad. He never quit a job but did take days off to spend time with friends.

Women potentially face reevaluation of their femininity when they work. Problems can arise from others' evaluations of their motives for working and the type of work they do. An office job is

consistent with notions of femininity but actions that others appraise as reflecting independence are not. Gloria's office job was
regarded as a good job where she could look nice and be paid reasonably well. But her motives for working were questioned when she
seriously considered accepting a promotion that would have necessi-
tated moving to another city. She turned it down and remained
living with her parents. It was the right thing for a young woman to
do, everyone said.

In modern society a job provides a person or family not only
with an income but with a status by which others evaluate the
person. Several studies argue that changes in an individual's work
situation often initiate additional changes. Work is considered an
important factor in making the transition from youth to adult
status. With the acquisition of a steady job (a legitimate opportunity and *prima facie* evidence of adulthood), involvement in delinquent (illegitimate) activities terminates (Cloward and Ohlin,
1960) and the necessity of hiding insecurity about manhood in delinquency and violence is removed (Matza, 1964). It is also argued that
women with jobs change their attitudes and behaviors; for example,
they shift toward egalitarianism in the home (Blood and Wolfe,
1960) and toward increased acceptance of female independence
(Mason and Bumpass, 1975). This chapter explores the validity of
these propositions for the work experience of the young men and
women of 32nd Street.

The acceptance of hard work is consistent with both the American dream and the honor code. For the former hard work is instrumental to success; for the latter, it is critical so that a man can
support his family in order to retain his authority and the respect of
others. Yet there are few good job opportunities available.[1] Most
residents work hard but are relegated to jobs in the secondary labor
market with all the problems attributed to those jobs: frequent job
loss, layoffs, poor pay, and little upward mobility.[2] To supplement
their wages, most residents engage in exchange of aid (mutual obligations) among a network of friends or family,[3] and some engage in
illegal activities. Among young unmarried men the peer group plays
a role similar to that of the expanded family network for married
persons.

While it is generally agreed that men should work at legitimate jobs to support their families, the jobs in the secondary labor market provide only a small degree of dignity as a basis for self-worth.⁴ The lack of confirmation of self-worth in the available jobs creates tensions between going to work and street activities and ties. Some young people have confronted the gap between their desire for success and their limited possibilities of achieving success by appraising work as necessary for survival, while others fail to confront this gap and continue without commitment to either a street or a conventional life-style.

It has become financially necessary for many women to work. The traditional values of womanhood and femininity, however, remain so strong that there has been little change in the local criteria used to evaluate a woman. Her moral worth still depends on her sexual purity, not her ability to support a family. When a woman uses her job to gain independence, she is negatively evaluated.

The work obtained by many young people has little impact on other areas of social experience. This may be explained by the inter-penetration of job characteristics and the normative expectations of the residents of the 32nd Street community. Good jobs are extremely limited for residents of the inner city, and the failure to find meaningful work sometimes reinforces alternative local normative patterns, which in turn further hinder success in the conventional job market.

The Need to Earn a Living

While few of the available jobs bring in much money, most youths make considerable efforts to find something. Most succeed or claim that it is possible. One unemployed twenty-three-year-old gang member argued that if a person looked seriously every day for a week or so, he could find a job. Many students also work after school and still find enough time to spend with their gang if they are in one.⁵ A steady job that pays much more than the minimum wage is almost impossible to find, and illegal enterprises and the mutual obligation network are considered acceptable means for supplementing wages.

Opportunities

Finding a job is often difficult without connections and with little
education. Rat Man, who never finished seventh grade and had an
extensive juvenile record, could not even get a busboy's job at $1.30
an hour: "I've been at four places this week. None of them want me;
they all give you the line about 'Don't call me, I'll call you.' They
never call. I thought it would be easy to find a job when I turned
eighteen." Rat Man learned carpentry in a juvenile hall and took
great pride in the elegant bar he built in the Lions' basement. He
claimed, "No carpenter will hire me—no education and a record.
How can I go into business—no one will trust me. I had to steal the
tools and materials to do this job."

Friends and relatives are usually little help in locating a job because everyone has either low status or a temporary job. Fred was
so proud when he found some of the other Red Shirts jobs at the
company where he was employed that he brought it up in several
conversations. Some youths even turn to the police for help. José
went to a police officer, who was aware of his extensive juvenile
arrest record and illiteracy, for a construction job. The officer finally
took him seriously and found him a job. In 1973 José was making
$7.15 an hour. He also worked locally on weekends and evenings,
painting homes and repairing roofs, porches, and driveways.

> I like to work; maybe I'll take some time off in a few years
> after I buy a few houses and make some nice apartments.
> I got to learn to read and write so I can get a driver's
> license. You know some of the dudes don't like to work
> much—they just hang around. I used to bring some down
> for jobs—some worked good, others didn't do too well.

Money

The value of a job is measured in dollars. Though Morse and Weiss
(1955: 191) argue that "working gives them the feeling of being tied
to the larger society, of having something to do, of having a purpose
in life," a job is little more than a means of economic support for
most youths on 32nd Street. The situation is similar to the one that
Gans (1962) describes for Italian men; work is a necessary expendi-

ture of time and energy to make a living and, if possible, to increase the pleasure of life outside the job.

The amount of money earned is generally seen as more important than the status of the job in the wider society. For example, Wolf could not understand why, when he could make $13,000 (1972) as a bus driver for the city and more if he worked overtime, I continued my education when I had no hope of earning much more than that. "Why should I go to school and earn less money? I'm not knocking education. . . . You know a lot of things I don't and have been a lot of places but you don't make any money."

Everyone is concerned about obtaining enough money to survive. Len, a Lion, asked me if it were possible to support two people on a wage of less than three dollars an hour. He was working as a shipping clerk. Six months later he told me:

> You know, Ruth, I've been working for more than six
> months and I only missed two days. Now I'm making $2.65
> an hour. It's beginning to look pretty good. When my girl
> comes back from Texas [she was finishing school] we can get
> together. I get along a lot better with my stepfather now
> 'cause I hated working for him. It was no good . . . he
> ordered me around too much. It feels good working 'cause I
> don't have to go jackrolling [stealing from drunks] with the
> dudes to get money to get high.

Ham, also a Lion, sat down on the grass near me in the park one day and asked me what kind of job was good for a man to have. "I want a dirty job which pays well." He had just finished his junior year at Tudor, was bored with school work, and wanted to feel some "real money" in his hands. "I'm tired of wearing these kinds of clothes; I can't style [dress well] in them. I need money so I can go into a bar and order a round. A man has to work." He later found construction work.

Supplementing Income: Illegal Activities

Working at a traditional job is viewed as the correct means to earn a living. Some people use illegal means to supplement income and, while they are not considered the proper means to obtain a living, they are often regarded as ethically neutral, that is, situationally adaptive.⁶ Some young people sell marijuana or steal merchandise from trucks or warehouses. Only a few of the young steal from drunks or steal ten-speed bicycles. While there are some major drug dealers on 32nd Street, most drug sellers do not sell full-time or make large profits.

Some young people accept the earning of extra money illegally but do not evaluate highly illegal means as a sole source of support. When Len got his job at fifteen, he called the Lions' attention to the fact that he would not have to rob drunks for his dues because he worked. His nonworking peers muttered in response, while those who worked nodded their heads in agreement. Enrique lectured the Lions on how it is wrong to steal from illegal Mexican residents. Most of those who earn money selling drugs also have a legitimate job. For example, Jock could have made more money than he did, selling drugs, enough to support his family while he attended school, but he would not do so. It is not the right thing to do, he said. It is acceptable to supplement income by illegal means but a man should keep at least one foot in legitimate enterprises. "I work hard but can't earn enough to support a family and buy the stuff a person needs to live decent, so I add a bit. Everyone does it," stated a nineteen-year-old father of two who worked for the minimum wage. All the other young men in the group agreed. Their image of the American dream demands that they work hard but does not prohibit them from helping themselves to some dividends that they feel they "deserve."

Those who live only by illegitimate means are criticized not only for giving up the American dream but for increasing the possibility of getting caught or getting others in trouble. "I'm smart," one of the Senior Greeks explained, "I work as an electrician and earn pretty good money. I also get some on the side but no policeman will suspect if I come with a new car because he knows I work. He doesn't know I paid cash. If he thought I didn't work, he'd be real suspicious."

Most young men try to hedge their bets for the future by balancing their legal and illegal pursuits. They maintain their hope of achieving economic success while continually experiencing the near failure that justifies their illegal economic enterprises. The sporadic working habits that illegal gain allows and the stealing of goods from employers in turn serve as justifications for employers to pay poor wages. One local employer said, "Stealing, stealing . . . that's why I can't afford to pay more." It is a vicious cycle.

Work and Self-Worth

To be evaluated as an honorable, moral person a man must maintain his authority over his family. To fulfill this role, he must be able to support them. While studies of gangs have found that members often shun work because it might jeopardize their street reputations (Short and Strodtbeck, 1965), on 32nd Street many youths, including gang members, work even prior to marriage and are respected for being able to handle a reputation and a job. Those who cannot find work lose the respect of their peers.

Though Anderson (1978) found that only the regulars at Jelly's Bar considered work a primary value, even the toughest gang members on 32nd Street value work. Gilberto, the leader of the Lions, was employed and made work more prestigious for the Lions. He worked in a factory for six months before he became a street worker for a local social service agency. Another Lion, Lou, worked after school and on weekends in a clothing store just outside the community for three years. During one wedding while he was drinking heavily, he kept reminding everyone that he had to be home early in order to be at work by nine. At midnight he left. Many of the Senior Greeks worked full-time. Mouse worked in a foundry at $4.50 an hour (1971), after starting work as a busboy at $1.05 an hour. Dagwood, with the reputation as one of the toughest men on 32nd Street, was a licensed electrician. Few have given up entirely on the American dream of succeeding economically.

A youth may even lose status if others think he cannot get a job because of a criminal record or lack of schooling. Rat Man was viewed as having forfeited alternatives for the future. According to one Lion, "He'll never be able to get a job with that record. I guess he'll never be able to make it like us."

A Good Job

While neither the jobs nor the wages available to members of the
32nd Street community are very good, some jobs—those more consistent with their image of themselves as tough and independent
men such as "dirty" jobs and jobs that allow some autonomy—are
evaluated as better than others. Other potentially positive features
are less important because to value these things might make the inability to obtain or keep them more painful.

One of the most important elements that 32nd Street men look
for in a job is freedom from strict supervision.[7] Pick explained the
advantages of driving a truck:

> I'm a truck driver out by myself, no one breathing down
> my neck. I do my job—earn around $13,000. I like driving.
> Had other jobs. I never had any trouble finding a job.
> Once I got laid off and went to collect unemployment. I
> refuse to stand in line waiting for some handout. I walked
> out and found a good-paying job. Can you guess how far
> I got in school? Never finished high school—too boring—
> and I went to Catholic school too.

Independence is consistent with their image of themselves. Moreover, independence allows them to avoid experiencing lack of
respect, which can be problematic to a man of honor. Youths are
sometimes fired after lashing out at a supervisor (either verbally or
physically) who has not demonstrated the proper respect in front of
others. Most of the places they work have no grievance mechanisms.

Jobs in which they can get dirty and use some strength are consistent with their image of themselves as tough men, and are considered good jobs. White-collar jobs are viewed with some
ambivalence. On the one hand, they may be evaluated as a "hustle,"
a good way of earning money because the employee is viewed as
doing little. Many residents assume that all people working in community organizations are hustling. They have desks and nice offices
and do not get dirty. Ten Pin explained, "All they do is bull-shit.
Yeh, they organize some things and helped me find a lawyer and set
up that game room but they don't get dirty." On the other hand,
white-collar jobs are hard to come by and striving for such a job is

likely to bring failure. Therefore, these jobs are often derided as "women's work." Women need the protection of an office with no strenuous physical labor. White-collar jobs are viewed with a combination of mistrust and lack of respect mixed with awe and envy.[8] To say publicly that white-collar jobs are better than blue-collar ones would be to admit their failures. The rejection of white-collar work is in part a rejection of something tacitly assumed to be desirable.

A "real man," according to many of the younger youths, needs to get dirty in order to show that he works. When Gilberto was working in the factory, he always arrived at the park in his work clothes and kicked the cement bench to demonstrate how hard his shoes were. He never did this with his dress shoes. After a short conversation he would announce that he was going home to relax, have a beer, and shower.

Although independence, dirtiness, and money are the most important criteria in evaluating a job, residents make few differentiations among their jobs.

Self-Esteem and Jobs

While the particular job generally has little meaning to most youths, they are sensitive to the status connotations of their jobs in the wider society. When asked about their work, they usually gave the location or name of the company, never the kind of job. Many of the youths knew only that their mother or father worked in a factory, not the kind of product the companies produced. One youth knew that his mother had been working in the same place for more than five years and made less than three dollars an hour, but he had no idea what product she made or what she did. Young women often knew how much money their boyfriends made and where they worked but nothing more. A person wears no "badge of ability" (Sennett and Cobb, 1972) for loading a truck or making paper cups. There is little feeling of accomplishment or status gained from any particular job.

The lack of a badge of ability becomes increasingly apparent when employers demand no work history. "Man, nobody even asks you where you worked before. They don't care," explained a nine-

teen year old to a sixteen year old. They were going together to see
about some jobs loading trucks. Both were hired and neither was
asked about his work history.

   The work situation rarely serves any expressive functions. As
most jobs are short-term and there are few workers of similar background on the job, there is little socializing at work. Few people
make friends or identify with anyone at work. According to some
young men, having friends on the job makes working more tolerable
and can increase loyalty to the job. "We get high in the washroom
together and then go back on the trucks and bull-shit. How the hell
can you find drilling holes interesting?" asked Ramón, a high school
graduate and member of the Red Shirts. Ramón, two of his
brothers, and several other Red Shirts worked together for over a
year. The job took on additional meaning when Ramón was nomi-
nated for the union stewardship. He read all the union rules and
brought the book to the park to show his friends who demonstrated
some interest. The possibility of election held his interest for a
while, but after he lost the election to an older man, he and his
friends quit.

   Some of the jobs obtained by the Lions in 1977 were perceived
as better because they allowed for peer group socializing on the job.
Rico, married and a father at seventeen, with a ninth grade education, managed a bar for his eldest brother where the Lions sometimes congregated. According to his friends he had a good position;
he worked when he wanted, with no supervision, and he could interact frequently with friends while working six nights a week. Both he
and his brother, who became a youth worker, worked steadily at
their jobs for three years and participated in peer group activities
while on the job. Their opportunity for sociability was the envy of
their peers. When a job is a sociable situation or demonstrates something about the kind of person one is, it becomes more than a
respectable way to earn a living; it gives a man some feeling of
importance.

Stolen Goods and Dependency: Potential Loss of Esteem

While some young people use illegitimate means to help support
themselves, they receive little approbation from peers for their en-

deavors because the behavior is situationally adaptive. Eventually the Lions could no longer condone Rat Man's illegal pursuits and failed to pay his bail. Though she claimed still to be in love with him, his girlfriend broke up with him for the same reason. Because the cultural system does not define illegal enterprises as morally correct, peers grant little approval for engaging in such activities, but no one will be criticized if illegal actions are used to supplement legal income.

Drawing on mutual obligation networks, while a morally acceptable method of receiving financial support, can be problematic if the flow of exchanges is not mutual. The recipient of too many resources is appraised as dependent. Al, at twenty, worked in a supermarket and was changed to the evening shift, which conflicted with the time he spent with his friends. After working for several months he began to wonder if he had any friends left. He quit but after two weeks had no money left. At first all his friends treated him to beer and he was frequently invited to eat at the homes of married friends. After four months of unemployment and no money, his friends started complaining that he had not bought a round of drinks in a long time. That continued for a while. Then Al seriously started looking for a job. An honorable man is able to support himself; therefore, while no one counts the rounds at the bar or meals, if an individual, whether friend or family, receives too often, he is perceived as dependent and treated as less than an honorable man. A man should try to work.

Tensions between Work and Peer Group

Sociologists often argue that employment is an indicator of adult status and plays a primary role in changing an individual's orientation from that of a youth to that of an adult (Matza, 1964). On 32nd Street jobs confer little status on the worker and consequently play a minimal role in the evaluation of self-worth or the confirmation of adult status. Feelings of self-worth must be derived elsewhere. But for most young men earning a living becomes increasingly important with marriage and fatherhood. A constant tension between the expressive solidarity of the peer group and the dull meaninglessness of earning a living remains. Frequently, youthful peer groups continue to play a major role in confirming self-worth on similar terms as before. Work provides few incentives to alter peer group affiliations or to shift a peer group's focus. "Worker" becomes an additional identity but does not replace others. Many continue their street activities while working.

On a daily basis most youths experience little difficulty in shifting back and forth between the conduct expected at work and on the street and generally follow the proper rules of comportment specified by each situation. There is no inherent normative conflict. For example, José, a skilled construction worker, still carries a gun and owns several but only for protection in the community. He never takes it to work.

> For a while I didn't carry a gun but once when I was near
> the El by a brick wall, I felt this car moving up the street
> slowly behind me; the motor died and I threw myself on the
> ground. They came in fast and fired five shots but missed.
> Ever since, I've been packed. It happened again a few days
> later but I got a few bullets into the car that time. I'm a
> pretty good shot 'cause I was the gunman for the Nobles
> when we started getting guns on 32nd Street. Before that, it
> was chains, bats, and knives.

This separation of work life and street life is common, but it is frequently not understood by members of the wider society. Enrique started in a job training program with Nico and had a perfect attendance record. Enrique and a friend were coming out of an alley on a Saturday night when a detective in an unmarked car stopped them. Enrique was arrested for illegal possession of a gun and released on bail. There had been an altercation with the Nobles earlier that evening and because Enrique was worried he had the gun. He told his supervisor at work that he had to go to court in December and was excused from work for that morning. He was given a continuance by the court but was dismissed from work the next day. No explanation was given. He could not understand why he had been dismissed before proven guilty or why what occurred in the community had anything to do with the job. "I wouldn't ever

bring a gun downtown; why should I want one there anyway?
There's no one there I got to protect myself against."

If the job interferes extensively with gang activities, however,
the situation becomes a problem. Pierre, a Lion, quit his night job
because he could not arrange his schedule to his own satisfaction.
He had to travel more than an hour to be at work by 11 P.M., which
ruined his evening with the Lions, and his girlfriend was upset with
the arrangement. He was not regarded as a failure for having quit as
long as he did not depend on others too long or on illegal pursuits exclusively to support himself. When a job becomes too time con-
suming, the peer group often wins out.

Peer groups with strong mutual obligation networks allow the
youths to survive financially if they are unemployed either by choice
or because of a lack of work. If most members of a group are
employed, then the others may take some time off; however, if for
any reason several should lose their jobs and most become unemployed, then some may need to go back to work to avoid a cash-
flow problem. When Fred of the Red Shirts found a job with several
of his friends, two other group members quit to hang around with
the unemployed. Several found jobs when Fred and his friends quit.
Particularly among the young single men there is always a group of
unemployed youths with whom to associate and a group of employed
friends to help out financially. In the case of the Red Shirts, several
of them also sold small quantities of marijuana.

It is important to work and the peer group supports those who
work. But peer group ties also permit and encourage absenteeism
and quitting by helping out financially and by providing the expressive values unavailable through work—a place to be someone. Many
young men continue to drift back and forth between commitments
to working and street life.

Marriage and Earning a Living

With the added responsibilities marriage and fatherhood bring,
earning money becomes increasingly important but the jobs available do not necessarily improve.[9] A man must provide his family
with essentials and be able to help others at times so that he will be

offered help when he needs it. Depending on others to meet the
needs of an entire family is almost impossible. The expanded family
or peer group network must be used only to meet emergencies and
to supplement wages through the exchange of services and loans,
not to support a family with an able-bodied man, which would
publicly display the man's lack of independence.

While age opens up a few more opportunities, the jobs available
are usually similar and the chances of being laid off just as great.
Only a few are able to obtain jobs that offer good wages or an opportunity for upward mobility.[10] Fredo, a Lion with a high school
diploma, worked at one job steadily for three years but had been laid
off twice, and during the summer of 1977 his time had been cut back
to thirty hours a week. The job paid slightly more than the minimum
rate. According to his wife, it was almost impossible to make ends
meet and a layoff was pending so she started working part-time in a
hotel downtown (for minimum wage and no benefits). Her sister was
caring for their daughter. Had Fredo not been married he might
have quit his job.

With the frequent layoffs and cutbacks in hours it is difficult
not to be tempted to earn extra money through illegal means; however, the increased risk of incarceration that comes with adult legal
status has consequences when one has a family to support. When
the wife of an imprisoned young man accepted welfare, several of
her friends expressed pity for her but thought that her husband was
irresponsible and deserved to be in jail for shooting a tavern owner
in a holdup attempt. Robbery is not regarded as a proper way to
earn money and the risks were too great. If a wife works while her
husband is in jail, not only do others judge him as having lost his
authority within the family, but she is self-supporting and may become too independent. The risks of losing dignity through unemployment increase with the need not to be subordinate to a wife.
The married man has too much at stake to risk incarceration frequently when he can work. The work becomes no more meaningful,
just more necessary.

Women and Work

Ferree (1979: 48) has argued in her study of Cuban women living in the United States that there is no "necessary conflict between traditional standards of female behavior and women's paid employment." On 32nd Street it is accepted that women work while men maintain their dominant position within the family. As long as a woman works to improve the collective economic position of the family and her job does not become a source of validation of self-worth, it remains acceptable for her to work. If work validated her self-worth, she might reevaluate the appropriateness of her dependency on men and the necessity of being concerned with sexual purity. It is considered legitimate for women to work only if the cultural status quo is upheld.

Work only rarely serves to encourage a woman to act independently. Most of the young women who work do so for short periods before they marry to make money to buy clothes and to go out with friends. Their jobs are, for the most part, as meaningless as the men's. Working women continue to live at home and quit work at marriage or when one salary is sufficient to support the family. Older women with families who work do so because they must and continue to be solely responsible for the housework, cooking, and children; they consider the double burden appropriate. Most quit when they can afford to.

The purpose of working, according to many unmarried young women, is to be able to afford the things they want, such as extensive fashionable wardrobes. One woman of twenty explained, "You should have seen the clothes I bought when I was working. I had shoes and a bag to match every outfit and several coats for each season. My mother couldn't afford to dress me so I went to work." Working for clothes remains consistent with cultural expectations for young unmarried women.

Office work and sales are considered the best jobs for women because they are perceived as feminine jobs: easy, clean, and passive. They allow a woman to be appraised as feminine since she can wear nice clothes and fix her hair to be attractive to men. Many young women, however, obtain less feminine jobs in factories. These young women never come out to meet their friends in their work clothes, but always return home first to change. Alicia at eighteen started to work at a factory for $1.75 an hour and after four months was making $1.90. She worked for almost a year before she had her second child and after a few months went back to work: "It's as good a job as any. I guess. I got to work to contribute to my kids' upbringing. My father's shop isn't making what it used to." She worked to help out and her relationship to her parents continued as before; therefore her working was appraised as appropriate.

Work is rarely an expression of independence, but when others appraise it as such, the evaluation of the woman generally is problematic if not negative. Taking a job away from home is an overt indication to others that a young woman desires to be independent. Most parents refuse to give their daughters permission to leave home because it reflects on their ability to control her behavior and maintain the public image of her sexual purity. Those who are determined to be independent and are old enough often enter the armed services. Amy told a group of women:

> I just decided I couldn't live at home any more and that I
> wanted to see the world. I applied for airline stewardess jobs
> and the Air Force. The Air Force acceptance came first, so I
> went. It was great. I went to Japan for a weekend and all
> over the place. I was always getting into trouble like coming
> back too late to the base but somehow I always managed to
> escape and never got into official hassles. I got married after
> a year. They gave me the pill but I didn't take it and I got
> pregnant. I didn't believe they'd find out so fast, so I got
> kicked out. It was fun while it lasted.

Another woman, Rachael, now in her late twenties, explained that she had to slip the permission paper in with other papers her father was signing. She felt she had to get away from home and did not want to continue at the local university. She disliked the armed services and after two years returned to finish her bachelor's degree in another state while working on several community projects.

The Job Corps offers an alternative for establishing independence. A Chicano recruiter, however, told me that it was impossible most of the time to persuade parents to give their daughters permission to enroll in the live-in facilities. Monica's and Dede's parents allowed them to enroll because they felt that they had already lost control of them. The young women were attached to an older male gang and were widely known throughout the community as "loose women."

Young women who work and appear to be using their jobs to assert independence from men or their families walk a delicate line and are often criticized. Some single women in their twenties have begun to use the money they earn not only to get together with friends for evenings out but to travel outside the city on unsupervised vacations. Some are divorced and others have not married. Many men are wary of these independent women, but some find them attractive yet are not sure about marrying them. Even some of the more sensitive men experienced in the wider society find women who openly act independently difficult to understand. After a long discussion about women's roles in a number of new movies, a very articulate twenty-four year old expressed his confused feelings about these independent women:

> You know Lola and I have been friends [itself a departure from the rules] for a long time and I like her a lot and know she is very smart, but I can't understand them and where we [men] fit in. They are always going places and doing things without us. They don't seem to *need* us at all. I get confused about how to act with them.

For those who have begun to use employment as a means to independence, the meaning of work has changed. The evaluation of these young women is not agreed upon; some view their behavior as deviant while others are uncertain about the change.

Getting a job is generally perceived in American society as an indicator of adulthood for young men that should refocus their interests and concerns and as an indicator of independence for young women. Within the 32nd Street economic and cultural context, working neither necessarily entices young men away from their peer groups and youthful activities nor provides the basis for female independence. Work is an experience in a specific job that is discussed and evaluated by a particular audience.

Most youths have jobs and many of them work very hard, but

few of their dead-end jobs give them any status. Because it is extremely difficult to get any other kind of job, better jobs are often devalued. A man of honor, however, provides for his family and does not depend on others, so men keep working even if they take time off or quit a specific job for a short period. There is no commitment to a specific job. Moreover, those with strong peer group ties who have failed to resolve the gap between the desire to succeed and the limited opportunities of doing so can avoid long-term commitment to the street or working.

For most working women, their employment is not regarded by them or by other residents as an indicator of independence. It is a way of helping their families buy what they need or, for many unmarried young women, a way of being able to afford the clothes they want. The working woman is made to fit within the cultural context. The positive evaluation of her identity is questioned only when her actions are regarded by others as indicating independence. While both men and women work, their jobs only minimally link 32nd Street residents to the wider society.

Adult Juvenile Gang Membership

Ronny, a Lion, charged with a felony, was urged by the judge hearing the case to join the army. He joined, was assigned office duty, and was sent to Germany. Drinking got him into trouble several times while in Europe but he received an honorable discharge. On his return, Ronny worked days and spent time with the Lions on weekends and in the evenings. After a year he quit working. During the summer of 1977 he was talking vaguely about getting some training. He developed a rationale for not continuing on to college: jobs for college graduates were scarce; he would have to work to supplement his GI benefits and thus would not have enough time to spend with his friends; and finally, he would be lost in the large, alienating classes. Playing ball, drinking beer, and talking with friends occupied most of his time. He asserted, "I'm still young." He was twenty-three and unmarried.

Sam was married, had a child, was living only a block or two from his mother's house, and had been working steadily over the past few years. It was rumored that he also sometimes sold as much as a thousand dollars worth of drugs in a week. He was with the other Lions almost every evening and was an important member of the softball team. He also had obtained a gun license and went to the firing ranges to practice. As they entered their twenties many of the Lions led similar lives.

Lou graduated from high school and started associating with some of the Chicano political activists. He dropped his street name and enrolled in college. By 1977 he had nearly three years of credits and regarded himself as an activist rather than as a member of the Lions, although he continued to have trouble with members of competing gangs who still thought of him as a member. He missed his gang membership and was frequently at the periphery when the Lions played softball on the weekends, but he did not play. Nor, when the gang members collected money for postgame beer drinking, was he solicited.

These three brief biographies illustrate some of the paths taken by youths as they move into their twenties. Most core gang members who are still in a gang at eighteen remain in a gang as Seniors, while fringe members drop out after relatively short commitments. Some gangs are destroyed when a high percentage of members are drafted into the armed services, are jailed, or are killed. Gangs such as the Lions, where only a few members are away from the group at any time and where core members are still in the gang at eighteen, continue their existence. When they marry and work, members do not completely turn away from gang activities. These young men, according to the American dream, should be certifying their competencies in the wider society, not in youthful peer group activities.

The fact of continuing gang involvement raises two related questions. First, why does this emphasis on male peer groups continue as the basis of sociability? And second, why do some gangs maintain their identities as tough and aggressive warriors after most of the members have achieved what is generally viewed as adulthood? On the one hand, studies of working- and lower-class communities, and Latin communities in particular, find that men and women tend to socialize in and receive emotional support from same-sex peer groups.[1] On the other hand, most studies of community and delinquency argue that gangs disappear with the onset of adult roles and responsibilities and that new collectivities form with new identities as social athletic clubs, where sports and socializing are the primary activities. Illegal activities, especially fighting, are not group related.[2] Other studies, however, indicate that Chicano gangs formed in the early teens continue as viable social forms.[3]

This chapter examines the social and cultural conditions that sustain the male peer groups as gangs after gang members have married, fathered children, and begun to work steadily.[4] First, it explores some of the reasons why some members leave and how some gangs disperse and disappear. Then it examines the factors

that allow and encourage other groups to remain together and continue as gangs. Gangs remain together because members have developed trust and strong bonds over the years and because there are
few other culturally accepted forms of affiliation in which they can
maintain close relationships and remain tough warriors, an identity
for which there are few alternatives.

Getting Out

Youths who rarely demonstrate public toughness, who have few
close relationships in the gang, or who have alternative contexts for
confirming self-worth can drift away from a gang with relative ease.
For those who have a long and deep involvement in gang activities
and relationships, leaving a gang can be a lonely and difficult experience. In some instances a gang segment (Littles, Juniors, or
sometimes Seniors) is destroyed when many members leave the
community whether through joining the armed services or im-
prisonment.

Peripheral Members

Some youths may associate with a gang for a short time without
developing close friendships or an identity as a tough gang member.
They may spend time at gang hangouts and, if they are asked, will
claim to be members, but after several months, particularly when
cold weather arrives, they disappear and fail to return. When other
groups become available or other interests are developed, others
drift away, largely unnoticed.

One summer when most of the Little Lions were fifteen and sixteen, three peripheral members stayed in the park with them. They
would talk, drink, and play ball with the Lions. Only one of them
was ever in a gang fight. By the end of October, when the temperature began to hit the freezing point, they all disappeared. Later one
of them told me that he had some other friends now who stayed
around his house. Most of the time they talked and drank just as the
Lions did but they did not get into gang-related trouble.

There were few ties to these peripheral members. The gang

members felt that the others owed them little and the ex-members felt little responsibility toward the Lions. None of the Lions claimed to know even where the three lived. They made little investment in gang membership and it took little effort to pull away. They did not have a chance to make public reputations as Lions and therefore found no challenge from those outside the group. With so few attributes and actions establishing their worth as gang members, peripheral members find the transition easy when alternative activities and groups arise.

The Disruption of Gang Continuity

Some gangs are broken up through external forces, as when a high percentage of members are drafted, incarcerated, or killed. If enough members are away from the community, the gang no longer exists. The continuity of the collective experience has been disrupted. Experiences away from the community may offer sufficient opportunity for a youth to develop a record of achievement in conventional or illegal pursuits and thus to change his interests and reevaluate former activities.

For example, prison provides opportunities for additional confirmation of toughness, for new citywide affiliations, and for new illegitimate activities, but if enough members are away from the community for an extended period, there is no gang to go back to. Some prisoners join prison gangs based on ethnic affiliation.[5] Their reputations become citywide and the conflicts more intense. A man returns to the local community with obligations to others all over the city and with additional criminal opportunities made available through prison connections. The liklihood of rejoining a local gang whose focus conflicts with other local gangs is greatly diminished.

The military draft can break up a gang. In one case several members of the Tigers, considered a tough gang and one of the first to use guns, were drafted and fought in Vietnam. That broke up the gang. When they came back to the community, some of them got together again as a social club, the Red Shirts. They collectively discussed their army experiences and developed a new concept of their identities and relationships. These Red Shirts thus differed from Ronny, described earlier, who went into the army while the other

Lions remained together. To stay away from the gang Ronny would have had to change the criteria upon which he constructed his identity without others to support him. None of his accomplishments was worth enough to him to enable him to do so.

The ex-Tigers frequently discussed the war and how silly the risk-taking was of the gang and how narrow were its concerns. Their club played baseball and gave parties. They made no attempt to develop a reputation. More informed about politics and their own place in United States society, they became concerned with class and ethnic divisions, not fighting other Chicano groups. Martin, a student at a local junior college, a draftsman, and a Vietnam veteran, decided not to die in the streets:

> You should grow up and out of violence, then if you don't bother anyone, they won't bother you. I can't go back to what I did before Nam. It's stupid to die without a war. It's better to fight the rich people. Politicians are corrupt. The change has got to be political 'cause guerrilla warfare isn't worth it. . . . We need leaders. Martin Luther King was brilliant and made sense but if you get involved, people step on your face and will think you're corrupt. . . . What I need to make me happy is money to travel.

The only time Tony, Martin's best friend, almost got into a fight after his return was when he wanted to maintain his family's honor by beating up the man who had made his sister pregnant. He talked about it but never followed through on his threats. Seven years after their return to Chicago, neither of them spent much time in the streets.

Core Members

Only a few core members turn away from street status once they reach eighteen. Some become more politically conscious, others turn to families, and a few become drug addicts. Lou, a Lion, was faced with a dilemma when his political friends argued that Chicanos should not fight each other but should fight the Anglos who controlled the system. The Lions maintained their identities as tough warriors by defining actions of other Chicano gangs as insult-

ing and responding with violence. Lou left the Lions. Not only did
the ideology of the groups conflict, but both demanded his time and
energy. He had good friends among the activists.

Len, who had always been concerned with supporting a family,
quit the Lions at nineteen when he and his girlfriend married. They
had two children in quick succession. Len tried very hard to support
them without depending on others or on any illegal means. "I don't
have much time to hang around," he said. He held two jobs at
various times in order to support his family.

Addicts are not acceptable gang members. They cannot be
counted upon to fight in the name of the gang and they cannot be
trusted. Many of the Lions experimented with acid in the early
1970's. While there had always been an older addict population on
32nd Street, the youths used little heroin until the mid 1970's. Gilberto and several others began using it quite frequently but only
Juan became addicted. "I guess the others didn't like it as much as
I did," Juan told me. He hung around with other addicts in the local
drug abuse clinic. He was trying to give up heroin, he said, because
his girlfriend's baby was due in a few weeks and he had to get a job.
The Lions knew nothing about his activities even though he spent
most of his time only a few blocks from the park.

One of the most difficult problems that the former gang
members experience is the termination of strong, long-term friendships. Always knowing where some of your friends are provides a
feeling of security and good fellowship. After two years both Lou
and Len still missed the friendship of the Lions. They still came on
weekends to watch the softball games and drink beer around the
periphery of the group, but they bought their own beer rather than
contributing to the collective fund. Lou tried very hard to reinte-
grate himself in the group by discussing events that had occurred
three or four years previously. No one paid attention. One afternoon
Len had his daughter with him. He and Lou discussed how difficult
it was to find someone to go drinking with in the evening. Len was
finding it particularly difficult because he and his wife were having
problems and they were thinking of separating.

Even after leaving the gang, many ex-members find that others
in society still identify them as gang members. A well-developed

and publicly acknowledged reputation allows one to deviate, for example, by not fighting with the group, but a big reputation can also cause problems when an individual wants to leave it behind. Even dropping the typical public symbols of an image promoter frequently fails. Tomás had been a member of the Lions and had a reputation as being very tough. Challenging and overcoming his claim to precedence would add to a challenger's status. Tomás was attempting to leave the Senior Lions in 1972 and really did not want to fight any more. Though he had been away from the gang for six months, he continued to be challenged. He grew his hair, changed his dress style, and varied where he spent his time. Still many people would not acknowledge that he no longer was in the street scene. He spent increasing amounts of time away from the neighborhood and attended junior college. He explained his problem:

> It's difficult when dudes are chasing you with a gun to turn around and say, "Hey, wait a minute, I'm not into that shit any more, would you lay off please?" You tell the dudes to cool it but they ain't going to believe you just like that. They think you're just saying it to put some shit over on them.

Once a reputation has been publicly confirmed, it does not fade away overnight. It becomes difficult for a former gang member to refrain from fighting when a breach of etiquette against him was meant as a challenge to his claim to precedence.

A year and a half after quitting the Lions, Lou explained his plight:

> They're still shooting at me. I don't have a gun now but a bullet just missed me last night and I'm going to get me a gun 'cause I get home from school late a couple of nights a week. My old man even moved out of the old hood.

Ronny's older brother lived away from the neighborhood for more than four years. He was afraid of being challenged and therefore afraid to go home. It was too easy, he felt, for him to interpret others' actions as intentionally insulting.

The problems of leaving a gang derive from a variety of

sources both internal and external to the gang. Not only is it
essential to form a new identity, but for most youths it is necessary
to find others to confirm their self-worth in new terms. They must
also be prepared to continue to be identified as gang members.

Remaining in a Gang

While many studies of delinquent gangs view the gang as unstable
or lacking cohesion, and as terminating with the attainment of adult
roles and responsibilities, many gangs on 32nd Street have senior
organizations of previous members now in their twenties, thirties,
and even forties. Most of them no longer hang on corners or in parks
but get together in taverns or in their homes. Like the Lions, most
are married, have children, and work at legitimate jobs (see table 1).
If asked, they still identify themselves as gang members and claim
the other members as their best friends. They are not constantly
prepared to fight nor do they go looking for fights, yet they are
involved in confrontations over collective claims to precedence and
some of them do get killed in such fights. Why do they continue in
the same male peer groups for so long, and why do they maintain
their status as gangs with reputations as tough warriors?

Why Stay Together?

It is not surprising to find male peer groups playing an important
role in the patterns of male sociability. Men and women are rarely
companions or friends in working-class, lower-class, or honor-based
cultures, and this community is no exception. However, as Suttles
(1968) argues, the membership of the adult male peer group (a social
athletic club) generally is different from that of the youthful peer
group (gang). Frequently adult groups are composed of relatives or
work associates.[6] On 32nd Street many of the gangs stay together
and factors in addition to kinship encourage their continuation into
adulthood. Strong bonds and intimate relationships within the gang
develop from trust and an extensive system of mutual obligations.
The ties are also ritually reaffirmed by creating *compadrazgo*
relationships among members. Moreover, most members continue

The Lions and Their Activities, 1971-1977

	1971-2	1973-4	1975-6	1977
MEMBERS (central)				
Location				
Army	0	1	2	1
Jail[a]	4	5	5	3
In the streets[b]	29	24	21	24
Total	33	30	28	28
Conventional Activities				
Marriage[d]	1	3	8	9
Fatherhood	2	5	11	13
Work[e]	5	6	9	11
School[e]	11	7	1	3
Mean Age	17	19.7	21.5	23.5
DROPOUTS				
Activities				
Illegal orientation	0	0	1	0
Legal orientation	0	1	1	0
Unknown	0	2	0	0
Total	0	3 (1974)	2 (1976)	0

a. All are juveniles or were in juvenile facilities, with the exception of three who have been incarcerated since 1974 on charges of murder and robbery.

b. These are the members who could be counted on to defend the reputation of the gang. Sometimes peripheral members "hang out" with the group for short periods of time. These peripheral members are not in the table. These data reflect those age-graded groups known as Juniors and Littles in 1971 that had evolved into Seniors by 1977. All of the 24 members noted for 1977 were members of the gang in 1971. Younger men took their places as Littles and Juniors.

c. Members in jail or in the army were still considered gang members and likely to rejoin the group upon release.

d. The number of each year indicates the total number of married members.

e. Included in the number of members working or in school are those who worked or attended school for a significant portion of the two years. Those not included in either category were spending most of their time just "hanging around."

Reprinted from Horowitz (1982: 7).

to live in the same community, with its limited opportunities for the development of alternative social networks with coworkers or because of the continued concern for male domination, with young women.

Over many years together, the members of the Lions have developed an extensive and intensive set of mutual obligations. Some of the exchanges are small and fairly inconsequential, such as rounds of drinks or meals, but others are much more important, are difficult to repay, and often remain unpaid for extended periods. These less tangible favors concern help in maintaining claims to precedence, taking the blame for someone else, and exchanges of personal information. Only through trust and the long continuity of social relationships can these obligations remain unpaid without creating dependency.

Trust is necessary to commence these mutual exchanges and trust is implied by the long lapses between fulfilling obligations. The longer the period until repayment, the more trust is needed and the more trust is implied in that relationship. Generalized reciprocity, where goods and services may flow in one direction over extended periods without disrupting the relationship, rather than balanced reciprocity, the constant exchange of similar goods and services, is usually found only among close family networks that are highly stable, autonomous, and large enough to satisfy most of their needs themselves (Sahlins, 1972). No formality in the exchange is necessary because everyone knows that it will be repaid. The system of mutual obligations found within the Lions resembles in intensity and extensiveness the type of exchanges generally found among family networks, not the type found among neighbors, who generally constitute a much more formalized, less stable network in which a rapid repayment of obligations is required (Lomnitz, 1977).

In many Latin American societies this trust is termed *confianza* (confidence). *Confianza* is a measure of the ability and desire to engage in social, economic, and informational exchanges. It is developed through subjective and personal evaluations of each other by the participants, the physical proximity of the participants (they must be close enough for exchanges to occur frequently), the similarity of the wants and needs of the group, and mutual knowledge of cultural and personal characteristics (moral character).[7]

The Lions have been together as a group for almost ten years and during that time there has been a continual exchange, both individual and collective, of goods, services, and personal information. Small exchanges have occurred continuously but the larger obligations often take years to fulfill. The constant lending of money or buying of rounds of beer provides a daily continuity of social relationships and the flow of exchanges. Whoever has cash pays for the beer; no questions are asked, no accounts are recorded. The same is true of small loans and meals. The more serious mutual obligations, such as owing someone for help in an ongoing struggle for precedence or for going to jail without revealing the names of the other participants, are often continued over an extended period. One member spent a year in a juvenile institution for a shooting and never revealed the name of the other Lion involved. Several years later that obligation had not yet been repaid. Several Lions explained that once members really become involved in gang affairs, they are constantly called upon to help out each other. There are always unsettled affairs of honor for which some gang members are obligated to help others.

Trust here implies equality of wants (such as willingness to fight for the gang and the exchange of fairly small economic resources) in addition to equality of moral character. The highly valued man in the gang is the tough and aggressive warrior who fights only when appropriate and is a good verbal negotiator. His most important moral quality is that he is an honorable man willing to stand up to support the gang's claim to precedence, without going overboard and causing fights in which the others have no desire to become involved. Only those who have this quality can participate in relationships with gang members and be part of the mutual obligation network. Len and Lou have a different moral character, having left the group voluntarily. They will not stand up in the name of the gang; their major concerns have changed over the course of the years away from the gang. Therefore, they no longer can be privy to gang secrets or belong to the mutual obligation network. While they are allowed to remain on the periphery, they cannot even participate in short-term exchanges. The gap between their past participation in collective activities and their present absence is too great. A drug addict like Juan cannot, by definition, be of good moral character. He will steal from anyone and thus can never be depended upon.

Sal's position and treatment by other Lions clearly reveal a number of issues concerning moral character, mutual obligations, and trust. Sal has always been considered a bit crazy by the others. He never seems to know when to keep quiet or not become involved in a useless fight or futile criminal enterprise. When he got out of a juvenile detention facility in the spring of 1977, Sam's mother gave him a place to stay and fed him. He had no money and made no effort to find a job. Moreover, he continually came up with half-developed schemes to get money illegally and often talked about attacking this or that gang. No one paid any attention. Sam told Sal in front of the others that he ought to start paying his keep. If he had been entirely trusted as a man of moral character, this flow of goods and services would not have required such rapid repayment. Others have had similar obligations go on for years without problems.

Further evidence of their lack of trust in Sal was demonstrated by how the Lions handled the following event. A gang shooting occurred in which a fourteen year old was killed. The police suspected that the killer was a Little Lion. Two detectives, who knew Sal by name, picked him up at the park, saying they just wanted to ask him some questions. Sam at first mentioned getting Sal a lawyer, but the Lions dropped the topic when the detectives drove off with him and they soon forgot about Sal. Sal did not show up for over a week and when he did, the others ignored him. He not only did things they considered crazy but also talked to the police. He therefore could not be trusted and was not allowed much leeway in the mutual obligation network. He was allowed to hang around because he was willing to fight. His moral character still had an element of good in it. But on several occasions when the Lions socialized away from their regular park bench, he was not invited. He was directly excluded when the others went to the Indiana Dunes one weekend.

Ties between gang members are often strengthened by adding

the relationship of *compadre* to that of friend. Many members ask co-members to serve as *padrinos* (godfathers) for their children, adding new responsibilities and commitments to the relationship. For example, the *padrino* of baptism is responsible for the child should the parents die. Not only is the gang tied together by a common stake in a collective reputation, but many of the members become part of one another's expanded family network.

Trust, or *confianza*, is both necessary for and implied in the mutual obligation network. If the members did not trust each other, they would not allow so many important obligations to go unfulfilled for such long periods, nor would so much personal information be exchanged. Though the exchange of personal information may seem guarded compared with the revelations that occur in modern group therapy and weekend retreats, in the honor-based subculture of 32nd Street, where revealing intimate problems is characterized as weakness, these youths share their fears and personal problems. The relationships developed among these young men are strong and long-term, more closely resembling lifelong friendships than the distrustful or sociopathic relationships often portrayed in the sociological literature about gang members.

The exchanges of personal information are not available to others.[8] While Klein (1971) has argued that frequently gang youths and their friends do not even know the real names of members, referring to each other only by street names, the Lions all know one another's real names and where they live, information often not available to people outside the Lions. Moreover, they slowly reveal information about their relationships to women and to their families. One of the Lions had a retarded brother about whom few people except for the Lions knew. The group as a whole also had secrets that were known only to members. That was one of the reasons they attempted to force Monk to join. They were afraid he had learned some of their secrets at a meeting, and only a member could be trusted with these secrets, which largely concerned future illegal escapades and weapons. Sharing secrets confirms the trust they have in one another, a trust that allows the development of close social relationships.

Most talk among the members is rough and, as in many street

corner communities, the common mode of interaction among young men, even good friends, is to "rap on" (verbally attack) each other's masculinity.⁹ Most confrontations are short and little offense is taken; others are prolonged and offense is taken. A physical fight is the only way to terminate the tension for an individual who is substantially less skilled at verbally attacking others; through a public display of physical strength, he can reassert his masculinity.

Rico found himself confronted verbally several times. He would lose a confrontation with Ten Pin, who would immediately turn on someone else; that person would tell him to go to hell. Rico would saunter off and return later. This is not what happened when the same type of verbal confrontation took place with someone, even a friendly person, outside the group. The Red Shirts, a group that did not fight, congregated with the Lions in the park and the Lions were always invited to their basement for parties. One of the Red Shirts and a Lion were "rapping on" each other until the Red Shirt was obviously losing in front of a rather large audience of peers. He fought and pinned down the Lion. Several days later they were talking to each other as friends again. Everyone's honor was saved but a fight had to occur because the verbal loser did not trust the winner not to question publicly his reputation.

Understanding and compassion within the gang have been shown through the members' consideration of those who are made to "walk the line." As punishment for violating a gang rule, members must run between two lines of members and are beaten with sticks and bats. One member, having failed to attend several meetings and a fight, was subjected to this punishment. When he cried after walking the line, he was permitted to leave the park unobtrusively and return the following day without further mention of the event. On numerous other occasions strong feelings among the members allow them to deal with the humiliation of fellow members by ignoring a situation that they would otherwise never ignore. No gang member has ever "lost" a fight. The fight was always "unfair" because the opponent had unfairly used a weapon or was much bigger.

Some discussions, particularly concerning problems with women, reveal the closeness of members' ties. Men should not have such problems because they are supposed to be in control of all situations. Admitting failure to dominate a situation is sufficient to lose face. Nevertheless, members of the Lions did discuss their failures. One member's former girlfriend cuckolded him by going out with others when she was supposed to be going steady with him. He publicly admitted being hurt and unable to control her; another member whose girlfriend walked out and married someone else made a similar admission. No one ridiculed either member. On another occasion, Tico told the others that he could not control his temper but he was working on it with a psychiatrist. Seeing a psychiatrist was generally perceived as weakness. On one occasion a judge had made seeing a psychiatrist a condition of probation for two Lions but they adamantly refused to go (their probation was not revoked). These are all things that men rarely discuss with other men because they all indicate weakness and dependency. To develop this degree of closeness is extremely difficult. There is no reason why these young men should give up this relationship with the gang when it proves satisfying and there are few alternatives.

As chapter 8 showed, work rarely allows young men to meet and develop relationships. Most jobs are too transitory. Moreover, marriage provides little companionship. It is culturally unacceptable for men and women to be equals, which is necessary for friendship to develop. The segmented sex roles mean that men and women have few common interests to use as a basis for companionship.

Few of the young men make friends on the job. Not only do they usually change jobs frequently, but many jobs are structured to limit opportunities for the workers to socialize. In addition, though the workers may perform the same unskilled jobs they may have nothing else in common. Only some men in their forties who have been working in the same plant on the same shift for more than ten years ever spoke of socializing with people outside the community whom they knew solely from work. None of the Lions ever socialized with anyone at work except when coworkers were also friends from the neighborhood. That is why people who worked with friends were so envied. Others claimed to have no one with whom to talk at work. Socializing occurs with friends from the neighborhood.

Women have their own female relatives and friends with whom to socialize. They generally expect relatively little companionship from their husbands. The women have their own parties, help each other out with "women's tasks," and go shopping together. Even at parties women generally talk with other women and men with other men. Women talk about children, men, pregnancy and marriage. The men discuss sports or the latest fights. Even on a Saturday night some husbands and wives may go to separate social occasions. The sexes shared few interests: the women have the home and children and the men have the streets, sports, and work.

Moreover, the cultural expectation of male domination discourages any public display of a man's dependency on his wife. Open displays of closeness to wives frequently lead to accusations of being henpecked or dominated. While it was acceptable for wives and children to watch the softball games on a nice day, any wife who came to the park too frequently was viewed as attempting to dominate her husband, who was seen as losing control of the relationship. I saw one member of the Lions and his wife all dressed up to go out together. He asked me explicitly not to tell the other Lions.

There are, then, both internal and external factors that help to perpetuate gang membership and allow members to develop close personal ties. While gangs may be fragile entities when the members are very young and the bonds new, the more time members spend together, the stronger relationships grow. As the gang evolves into adulthood, internal cohesive mechanisms become more important and more intense. Exchanges cannot be seen as purely utilitarian; they are in part symbolic of their ties.

The Continuity of Groups as Gangs

The Lions, Greeks, Nobles, and several other gangs have senior components who still get into fights over breaches of etiquette to maintain their reputation as tough and aggressive warriors. Why should employed and married men still be sensitive to other gangs' claims to precedence? Why have they not become social athletic clubs, as Suttles (1968) describes, concerned only with sports and entertainment? Much of the literature on gangs argues that the style of presentation of self that includes violence as an expression of manhood should and will change with the onset of adulthood and its roles and statuses.

On 32nd Street male adult roles do not necessarily imply a

change to identities based on occupational or parenting competence. The jobs available to most gang members are not jobs against which one might voluntarily measure self-worth, nor in this sub-culture do men play a critical parenting role. They have little with which to replace the image of themselves as tough warriors, and little incentive to confront the gap between their limited economic success and their desire to do better. They continue to straddle the worlds of the street and the wider society. By maintaining their street identities, by sharing a vocabulary of honor that situationally justifies the use of force and appraises any public demonstration of intimacy or dependency as dishonorable, they maintain local status and their self-image as tough warriors.

The continued commitment to gang affiliation is dramatized by the lack of change in symbolic devices used to express membership. While the Lions play softball regularly and have a winning team, their clean and pressed uniforms are in their traditional colors and have "Lions" emblazoned across the chest and "David's Tavern" across the back. Nico's son has a uniform and several of the wives have matching hats. A number of the Lions have new gang jacket-sweaters with more elaborate emblems. Their dress continues to affirm their identity, as do their remaining on the same park bench and their public recounting of past events.

Violence continues as an acceptable response to a challenge to an individual's honor or to a collective insult. The Lions often do not hesitate in defining breaches of etiquette as intentional and threats to their claim to precedence. Pete, for example, explained how he got into a fight the previous week: "This dude and his girl were sitting together in the park. . . . He called me a punk, so I let him have it. . . . Pow, pow." Every third sentence continued "pow" or "I let him have it." This conversation was a bit overacted because Pete was high on drugs, but his girlfriend confirmed this fight and the fact that he fought frequently. Both the reputation of the individual and the gang continue as central concerns of these young men, for dishonor is still experienced as a loss of manhood.

Historical events also perpetuate intergang warfare. Tico of the Lions explained that several insults have never been redressed sufficiently. Sometimes it takes years to settle an affair of honor, but men of honor must do so. The continuity of gangs is thus tied, in part, to maintaining self-esteem in terms of the moral qualities of a man of honor.

With their reputations well established and highly evaluated, the Lions need not respond to each potential insult as if it were intentional. If they choose not to view an insult as intentional, there is no necessary loss of prestige. Many incidents are not viewed as a challenge. They felt no need to become involved in Little or Junior problems, nor to fight when the rival team at a ballgame commented on their state of inebriation (Nico could barely stand). Instead, after giving up a number of runs in the first few innings, they came from behind to win the game. Then they proceeded to get drunk again and everyone left them alone.

While it may not be necessary continually to reassert one's claim to precedence, and while fights in the name of the gang or the individual may be fewer as the young men enter their twenties, there still are fights. With the participants more skilled in the use of guns, the possibility of a death becomes greater. Three Senior Greeks were shot and killed in a bar and several others wounded in a gang-related incident that was part of a long history of confrontations, as was the death of the president of the Lions, Gilberto.

This continued commitment to an identity as a gang member does not mean that all alternatives have been eliminated. With the marginal status of most of the jobs, the chances for financial success through a good job are severely limited. However, youths continue to work even when they could be earning much more at illegitimate enterprises. Over half of the Lions who were not in the army or in jail in 1977 were working full-time or attending school. Half were also fathers. Those who were working all had well over a year's time invested in a job, but work itself does little to enhance the self-esteem of members; that must be confirmed through the gang interaction and activities.

Even if the value of a particular job did not allow a young man to distance himself from a perceived insult, it might seem that marriage and fatherhood would increase the commitment to a conventional response. However, while marriage may decrease the chances of interpreting an insult as demeaning, it is not sufficient for most to make that commitment. While fatherhood does offer a basis of self-esteem, and while most young men who become fathers are extremely proud and play with their babies when wives and children come to the park, for most fatherhood too is an insufficient basis for commitment to purely conventional activities. For Len, his new family was enough to pull him out of the gang, but when that relationship became tenuous, he appeared ready to return, often hanging around the Lions. Rico and Enrique, both married to their long-term girlfriends, spent less time at the park with the others and were less likely to be available for an immediate response to an incident. Nonetheless, as men of similar moral qualities they are considered, and consider themselves, members of the gang and ready to fight for it.

From Image Promoter to Image Defender

Underneath all the symbols of continuity, change has begun to occur, but it is never publicly articulated. To acknowledge the change would be to admit that the members are not as tough as they were and that the reason for staying together has changed. In fact, from self-image promoters they have become self-image defenders. While a number of relatively superficial symbolic devices (clothes, gang location, and verbal bravura) continue to dramatize their commitment to their identity as tough and aggressive warriors, in fact their concerns have shifted and the meaning of violence has altered. The relationship between reputation and violence has begun to seem a problem, but this never becomes a public issue.

The switch from image promoters to image defenders is illustrated by Sal's failure to understand this change, which occurred during his absence. He was not quick to notice this subtle, private change because no one talked about it. Sal continually proposed that they go out and provoke fights. No one would tell him directly that the gang had no interest in provoking new fights. They just kept refusing. His failure to comprehend the change was part of the reason for the attempt to ease him out.

A few other changes had occurred. For example, some members of the gang referred to Ronny by his real name rather than his street name. No one except his oldest brother had ever before called him by his real name. Most of the other Lions were still referred to by

their street names. Another example was a Lion who had been in a
juvenile center for a year and seen a psychiatrist twice a week: he
was able to give a complete analysis (two hours worth) of his person-
ality in correct psychological terms and boasted about the experience.

To acknowledge publicly the change from promoters to defenders would be to admit that the members are together no longer
because they are tough men but largely because of the friendship,
intimacy, and companionship that have developed over the history
of the group. This is inconsistent with their image of themselves as
tough and aggressive. Since they have developed no other acceptable identity, they continue to remain a gang to maintain that
image in their own eyes and in the eyes of those around them. However, their relationship has changed. *They remain tough so that
they can be together rather than being together because they are
tough.* The meanings of toughness and violence have changed.

Core gang youths remain together as gang members on 32nd Street
beyond the period hypothesized by most sociological studies. There
is much more to gang membership than the maintenance of their
social identity as tough and aggressive warriors, though it is this
image of themselves that is the source of group continuity as a
gang. Without the strong friendships developed over time among
the members, gang membership might deteriorate, but the intimate
relationships and the lack of alternative relationships keep the
group together and expand the relationships to include *compadrazgo*. The Lions, like everyone else, need intimacy, trust, and
friendship. Mutual obligations form the basis of this relationship
and are symbolic of it. The gang is the perfect social group for
intimacy and dependency since it maintains the public myth of the
aggressive warrior but in reality offers a comfortable place for tough
warriors to develop close ties.

The sense of self found in the gang relationship is unavailable to
most members elsewhere, yet adults indicate some tension about
having juvenile identities. They asked me whether they had
changed. When I returned the question to them they hesitatingly replied: "We're older now," or "We should get together for good
things like housing and jobs," or "We shouldn't kill our own
people."

Some community members are more tolerant than others of older gang members. Some excuse them as still young, others call them "good for nothings." Most people ignore the gangs. It is only when an acquaintance gets hurt or a public incident occurs that evaluations are made. While most residents understand the motives of the honorable man, the exaggerated violence that gang members use to obtain status as tough men is considered intolerable by many in the community. A grown man should express his domination and independence not through gang membership but through his family relationships. As a man of honor, however, he would remain sensitive to others' efforts to demean him.

10

The Consequences of Being Different

Looking back on all her responsibilities and problems—taking care of seven younger siblings, working after school from the age of fourteen through college, saving her money, and studying hard—Louisa, a college graduate with a job in the business sector, was not always sure it had been worth the effort. Living alone in a small apartment away from 32nd Street, she was often lonely even though she had made a few friends. She now had little in common with her family or the women with whom she had grown up. She spoke differently, acted differently, and dressed differently. Her mother would have been upset had she known what Louisa paid for her business suits.

Switching language and dress for home visits was easy compared with the adjustments she had made in her perception of herself and the nature of her world as she grew up. During high school she told her mother that she never wanted to be a mother; her mother did not speak to her for weeks. At nineteen Louisa made the critical and very difficult decision to accept a full scholarship to a college away from home over the objections of her mother and many of her relatives. "Nice girls" did not move away from home until they married. This argument was repeated every summer when she came home to work and would not live in her family's apartment.

During her first year away at school Louisa made few friends, but later became more involved in campus life. Upon returning to Chicago after graduation, Louisa found that her mother expected her to handle many of the emotional and financial problems of her younger brothers and sisters. Although no longer much a part of the 32nd Street world, she is still responsible for resolving many of its problems. At the same time she is trying, as a Chicana, to find her way in a wider society that does not always accept her, even with her educational certification demonstrating organizational ability, hard work, dependability, and verbal and social skills. That Anglo world offers little social life and social support for a young woman from a different social and economic group. Louisa found it difficult to make friends at first, to find a good job, and to deal with her familial demands. She was often depressed.

Linda, like many of her friends, has been a political activist since high school. Always involved in a myriad of activities, Linda did not do well in high school but was determined to work her way through college. Lacking funds, she had to drop out of college for a semester several times, but she did well consistently. Unlike Louisa's friends from high school, the majority of Linda's friends attended college and some, like Linda, came back to live and work in the community.

From the time she was fourteen or fifteen, Linda was constantly made aware that she was different from other community residents. She moved out of her parents' home before graduating from college. Her parents, who could not afford to help her financially, were hurt and angry. Not only did they believe her behavior irresponsible because she lacked the money to live alone, but her father believed it morally wrong and ignored her for a long time afterward. After graduation, when she returned to the community to work, she lived with other community workers.

Linda experienced some strains in her relations with other community residents. Her younger sisters felt uncomfortable talking with her and criticized her dress and behavior. Linda frequently violated sex role expectations; for example, she beat a male friend at pool. While she remained in the community, Linda was continually confronted by how much her standards differed from those of the community. She found it necessary to separate her public and private life. After several years she found an apartment outside the community although she continued to work there. But the tensions created by her standards for social relationships and the constant mix of social life and work were overwhelming, and she stopped working in the community.

The pressures Jesse experienced from his peers were almost

enough to defeat his attempts to change his local orientation. He had been not just a gang member when he was younger but gang president. Though he left the gang at sixteen, he remained deeply committed to local peer group relationships. He became involved in a drug-using group for a short time but realized what he was doing before it was too late. He started his own drug program while attending classes at a local junior college.

Relations with his 32nd Street peers took most of his time, energy, and money. He would lend them any money he had and would spend hours talking. His apartment was always open to anyone who wanted to talk, party, or "crash" (spend the night). If a friend asked, he always went out drinking. Caught in the male world of continuous exchange and excitement, he found it difficult to pursue his studies. However, the further he got in his career, the more unequal the exchanges became. He was always the one giving the parties and helping out.

As a paid community worker he had control over scarce resources. Resources received from him could never be returned, and a *patron-peon* (dominant-subordinate) relationship would develop if his resources were accepted. To deal with this situation, many of his friends defined all of Jesse's resources as belonging to the community organization, which meant the exchanges need not be reciprocated. As a result, neither his time nor his money were ever his own. After several years, he felt he could handle the situation only by leaving the community and the city to try to succeed in the wider society. He later moved back and took a job in sales.

These three brief biographies focus on some of the problems young people experience when their behavior and appraisal of social relationships—their balances of honor and the American dream—differ from the local moral order. Some choose to leave the community in pursuit of economic success, while others work to improve the resources available to the community. A commitment to pursue the American dream or to political activism creates tensions with some of the expectations that follow from the code of honor. Familial and peer relationships exert pressure toward conformity to the local moral order.

Individuals who choose to measure their competency in terms of the wider society rather than in terms of local identity risk a loss of social and emotional support from peers and kin. Trusting and close relationships must be developed with new people and on different terms. The movement away from the traditional sources of support and the traditional basis of social relationships can create feelings of acute loneliness. Little within the Chicano community prepares them for the competitive, individualistic Anglo world of social relationships in which they must face lack of acceptance and some degree of discrimination. They become caught between two worlds.

Those who choose to become political activists must retain an identity rooted in both worlds. On the one hand, to organize and represent the community they must maintain some traditional bases of social solidarity and membership in community networks. On the other hand, they must be able to negotiate their way in the wider society: the world of grants, bureaucracies, and politics. Instead of full membership in either world they are between two sometimes conflicting worlds, each with its own expectations and social relationships. Unlike the upwardly mobile individuals, the political activists form their own social group and subculture. Many of the local activists live together in one area of 32nd Street developing their own life-style, which accepts some and rejects other symbols of both worlds. An activist's world here is a localized version of the world of other community political activists outside the traditional political system.

So far this book has examined how young people whose identities remain locally rooted have constructed their lives. This chapter concerns the processes that help and hinder the efforts of some young people to be different as well as how they develop and manage these differences. Generally, the difficulty of moving out of a subculture (particularly lower-class, working-class, and ethnic subcultures) into the wider society is explained by the degree to which norms are internalized and whether the meanings of norms are largely determined by the socioeconomic position of the group or tradition.[1] The more the group is socialized into a traditional value system, the more difficult it is to change. On 32nd Street the movement away from relationships based on specific moral and cognitive categories is possible but not easy. Integration into the wider society requires more than merely doing well in school and getting a good job. It involves new definitions of relationships, as well as efforts to develop new solidarities in a rather hostile environment. Culture is not static or unambiguous, nor does its content depend solely upon socioeconomic placement. It is possible for people to redefine their priorities and social relationships, but beyond certain limits an individual who is "different" experiences difficulty in adjusting to a new subculture and does not feel a part of the old. New social supports that allow for feelings of belonging and understanding must be developed. The lives and relationships of those who move out of the community in pursuit of economic success and those who are politically active on behalf of the community illustrate the difficulty of becoming and being "different."

The Costs of Social and Economic Success

If a person is a good student, encouraged by teachers, given scholarships to college, and able to obtain a good job, then why should leaving 32nd Street still be such a difficult and tension-ridden process? Why are some people not particularly happy when they are succeeding? A change means not only that they must appraise and evaluate their own behavior on different terms but that their families and peers will appraise them as "different." Many are without a supportive friendship network and find that their families no longer understand them and cannot give them support. Frequently, mobility means succeeding alone and, in the end, possibly not belonging to either world.

Pathways to Success

For some youths, opportunities are presented and encouragement begins early in their school career and they readily acknowledge to themselves and others that they are different. Others are more uncertain about how they see themselves and attempt to hide their differences from their peers, sometimes refusing all efforts to help them along in school. A third category of youths has little desire to be different when young, receives little encouragement, and has few opportunities, but later experiences make them want to be different.

Commitment to achievement in terms of the American dream can be demonstrated by public efforts to do well in school. These youths announce their desires to be seen as scholarly and hard working; they wish their self-worth to be measured by the standards of academic competence. They open themselves to exclusion from most peer groups by their open declaration that being a student is an important aspect of their identity. While education is viewed as important by everyone, good students who do not make an effort to be like everyone else can be evaluated as trying to be better than others. Few groups will accept them as friends. To be accepted they must not publicly demonstrate their scholastic achievements, which therefore never become part of their public identity. If those achievements are minimized publicly, these students make less of an investment in school. One young woman did very well at school unbeknownst to many of her friends. She was often in trouble—not enough to be perceived by the school as a troublemaker but enough so that her friends felt she was like them.

The meaning of scholastic achievement may differ. An individual may use the identity of good student to claim to be a particular kind of person, as Louisa did, while another may make no such public claims about academic achievement, as the young woman mentioned above did. The latter invested less in her school achievement. While she was proud of her achievement in private, it never became part of her identity. She became pregnant during her junior year, dropped out of school, married, and stayed in the community.

Other youths lead rather average local childhoods. They belong to gangs or tough peer groups, do not do well in school, and spend much time partying with their friends during school hours. For them the movement away from local standards and social relationships necessitates a redefinition of identity and, unless they receive full scholarships to out-of-town schools, they must continuously deal with previous relationships based on former standards. It takes a while for others to believe that a change has occurred. One young man was able to avoid these problems. He led an active street life but did well in school and attended boarding school on a scholarship. Upon his graduation from a major university he claimed that the transition had been relatively easy. Neither prep school nor university was difficult; working on 32nd Street was. Some men after returning from the armed forces and examining the life-styles of their friends decide to go to college, not wanting to spend their lives on the streets. Others work in a factory for a while, decide that they do not want to spend their lives there, and begin to attend local colleges.

The process of redefining one's identity is difficult and sometimes impossible, particularly for those who remain in the community and keep up old associations. For example, one young man who was very intelligent and skilled verbally had so much trouble reading and writing that after two years of constant failure in an adult education class for high school dropouts he gave up and returned to street hustling. His lack of academic skills was not the only problem. He was also trying to support his family, who wanted nice things—a decent kitchen, some furniture, and good clothes. His wife was unwilling to wait until he got through school; her relatives were beginning to think that her husband was less than honorable for failing to support his family properly.

Being Different

People who base their identities on nonlocal criteria are evaluated as different from most local residents. Such people judge their competency in terms congruent with those of the wider society, that is, almost entirely according to educational and occupational accomplishments rather than honor. Sometimes they remain outsiders to the middle-class community and become outsiders to 32nd Street as well. Their relationships to their former friends and family change, yet most never experience complete social equality in the wider society and find it difficult to develop close ties.

For some young working women, independence is unnecessary and they continue to live with their parents or husbands. Others who choose careers often begin to act in ways regarded as independent. Decisions to attend school away from home, which are seen as symbols of independence, also give young women an opportunity to experience independence. Because they must proceed on their own, overcoming much opposition from family and friends, the young women become increasingly independent and more sure of their ability to stand on their own. Louisa nearly did not go away to school. On the day she was to leave, she decided she could not possibly go. She finally went but nearly left school several times during the first year. When she returned for the summer she was able to withstand the criticism of her family and not move back home. In fact community feelings against unmarried women living away from their families are so strong that many landlords will not rent to them unless they are welfare mothers.[2] Many believe that any single woman living alone is no better than a prostitute. This can bring shame on the entire family, as a daughter's sexual purity cannot be established if she lives away from home, whether or not she actually remains a virgin.

Social relationships not only with her family but with men often change. A woman who is independent and more sure of her skills may expect to be equal to men, not submissive. This change raises the issue of control over a woman's sexual activities and her sexual purity. If women should not be dominated by men, then the dilemma between passion and virginity need not exist. A woman who is independent does not submit to a man but decides with him. She does not give in to him in a moment of passion but engages in sex when they mutually agree to do so. This changes the meaning of birth control, motherhood, and virginity.

The importance of motherhood remains intact, as it does for many Anglo feminists (Blake, 1972); however, the meaning changes. Most women from 32nd Street have children, but they argue that they have them by choice, not as a requirement to fulfill their identity as women. Women should have children when they want to, even if that means waiting until they are in their thirties. Although many women delay having children, they still highly value motherhood.

Virginity too has a different meaning. A woman does not remain a virgin to protect her sexual purity and the honor of her family but remains a virgin by choice. The decision about her virginity is defined in terms of control over her own body and freedom of choice, not in terms of the importance of virginity and submission to men. One young woman of eighteen claimed that she was still a virgin because the right man had not come along yet.

Others, now feminists, agreed with her position, though they had felt differently at the time they gave up their virginity.

The meaning of birth control is also altered. Because birth control can be appraised as the means to allow women to control their own bodies and to participate actively in sexual decisions, its use does not mean sexual license (unbounded sexuality) and the denial of motherhood but rather freedom and independence. The women's appraisal and evaluation of their own actions have changed. The rest of the community continues to evaluate these women largely in terms of the traditional moral categories. To the community these young women violate notions of femininity and sexual purity.

Young men have different problems in developing an identity in terms of the wider society. The more a young man defines himself in terms of education and economic success, the less he needs to define breaches of etiquette as demeaning and the less he can afford to risk defending his honor. Defending honor heightens the potential of incarceration or suspension from school and thus jeopardizes his success and educational choices. If he still resides in the community, however, the likelihood of being seen as a coward if he refuses to defend his honor remains a concern to most youths.

For a rep avoider to maintain an identity as an honorable person by community standards is difficult. Any male who runs home to avoid responding to an insult would be regarded as weak and dishonored. For example, Beto's complete refusal to fight when another young man publicly called him names several times and even insulted one of Beto's sisters was considered cowardly even by several of his friends who were themselves rep avoiders and rarely fought. Being a rep avoider does not necessarily bring a poor appraisal, but in some situations it is judged that *anyone* should fight to maintain some semblance of honor. Total removal from the honor code is not possible within the community standards. No matter how much youths use educational competence to evaluate self-worth and avoid situations where they might have to fight, they are affected by community standards. The possibility of remaining completely unconcerned with honor, even if a young man is committed to getting ahead, is inconceivable unless he totally disregards his peers and his family.

The basis for trust among peers or neighbors is absent when a young man or woman is perceived as having a different set of cognitive and moral categories, when they publicly demonstrate a desire to be appraised and evaluated largely on the basis of academic or job achievements, and when their wants and needs are no longer in accord with those of most of the community. These young people feel little desire or impetus to become involved in a mutual exchange network. They have few interests and problems in common with other residents. The social and symbolic forces that lead to the development of trust are absent and consequently so is the cohesive force. Some of those who are different have very little peer support. Occasionally, small peer groups of upwardly mobile youths are formed, sometimes brought together by an outsider or an activity. One such group was created when a grade school teacher took a group of young men to various events around the city. Another group of both young men and women developed around their common interest in a student radio station.

It is often difficult for 32nd Street residents to develop close ties outside the community. When these young people move out of the community to attend school or work, the transition means more than just being judged by a new set of standards and learning new skills. The experience of social competency is elusive for many. It is not that these young people do not know how to dress or are unaware of the rules of social comportment; to the contrary, most of them have an excellent knowledge of polite social skills. However, developing friendships and dating relationships in a middle-class Anglo world takes much more than good manners.

Though there are few hard and fast rules about friendships, or dating relationships in today's middle-class world, most middle-class young people have discussed their expectations in high school. For the young 32nd Street person who moves into this world at eighteen or nineteen, expectations are either nonexistent or culled from the media. While social relations always contain a potential for misreading of signs, the potential is greater among people of diverse backgrounds. Signs of affection can be mistaken for signs of commitment. Signs of insecurity can be mistaken for signs of dislike.

Moreover, individuals who date non-Chicanos must consider the importance of their ethnicity. Many do not wish to subvert their ethnicity through intermarriage. On the one hand, some of the independent Chicanas have a difficult time locating Chicanos who find women's independence desirable. On the other hand, many Anglos will not go out with a Chicana.[3]

Freedom, independence, and success in the wider society encourage changes in family relationships. The family honor can no longer be linked to a daughter's sexual purity, although some members of the expanded family may continue to try. One young woman's aunt constantly complained about her niece's behavior long after the parents had come to support their daughter's new life. In other cases the upwardly mobile youths become the dominant and supportive member of the family. The flow of resources becomes one-directional: information, money, and emotional support move from the youth to the family. One mother depends on her son to help pay the school tuition of the younger children as well as to resolve all the legal, academic, and emotional problems of the younger children. The drain on the son is overwhelming and he receives only a little of the support he needs. No one can really understand his problems at home anyway, he claims. They are not problems that others in his family have ever experienced. Helping to support a family may create additional problems for beginning workers in the corporate world where they cannot afford to live in the style of others making similar salaries. However, unlike the relatively fragile bonds of the peer group network, the family bond and expectations remain strong though often tension-ridden. Few young people reject their families or are rejected by them.

In Neither World

The upwardly mobile have few places of real support where they can be themselves and where trust and understanding can be developed. Though they evaluate themselves and others in terms of professional competencies and are successful, this does not mean they can move easily through the middle-class Anglo world. Yet they do not find it easy to be in the world of 32nd Street.

These young people are different from middle-class Anglos:

they are Chicanos and most claim that allegiance. While many of their work problems may be similar to those of young Anglos, their problems of living in a new world are not understood by the Anglos. The social differences are significant, and while many Chicanos have Anglo friends, only a few such friendships are close.

At the same time many local ties, except for family ties, have been severed. Many of these young people no longer have much in common with their old friends, and the potenial for violence now makes them uncomfortable. One young woman who had known several of the older gang members well during high school felt uncomfortable with them three years later. One man is afraid to return to 32nd Street for fear that he may be provoked into fighting. Consequently many of these young people are lonely. There are so few of them that they rarely find each other in the wider society. In this they are unlike the political activists, who have developed their own local subculture and solidarities.

Political Activists

During the late 1960's political activism became a way of life for some community residents.[4] The number of those deeply involved on occasion reached close to one hundred young people in their twenties and thirties. Many were employed by social action and service programs. Others were volunteers for many community and political activities and were employed at regular jobs or were students. It was not until the late 1960's that Chicago Chicanos began to interact regularly with Chicanos from California and the Southwest and several national leaders visited 32nd Street. During the early 1970's the federal government made funds available for the Spanish speaking—a group that had been largely passed over by federal programs during the 1960's. Residents of 32nd Street were able to take advantage of these funds with the help of a team from the state's mental health facilities. They brought a large number of federally funded programs to the area: drug abuse, recreation, college courses, tutoring, language programs, and a bilingual library. The activists worked as staff for these programs and used

210   *Honor and the American Dream*

their skills to develop public interest in the social programs, to organize proposals and protests for more jobs, and to work for better education and against immigration policies.

Pathways to Activism

Many of the activists were born in the United States, many of them in Chicago. Most spoke Spanish while growing up but as adults some were more comfortable in English. There are several pathways to becoming an activist. One group of males came from the streets to become youth workers in traditional settlement houses and then activists, while many of the women started by organizing for better schooling for their children. A second generation in the mid-1970's attended college first and then returned to work in the community. While some of the first generation activists graduated from college, others did not finish high school, yet all feel education is important. Most live in the community and many grew up together, which gives them a long common history and emphasizes and reinforces their solidarity as a group.

Many of the young men grew up in what they considered real poverty in an area near 32nd Street that was largely demolished to make way for urban renewal. Most, though street-wise and very tough, were not gang members, which enables them to move among many groups. While working as recreation and gang aides in the community, several attended a national Chicano political conference in 1969. Caught up in this political and social movement, they began to turn to organizing and to developing more instrumental programs and organizations. They learned how to write proposals for funding and how to manipulate government officials.

Many of the women became active as a response to the poor education their children were receiving in the community schools. Some started by using conventional channels, and when that failed to have an impact on the schools, they organized rallies and sit-ins to protest poor teachers and administrators, continued utilization of condemned buildings, and the lack of bilingual education. With their commitment to social change and activism, they needed day care centers for their own children and saw that other women who needed or wanted to work also needed such facilities. They organized a day care center and a women's center. Several of the female activists were or became involved with their male counterparts, which further solidified the activists as a group.

Still other youths, like Linda, who became involved in radical politics in high school and continued to be involved in college, felt a commitment to the community and came back to 32nd Street to work. They wished to improve the social and economic position of the community and expressed no desire to accumulate the traditional symbols of middle-class status or to work in traditional white-collar jobs, which encourage separation from the community. Several had good job offers outside the community. They chose political activism over the American dream of individual economic and social success.

Being a Political Activist

Political activists do have a different orientation from that of the average community member or the upwardly mobile person. A successful activist must be especially skilled in impression management in order to deal with a variety of people in different social worlds. Good contacts in many different settings both inside and outside the community are essential. Success depends in part on knowing who has the resources outside the community and on being able to obtain them. But activists must be able not only to provide large numbers of community residents with services but also to mobilize large numbers of people and to mediate between community factions. For this they must be trusted by community residents. Activists must be appraised as being "of the people" both by the community and by the representatives of the wider society who wish to deal with the community. They must not define their actions in terms of honor or the American dream of individual competition and economic success. Yet they must appear to do both in order to be acceptable to both groups.

Although activists spend time in the streets, their orientation toward street life and activities changes. They still use the verbal skills and street knowledge they learned during their youth days, but they are no longer attracted by the excitement of street activities. They cannot be drawn into contests of honor, although they must understand street youths if they intend to turn the gangs away from fighting each other and toward more constructive political activities for the community as a whole. Activists involved gang members in weekend retreats where political activism and ethnic identity were discussed in marathon sessions. They also organized several mass meetings of all 32nd Street gangs and negotiated a peace among them for several months in the early 1970's. When one of the leaders of the peace movement was shot and killed on a street corner while mediating a problem between two gangs, peace ended. While activists no longer find the honor confrontations of the street alluring, much of the status, prestige, and power they have is based on their ability to direct the activities and the energies of the street-oriented residents.

Despite their different orientation, the activists still like to think of themselves as typical community residents and not as leaders. They are different, however, because they are working not merely to maintain their family honor or for their personal advancement but to mediate between the community and the wider society for the social, political, and economic benefit of the community at large.

To deal with the members of the wider society, they must understand them well enough to manipulate them. The ability to manipulate symbols of identity and affiliation is central to the activist's success with the wider society. This means acting sometimes like a middle-class person and sometimes like a street tough. The identity an activist projects shifts with the situation being negotiated.[5] They use language, dress, aggressiveness, degrees of educated speech, and skits to create an atmosphere. Sometimes, wearing Mexican ponchos, hats, or sandals with their jeans, they threaten the representatives of the wider society. They may speak a few words in Spanish to increase the tension. In some skits one plays aggressor and demands a particular resource while a second person, in educated tones, attempts to placate the first person while saying that he really cannot control the first and perhaps the official ought to do what is asked. All these presentation-of-self skills are extensions of the verbal and dressing skills learned in the street. Toughness is not, for the activist, a direct indicator of his manhood but a tool to manipulate an outsider for the benefit of the community. The meaning of many of these actions has changed from largely expressive, identifying who the person is, to mainly instrumental, a means for obtaining resources and power.

In other situations divisions between Latin groups must be overcome in order to improve the bargaining position of 32nd Street. Symbols of allegiances must be manipulated to take advantage of opportunities. For example, the people are 32nd Street residents when they are negotiating with the city for better garbage pickup; they are Latinos when negotiating along with Puerto Ricans for bilingual education; and they may be Chicanos when speaking to the nation political scene.

Men have traditionally taken the leadership roles while women have taken helping roles such as secretaries and aides to the men. Local expectations were violated in the early 1970's when local women began to take leadership roles as well. With the increasingly important activist roles, the study of women in Mexican and Chicano history, and the connections with Chicanas throughout the country, these women, like Anglo activist women in the 1960's, realized that women have been, can be, and should be leaders. While the Chicanas' concern for independence parallels that of the Anglos, it is not derived from it. Local female activists were invited to national meetings where they met other women in similar situations. In the early 1970's a woman's organization started on 32nd Street and sponsored a conference about Latin women. Moreover, the national interest in past and present Chicano affairs led to a new analysis of the role of women in Mexican history. Mirandé and Enríquez (1979) have argued that there have been a number of strong, independent women in both Mexican and Chicano history, despite the traditionally subordinate role of Mexican women. This gives female activists good precedents for their change from supportive roles to independent leaders. Through these meetings female activists were able to develop support networks and collectively devise new evaluations of the identity of women.

While these men and women are working on behalf of the community, they differ from the average community resident. These differences sometimes make relations with community members difficult. Tensions are experienced in the evaluation of the sexual purity of women, in the evaluation of community work as nonwork, and in the ambiguous nature of their participation in mutual obligation networks. These tensions create potential problems in the daily interaction of activists with others, problems that affirm to the community residents that activists are a different kind of people.

Because women activists live and work in the community, their behavior is more public than that of upwardly mobile women and therefore more likely to receive criticism. Moreover, while the women working in the wider society receive some prestige for their relatively high status positions and good incomes, the political activists have neither. Many of the activists have children, and the community sometimes perceives these women as poor mothers both because they are too independent and because children do not appear to be their only concern. Although as a group female activists are negatively evaluated as mothers, individually many were appraised by community residents as very good mothers. In terms of community moral categories, the behavior of female activists is always open to question.

A second area of tension between the community and the activists is the nature of their work. Some residents argue that activists are being paid for doing nothing and equate them with welfare recipients. One mother of a very successful activist told him to go out and get a real job. Organizing cannot be work. Organizers do not get dirty, do not keep regular hours, spend time hanging around, and make no visible product. Many of their activities—finding jobs for people, talking to people who need someone to talk to, transporting people to hospitals or courts, and helping to get youths back into school—are favors (mutual obligations) that members of the expanded family do or try to do for each other. Therefore their actions are not seen as work.

However, if the relationship between the activists and other community members is seen in terms of mutual obligations, other problems arise. The exchanges are not between equals. Resources flow from the activist to the client (a dominant-subordinate relationship) and secret or personal information flows only from the community member to the activist. People who are trying to help others without themselves being helped in the same manner do not exchange information, discuss each other's problems, and thereby build trust. The activist has control of resources and information that for most are too extensive and expensive to repay.

Unless the residents are willing to be constantly in a subordinate position, they must redefine the relationship. Many residents do not wish to give up the resources to which activists have access, so they define all of the workers' resources as belonging to some government agency, not to the workers. Frequently this means that residents define *everything* activists have—time, energy, and money—as belonging to the program, so that anything can be demanded at any time or place. The pattern of constant demand becomes very difficult for the activists. They are on call night and day and have almost no privacy or personal possessions. One worker had youths in his apartment every evening and often through the night. They ate whatever he had, borrowed his money, and sometimes wore his clothes. The government was paying, one youth explained. Other workers are often called in the middle of the night to bail someone out of jail or to take someone to the hospital. Nothing belongs to them personally.

These constant demands, the often confused relationships with other community residents, and their distinctiveness from other community residents all provide impetus for the activists to retreat from community social life, largely to their own enclave but sometimes to other cities or to jobs in the wider society. Activists are marginal members of a marginal community. They must be seen as members of the local community and the wider society, but they are neither.

An Activist Life-Style

Unlike the upwardly mobile, who have no group to which they can retreat and feel at home, there are enough activists to form more than one social grouping and to develop symbolic devices that distinguish them from both the community and the wider society. Many of the activists live in the same area of the community and several in the same building. Many are related or have been friends since childhood. Others are connected through the *compadrazgo* relationship. They spend extensive periods together at work and at

play. In fact, their life-style makes their relationship with older
community members more problematic.

   Though the activists continue to live in the community and are,
in general, no better off economically than others, they differ from
the community in dress, language, apartment furnishings, and often
what is done for fun on a Saturday night. Moreover, many of them
have intentionally given up all the symbols of economic success.
Their life-style is, in part, a local version of the counterculture of the
1960's and early 1970's, for example, in their public disdain for
"appropriate" dress and furniture, a suburban home, a midsize
American car, and other symbols of middle-class status. They wear
old, unpressed blue jeans or painters pants and work shirts. They
live in apartments furnished at the Salvation Army store with
street signs or political posters as decorations. Most community
residents would be embarrassed to live that way: they want smooth,
nicely plastered walls, not exposed brick; bright new matching
furniture, not old pillows and rickety chairs; and a matching bed
and dresser set, not a mattress on the floor. In distancing themselves from these aspects of mainstream America, in rejecting the
American dream, the activists also distance themselves from the
local community. Some community residents see these activists as
outsiders even though they grew up and live in the community.

   These young people have chosen to place their identity as
Chicanos ahead of everything else. Yet many of their interpretations and evaluations of situations and social relationships are at
variance with local ones, particularly in the area of sex roles and
achievement of the American dream. They prefer to work to raise
the socioeconomic level of the community by obtaining more opportunities and resources from the wider society and by social change.

Both the upwardly mobile and the political activists have resolved
the dilemmas that are faced by everyone in the 32nd Street community differently from other residents, so differently that residents have doubts about their being like them. Both sit on the
margins, many not wanting to be excluded but feeling not quite
comfortable when included.

   The upwardly mobile young people have chosen individual

competition over local social solidarity while maintaining some ties with the family. The meaning of those ties has changed. The flow of aid comes from the upwardly mobile to the family instead of being reciprocal, and it usually goes just to the nuclear family rather than the expanded family network. Other members of the network sometimes evaluate the upwardly mobile person, particularly if a woman, as suspect. This is exacerbated if she moves out of the family home, publicly flaunting her family's lack of control. She sees no dilemma between virginity and passion. The meaning of sexuality is couched in terms of freedom of choice and equality. For a young man, the dilemma between convention and violence is usually resolved in favor of convention; the risk of violence is too great and the need to be tough is experienced as negligible. Others may on occasion evaluate him as a coward because he ignores things that others would evaluate as demeaning, not only to him, but to his family.

The public self of the upwardly mobile person is different from the public self of other community members. They appear determined to succeed in terms of the American dream and often in disregard of local standards. Privately, however, many are afraid of the loneliness of independence and individualism. They are not quite accepted in the middle-class Anglo world, nor do they want to lose their Chicano identity. They still consider themselves Chicano and linked irrevocably to 32nd Street and their families there.

The political activists have resolved these dilemmas in another manner. Though they continue to live and work on 32nd Street, their relationship to the rest of 32nd Street remains problematic. They are not like everyone else. They have been able to develop a new collectivity so that they do not struggle alone. They are working not for themselves but for the community of local Chicanos. They have given up individual competition to a greater extent than the rest of the community.

Neither convention nor violence is expressive of the activists' identities. Both are utilized only to better the position of the community. In public activists manipulate their identities as local residents and as leaders of the community familiar with middle-class mores, but in private they are both and neither. They are tied through extensive mutual obligations networks to community residents, yet even the overt symbols of their life-style separate them from other residents. The women have become independent and the men are not overly concerned with violations of etiquette. While the symbols of their life-style resemble those of the Anglo middle-class radicals of the late 1960's and 1970's, these activists are different: they are Chicanos rooted in their tradition and in 32nd Street.

II

Community Culture and Locally
Rooted Identities

The residents of 32nd Street meet the universal problems of life—earning a living, starting a family, bringing up children, and enjoying leisure time—in a distinctive manner. The explanation for this uniqueness lies, first, in the community culture; second, in the importance of local solidarities; and third, in the relationship between community culture and social order. These three intertwined sociocultural processes are embedded within the primary symbol of Chicanismo, a political and cultural affirmation of ethnic identity.

Chicanismo best expresses the dilemmas that 32nd Street residents face and the dialectical processes through which they experience and act out these dilemmas. Chicanismo symbolizes the choosing of Mexican and United States cultural elements, an active process whereby people attempt to control their lives through and within a myriad of complex United States urban institutions. These institutions both help and hinder the development of the Chicano identity. Chicanismo symbolizes the Mexican-American desire to be neither black, nor Anglo, nor "deprived," but to be themselves: to encourage the traditions that they brought from Mexico and to demand the rights guaranteed them and the respect they deserve as hard-working residents of the United States. Embedded in the intertwining of the cultures are the difficult choices between virginity and passion, the public context and private actions, violence and convention, and close familial ties and individual competition.

The uniqueness of life on 32nd Street is reflected not only in clothing styles, music, gestures, and language but in the particular meanings attributed to actions and relationships. For example, motherhood remains the most valued role for women even when they work. Working does not mean independence; it means only additional money to make the household more comfortable. Moreover, a woman's social world remains largely limited to her female expanded family network. A man works to remain honorable, that is, to support his family and to be able to engage in mutual exchanges within his expanded family network. A man's social world consists primarily of men in his expanded family network and often the men with whom he grew up. Sometimes this means that he remains a gang member.

Life on 32nd Street is often tough. Any romantic notion that it is an idyllic setting where everyone gets along and develops deep and long-lasting friendships without any conflict, confusion, or mistrust should by now have been dispelled: there is fighting, poverty, and social conflict on 32nd Street. This does not mean that there is no order or that the local culture does not provide for the development of trusting, strong, and intimate social relationships. Only a few residents on 32nd Street leave and try to make their lives elsewhere. Symbolic and existential forces impede mobility, both geographic and economic. Moreover, there are particular satisfactions to staying. Leaving means loss of many close social ties and an often lonely fight for greater economic and social success. Staying means strong social support and a positive sense of self but often some economic sacrifice and very hard and unrewarding work.

Community Culture and Moral Order

The concept of community culture is used here as a guide to discovering an important facet of community and social life rather than as a condition for or model of community. It is not meant as a basis for a typology of communities, such as Suttles's (1972) defeated and defended communities or Janowitz's (1967) limited liability model of community. Nor is it meant to specify those variables necessary for "belongingness" (that is, sense of or interest in community), such as length of residence, stage in the life cycle, or socioeconomic class, which Kasarda and Janowitz (1974) discuss.

Those works view the community as having relatively little social or emotional importance in the lives of most residents.

The concept of community culture incorporates a model, whether a social ecological model (Janowitz, 1967; Kasarda and Janowitz, 1974; Suttles, 1972) or a subcultural one (Bergen, 1968; Gans, 1962; Liebow, 1967), of how the larger social system affects the lives of local residents and an ideological model of what community should be (Gusfield, 1975; Redfield, 1960; Toennies, 1957). It incorporates the formal and informal organizations of social relationships, their evaluation, and what they should be. It takes as data the meanings of actions and relationships and sees as problematic the origin of the meanings.

Community culture is what allows people to say "Those people are like us and those others are not." It contains criteria for inclusion and exclusion. It allows people to say that a person who wants to be included ought to behave in a specific way. The ties on 32nd Street, particularly expanded family networks and peer groups, are sufficiently close that people can tell others how they *ought* to behave because these people are perceived as having some rights over and responsibilities for the others.

Just because people are poor and do not measure themselves against the standard socioeconomic criteria of middle-class America does not mean that they have no generalized standards, that is, symbolic devices that identify them as certain kinds of people with certain values, nor does it mean that a universally applied moral order is formed only when the social order is complete (Suttles, 1968). Urban life can be rich in symbols, norms, and values that give meaning and importance to particular social relationships. The study of community culture allows us to study the content of people's lives: the activities and social relationships to which they attribute importance. As we have seen, symbols, norms, and values can have powerful effects on social relationships.

It is through local organizational arrangements that these symbols, values, and norms of the community culture become articulated and evolve out of repetitive interaction. At one level of organization are institutions which are generally task-oriented. Such institutions include schools, work, community agencies, and political groups. Some are locally controlled while others are linked directly to the wider society. On a second level of organization are leisure-oriented, informal groups such as social and athletic groups, gangs, and romantic relationships. The last level is that of the family. Families have a relatively strong investment in the immediate area because it is not only where they live but where they must bring up their children.

The 32nd Street community distinguishes itself from other inner-city communities in three ways. Its uniqueness can be seen through the two-dimensional view of culture, in the intertwining of honor and the American dream and in the conception of culture as shaping life and as continually being created and recreated through interaction. First, the local institutions are articulated with the larger social structure of the urban area in a unique way. For 32nd Street residents these institutions do two things at once, and do neither very well; they are often at cross-purposes with each other. They train people to be members of the local community and also to be something else, to turn toward the wider society. Schools and to some degree families accomplish neither very well. The culture continues to be a very complex and sometimes confusing amalgam of honor and the American dream. Second, 32nd Street is a segmental society based on gender, age, and orientation to the wider culture. Finally, the importance of local community solidarities is normatively, ecologically, and symbolically determined. The attractiveness of residents to each other is powerfully determined and understood; obligations and necessities push and guide; and norms affirm what is proper and respected. Relationships, however, must be negotiated constantly in a life that is not rich in conventional resources: money, job opportunities, political power, and good schools.

Community Culture and the Wider Society

Community culture is not immune to the allure of the culture of the wider society, unchanging, or always clear and unambiguous; 32nd Street is not a traditional little village cut off culturally, socially, and ecologically from the wider society. Its culture cannot be equated with that of a Gemeinschaft (Toennies, 1957) or a folk community (Redfield, 1960). As we have seen, the community's unique articulation with the institutions of the wider society affects the meanings of local relationships. Some symbols and norms are altered significantly from their traditional state while others are changed only slightly. Sometimes expectations conflict or normative ambiguity is created. Some expectations are situationally adaptive and nonevaluative. Little behavior is purely reactive; each experience is interpreted through existing moral categories. Community culture is not just a reaction to the socioeconomic position of community (Gans, 1962; Liebow, 1967). Neither is its content determined solely by the way the community has been cut off from or linked to the wider society (Suttles, 1978), nor its distinctiveness merely a reflection of its degree of provincialism (Suttles, 1968). Its articulation with the wider society is unique because of its own traditions, which have evolved through the experiences of residents and their continuing interaction with each other and with representatives of the wider society. The youths have their most continuous interaction with members of the wider society through the school system and only later become involved with employment and the political system. Most other experiences are filtered through television and the movies, though many of the older youths frequent the downtown and night spots around the city.

School: Limits on the American Dream

The value of getting an education is clearly understood and positively valued by all local residents; however, as a value it is not powerful in orienting the actions of most 32nd Street students. The schools that local youths attend articulate poorly with both youths and their families and fail to mold the youths into individualistic economic competitors. From the perspective of school personnel, disorder reigns and the students are "impossible." From the perspective of most youths, certain situations merit disruption and students are neither stupid or dangerous.

School personnel tell youths that they need to do well to achieve. At the same time teachers and counselors make little effort to help students yet complain that students are not succeeding. Parents often encourage youths to stay in school but few have the skills to help. They are also frequently caught in normative conflicts, for example, over a son's need for independence and their own desire for control. There is no clear message to stay in school, nor encouragement to graduate.

There is little reason to stay in school in order to get a better job, and lack of interest becomes the collective expectation. Peers often convince friends to cut classes or drop out. Moreover, with the high risk of failure and the lack of investment of self in school, youths, instead of defining violations of social etiquette as awkward encounters, define them as calculated disrespect, placing their honor at stake. Violence becomes the only means to resolve these situations and keep their self-respect and the respect of their peers. Combined with the probability of failure, the result is often the triumph of peer group solidarities over individualistic success for many young people.

Marginal Success

Normatively the world of work links the American dream and the honor code. Men should work. The meaning of work, however, is rooted in the local code of honor. A man of honor must work to support his family, while a man in pursuit of the American dream must work to get ahead for status. When young men take on the responsibility of a family, there is increasing local pressure to work consistently, even among gang members. Most young men do so to maintain their status as respectable men, though the jobs available provide little more than economic subsistence. Aware of the low status of their jobs and the minimal investment of self in the task, they gain little respect from holding a particular job. In fact, these jobs indicate something less than success by any criterion of the American dream.

Work has marginal expressive value to the young men trying to make something of themselves. There is little incentive to sacrifice local identity as honorable men when the chance for success in terms of the American dream is so slim. A man maintains respect largely for his ability to support his family and help his expanded family network. The meaning of work is constructed within the honor framework. Work fails, therefore, to link 32nd Street residents to the larger culture.

One Person, One Vote?

Local political activists have been largely unsuccessful in becoming integrated into the local political machine and have developed their own subculture of Chicano politics and protest in order to gain influence. Only by going around traditional patronage channels to federal agencies and by using nontraditional tactics, have they made the community's influence felt.

The back rooms, the patronage jobs, and the elected positions are unavailable to 32nd Street residents. Local politics are the politics of proposals, noisy negotiations, protests, and violence, not necessarily out of choice but out of necessity. Success depends on the activists' abilities to deal with and be part of both the local community and the wider society but to be immersed in neither. They must remain in a marginal world. However, to be part of the wider society is to be alienated from the local community, while to be part of the local community is to be enmeshed in local relationships and to use toughness as an expression of self rather than as a means to an end. Politics does little to channel the culture of the wider society into the community; rather, residents use politics to obtain what they believe is rightfully theirs as hard-working and respectable Chicanos (jobs and educational opportunities and bilingual-bicultural programs).

Experiences within the institutions of the wider society have broad ramifications on social and cultural life throughout the community—on the family, peer groups, mutual obligation networks, and the construction of identity. These experiences create and deepen dilemmas that all must face and resolve.

Segmentation by Age, Sex, and Orientation

Suttles (1968) argues that age and sex segmentation in inner-city communities is a territorially protective response to the untrust-

worthiness of neighbors, while Gans (1962) argues that such segmentation is a result of a class-based belief system. Here I have
argued that segmentation becomes meaningful through the expectations of the local community culture, based on ethnic tradition
and class. Only those considered outside the community culture
accept both males and females in a peer group and alter the relationship with parents by one-way (child-to-parent) rather than reciprocal
aid. The segmentation by sex and age is based on symbols and
values of manhood, femininity, and respect. Within age and sex
groupings are further social and cultural divisions by orientation
toward honor and the American dream, that is, by moral character.
Within those groups close ties can be developed and identities can
be constructed and validated by peers in the pursuit of leisure activities. How does one build a self in this context? How does one
maintain a family, make and keep friends, and carve out a stable
life? On 32nd Street it is done well, and done in a variety of
acceptable ways. People resolve these dilemmas in different
manners, not all of which are equally successful or equally evaluated
but which are rooted in the local community culture.

Leisure Activities and Peer Groups

Leisure activities and peer groups are segmented by age, sex, and
orientation. Street-oriented males are divided into age-segmented
groups (gangs or social groups). Female peer groups do not divide as
readily by orientation or age. Some young women join gangs, others
congregate in groups in the parks or on particular blocks, and others
mainly stay around their homes. The upwardly mobile youths form
the only peer groups that are not segregated by sex. With the possible exception of the upwardly mobile, much peer group activity, as
in any community, is concerned with sex role identities. Different
peer groups have different stances concerning the way to become a
respectable man or woman. The variations are acceptable within the
context of the local community culture.

The most controversial male groups are the gangs. The gang as
a single-sex peer group is not viewed as problematic, because single-
sex peer groups, often made up of expanded family members, are
the accepted form of friendship and solidarity among males and fe-

males alike. However, honor has become encapsulated in the gang rather than in the family and has become increasingly linked to an exaggerated notion of toughness and aggressiveness. Although many of the older residents agree about the need to fight, people outside the gangs rarely approve of the use of fighting skills and jail terms as criteria of status and identity, particularly when the gang members get older and take on familial responsibilities.

Those gangs that remain together as the members mature become almost primary groups with little internal stratification. While gang fights remain the ritual that certifies them as a group of men of precedence, the meaning of that ritual changes. Gang members no longer remain together because they are tough but remain tough so they can be together and depend on each other without losing face. Even though they have much less enthusiasm for fighting, with the high risk of failure in terms of the American dream, they continue to flirt back and forth between convention and violence without making commitments to either. Because their identities remain invested in gang relationships, they must remain warriors; otherwise, their intimacies would be publicly revealed. The persistence of gangs is a function of intimacy, culture, and perceived lack of valued economic success. Gang membership becomes a very comfortable and secure relationship but also continues to promote violence and to deter individual commitment to economic success.

While a high proportion of males join gangs, most do not remain members for long and their honor is not encapsulated within the group's. Toughness does not generally become the basis of an identity. Peer groups composed of image defenders or rep avoiders tend to be smaller and much less visible than the gangs. A few groups based upon athletic skill or interest are formed but most youths seek to establish their identities in the pursuit of women and in fashionable dress. Most of these young men and many of the gang members come to resemble "routine-seekers" (Gans, 1962), hanging around with a few friends or relatives after work or on weekends. To achieve respect, they are concerned primarily with maintaining the honor of their families by supporting them and protecting the sexual purity of their women.

In most groups, including the gangs, ties are built up in mutual exchanges of material goods and services. These material exchanges initiate social relationships but the exchanges become more symbolic as trust is developed through the exchanges (Henry, 1978). Mutual exchanges in this community have become ritualized as expressions of social solidarity but are also utilitarian because most community members have poor access to necessary services and goods.

A young woman's femininity is linked to virginity, the expression of passion, and her relationship to men. Traditionally, in order to maintain their honor young women had to maintain their virginity until marriage, thus keeping their passion in control. Even today, rumors keep young women "in line." Everyone seems to keep track of the relationships and actions of many people—their friends, pregnancies, separations, and marriages—and everyone is aware that most men want to marry virgins.

Few women actually remain virgins until marriage. A woman faces a dilemma when she is in love and her boyfriend wants to engage in sexual intercourse. Men are supposed to dominate the relationship. The resolution of this situation, once it becomes public knowledge, forms the basis of her evaluation by others. Some young women are able to maintain their identities as virgins and are seen as remaining under the control of their families. Others claim that in a moment of passion they had to submit to their boyfriends. Their sexuality remains bounded, but to maintain the traditional ideal state they must stay away from men except under supervision. Just spending time with men may change their identities.

Motherhood is the most highly valued role for women and can resolve both symbolically and existentially the dilemma between virginity and passion. Like virginity, motherhood, wed or unwed, *can* bound a woman's sexuality, as long as others appraise her as making motherhood her central concern. That must be negotiated. The function of the symbol of femininity remains the same, to bound sexuality; only the content of that symbol has changed.

Young women who spend too much time with young men and who do not become mothers are suspected of using birth control—an open expression of passion and a denial of motherhood. These young women tend to have their own peer groups and their relationships to young men are very different from those of other young women.

The basis for sex segregation of social groups can be found in the notions of femininity and masculinity. To fulfill their sex roles females must demonstrate submissiveness to men and men must demonstrate control. This means that their provinces of action are separate—women within the protective environment of the home and men in the streets or work—and that men and women cannot readily form friendships because such relationships require equality. The mutual exchange of personal information, necessary for developing trust and symbolic of trust in a friendship, cannot occur when one person is in control and dominates the other. Consequently, most peer groups and sociable activities remain sex-segregated. Because of the expectations concerning men and women, any male-female relationship is suspect. Men who do women's work (cleaning or cooking) or women who do something within the male's province (use violence) are criticized, and there is no generally acceptable resolution. A cultural resolution, however, has been negotiated for working women. This situation is explained in terms of the honor of the family, the lack of job opportunities, and the man's continued control of his wife or daughter by allowing her to work.

Except in the male senior gangs, age segmentation among young men and women, but particularly women, largely disappears with marriage and parenthood. Friendships are often solidified into *compadrazgo* relationships as children are born and friends are asked to be godparents. Social life becomes increasingly an expanded family affair. Respect for elders is considered critical in social relationships.

Those who violate local standards by opting to pursue the American dream often experience the tensions between peer group and familial solidarities and the individualistic success ethic when they are young. Some resolve it early; others hang on to old relationships, keeping their public presentation acceptable by local standards while their private selves struggle to succeed, frequently without much social or emotional support. Others manage to get together with upwardly mobile peers and develop a strong friendship network. Growing up often means moving out of the community.

If the youths who are pursuing the American dream flaunt their lack of concern for honor, they are often criticized by peers and family. Their actions are evaluated as unacceptable. Failure to respond to what is perceived by most as a public insult can result in a young man being appraised as a coward or fool. A young woman, whose honor is encapsulated in that of her family, dishonors them by moving out on her own, regardless of her actual sexual status, because it is assumed that neither she nor her family has control over her behavior. Most youths who succeed have made many conscious, often unpopular choices while growing up. Others appear to drift out of the culture and community rather than plan their departure, but those are few. It is hard work and risky, because it is easy to fail and difficult to be marginal in a marginal community.

The Expanded Family

An active, extensive family network is highly valued by community residents and is critical to the maintenance of the code of honor. An honorable family has a generalized reciprocity network. However, there are also pragmatic benefits to having a large kinship network because of the marginal economic situation of most families. Expanded family members help each other through emergencies and periods of unemployment and provide temporary child care.

The expanded family network reinforces both symbolically and existentially the continued sex role differentiation both inside the family and in the wider community. The women provide emotional and social support through their own social network for the wife and the men do the same for the husband, which means that the husband and wife need not depend on each other for such support; the husband remains the provider and the wife, the mother. More egalitarian, task-sharing models need not develop. There is no symbolic reason to violate the sex role expectations, as the mother is highly valued in her role and has a strong group of women to support that ideal, while a man who supports his family and protects their honor is highly respected. Any man who is appraised as unnecessarily relying on his wife or welfare to support the family is dishonored.

Families, no matter how strongly bonded, are subject to the many strains of being poor and living in the crowded inner city. Any time a man asks for financial aid or services from a member of his network, he places a burden on the donor's family unless he can return the favor or money rapidly. Tensions can easily arise because few families have surplus money. Bringing up children is made difficult by the parents' lack of control over their children's education and their lack of skill and resources to help their offspring get ahead economically. Moreover, the world of the street encourages actions not totally approved of by parents.

The realities of inner-city life are such that it is surprising that families stay together and that Mexican-American families in particular continue to have significantly lower divorce rates than blacks or whites (Frisbie, Bean, and Eberstein, 1980). This situation must be explained in part by the high value given to the cohesive family and the support of the expanded family network. Their importance is continually reaffirmed in the rituals of the large cotillions, weddings, elaborate funerals, and more intimate family celebrations.

Social Order and Respect

The question of how social order is created and maintained, particularly in the inner city, is continually debated. While Wirth (1938) decried the lack of order due to the size, heterogeneity, and density of cities, most studies agree that some degree of order exists (Anderson, 1978; Gans, 1962; Liebow, 1967; Whyte, 1955). The question arises whether order is created through the structural arrangement of social relationships such as ordered segmentation (Suttles, 1968) or through internalization of "norms" (Gans, 1962; Liebow, 1967; Miller, 1958).

Suttles (1972) argues that the model of social order of consensus based on old customs and traditions and reinforced by the "natural" close ties of the group is an overly romantic notion of community and certainly not useful in understanding urban America today, if such idyllic communities ever existed (Gusfield, 1967; Lewis, 1967). Today, Suttles states, people in the inner cities perceive each other as untrustworthy and dangerous and, unlike middle-class people, they are unable to evaluate each other in terms of educational attainment, job status, and financial success. As a result, the moral order, which is based on individual judgment, is tenuous and lacks applicability to "real people" (Suttles, 1968: 231). Social order is maintained primarily thorugh the retreat of individuals to their own ethnic, territorial, gender, and age groups. For example, gangs form with individuals of the same sex, age, and ethnicity to protect their territory. Fights occur when that territory is violated. As this book has demonstrated, intergang and most interpersonal violence is linked first of all to the code of honor and the meaning attributed to others' actions, not directly to the defense of territorial boundaries.

The subculture theories view order as emanating from socialization to "value" systems. There is a very mechanical relationship between values and behavior. According to subcultural perspectives on unwed motherhood, because women in some subcultures value unwed motherhood as highly as motherhood within wedlock, many women become unwed mothers (Henriques, 1953; Stycos, 1955). Goode (1960, 1961) argues that when the possibility of marriage through proper means is limited, then the rules break down (anomie) and young women seek any means available, including the deviant action of unwed motherhood, to obtain a husband. Values are seen as unchanging, and when values cannot be achieved, deviance is the result. The analysis of unwed motherhood on 32nd Street has demonstrated that neither of these explanations is applicable here. The importance of symbols of femininity can be changed through interaction, and there is a complicated relationship between behavior and evaluation.

Social order, from the perspective presented here, is rarely complete; however, there is a problematic, complex, and dynamic relationship among symbols, values, norms, and social order. Social order must often be negotiated among residents but it is informed by local, collectively understood symbols, values, and norms.

Most people want to be "respectable." Most also want the affirmation of self that others provide. People are social animals and selves are developed in interaction first within the family and then with peers, the schools, and other agents of the wider society (Karp, Stone, and Yoels, 1977: 33). It has been documented that urban life does not necessarily lead to increasing individualization (Anderson,

1978; Fischer, 1976; Gans, 1962; Liebow, 1967; Whyte, 1955). Close ties are in evidence on 32nd Street, though what is evaluated as respectable and reasonable is sometimes problematic.

Symbols are generally abstract and do not tell people how to behave. They do, however, provide an orientation for the man of honor and for the man who pursues the American dream. Values are incorporated into the organizational arrangements within which everyone interacts, yet they also frequently provide only a rather vague framework for everyday interaction. Moreover, the relationship between values and action becomes increasingly complex when values are inconsistently articulated throughout local institutions.

The two codes articulated on 32nd Street, honor and the American dream, often frame different orientations to the same situation. For example, a young woman who becomes involved in a sexual relationship can place her decision to use birth control in different contexts, either as a woman who is postponing motherhood to increase the possibility of upward mobility or as a woman whose sexuality is unbounded. Others may or may not agree with her choice.

Even when the normative codes are quite specific concerning how an individual is supposed to act, the two codes may specify different interpretations of the situation and different sets of actions. Because there is no higher order of values to decide between them, a situation of normative ambiguity exists. For example, when a young man is tripped, he may interpret that as an insult to his manhood and respond physically or he may attribute it to the crowded room and apologize. In other situations values within a framework may conflict when translated into normative expectations. For example, it is impossible, without chaperonage, for a woman to submit to men *and* to remain a virgin if her boyfriend wants a sexual relationship.

How individuals resolve such situations is critical to others' evaluation of them as respectable. Exactly what is considered respectable does vary from group to group and is negotiated between the individual and the group. Sometimes it is difficult to reach an agreement even within a group, as behavioral specifics are often not laid out. For example, becoming a mother does not mean that a woman becomes respectable. Respectability depends upon what characteristics of motherhood are emphasized and how others see those actions. Nor are there specific limits for how much flirting is too much. It is not easy to act solely on the basis of abstract values and to be appraised as having done so properly. There is a problematic relationship between what a person does and how it is evaluated.

Local audiences vary somewhat in defining what is proper, and institutional contexts vary. Moreover, behavior may be seen as an isolated act or as part of a larger context of known behaviors. The community culture provides the context in which close ties, intimacy, and selves that engender trust and respect can develop, but there are times when unknown people appear dangerous.

Much of social order must be negotiated. Different groups evaluate behavior in different ways, depending on how they collectively decide to resolve the ambiguities and conflicts. Symbols, values, and norms *do* orient action and allow moral judgments to be made that extend beyond face-to-face relationships. However, the relationship between culture and action is complex and often ambiguous, so that it is sometimes difficult for community residents to interpret the behavior of others and conflicts arise.

The Future of Chicanismo and 32nd Street

Though social scientists have long noted the inadequacy of the "melting pot" image of United States society, and though people have become more concerned with searching for their roots, there remains an undercurrent of thought that Americans should all act and be alike. Only if people become "like us," the middle class, by moving to the suburbs, by drinking the appropriate cocktails, by furnishing a home as the magazines decree, by adopting the nuclear family ideal, and by emphasizing the individualistic success ethic, will they be fully American.

Many outsiders ask why the 32nd Street residents are not like others. In part the answer lies in the lack of resources and opportunities for upward mobility and in the poor school systems. These are all class-related factors. If these problems changed, some aspects of life would be readjusted. There are, however, other elements of their social world that are ethnically based and freely chosen. These would not necessarily change if the economic situation shifted. For many residents, 32nd Street and ethnic identity offer them something of value.

The critical mass of residents in an inner-city location is also significant (Fischer, 1976). If the plans for urban renewal finally include 32nd Street, people will be forced to relocate and more than the present trickle will move to the suburbs. This will fragment the community, as it did the West End (Gans, 1962). The 32nd Street residents do not seem to have the resources of some other urban ethnic groups, who are purchasing sections of suburban communities and planning to move to them. If territorial fragmentation does occur, there would be more change. Culture adapts to new situations.

Some aspects of culture, such as the expanded family network, will survive, even if their content alters slightly by ecological or class changes. Not only do Mexican-Americans have a low divorce rate compared with other ethnic groups, regardless of the length of United States residency and location, but the expanded family network remains the valued and predominant family form. Some traditions may persist much longer than any class-based theory would hypothesize, while other symbols, values, and norms may change as community members achieve greater economic stability and begin to spread through the city and into the suburbs. The United States as a melting pot may not only be unachievable but undesirable. Why should everyone be the same?

Notes

Chapter 1. Introduction

1. In this book I refer to all people of Mexican ancestry in the United States as *Chicanos*. While not all those of Mexican ancestry prefer this term, it seems best to embody the varying mixtures of United States and Mexican cultures today in the United States. For an excellent discussion of the origin and meaning of the term *Chicano*, see Montenegro (1976).

2. This is a pseudonym, as are all names used in this book. I have left vague some of the community characteristics that are less relevant sociologically. I have also slightly altered some of the less important characteristics of individuals and groups so as to maintain their privacy.

3. Throughout this book I refer to groups of young people who fight to defend their name as *gangs* in accordance with the sociological literature; however, members and others within the community often refer to these groups as *clubs*.

4. This is the number used by local community activists when they discuss the "gang problems." Because of the disputes with the police over what constitutes a gang fight and the fact that the community is a small part of two districts, I have decided to use the number the community residents use, though it may be high for most years. There is always a possibility that deaths over a period of more than one year or outside the immediate neighborhood are included in the statistics.

5. All conversations were in English, unless otherwise noted.

Chapter 2. Culture and Inner-City Neighborhoods

1. For example, see Hunter (1975), Leach (1961), Kornhauser (1978), Parsons (1951), Suttles (1968, 1972, 1978), and Thomas and Znaniecki (1918).

2. Durkheim (1964), Toennies (1957), and Wirth (1938) have all argued that urbanization produces disorganization and the loss of the importance of the local community.

3. See Peterson (1979) for an extensive analysis of expressive symbols and material culture.

4. She strongly criticizes the notion of delinquent subculture (Cloward and Ohlin, 1960; Cohen, 1952; Miller, 1958).

5. Suttles (1972), for example, views what he calls "vigilante groups" as occurring only in conflict with other groups. Klein and Crawford (1968) argue that the delinquent gang is maintained only through the continuation of outside contingencies.

6. Liebow (1967) argues that the street corner men he studied only have a "shadow culture" because it is entirely dependent upon their economic position. Gans (1962) in his analysis of an Italian community argues that beliefs are determined by the socioeconomic and political position of a group.

7. Cf. Peterson (1979).

8. For an excellent analysis of the importance of culture see Fine (1979) and Fine and Kleinman (1979).

9. For a similar analysis see Manning (1973) and Abner Cohen (1974: 37), who argues that symbols are continuously interpreted and reinterpreted.

10. For an excellent analysis of form and function of symbolic formation see Cohen (1974), especially pp. 26–34.

11. See Douglas's (1971) and Williams's (1960) differing views on the American value system.

12. See Schwartz et al. (n.d.) for a comparative analysis of education in a number of American communities.

13. See Schwartz et al. (n.d.) for an analysis of adolescent peer group relations in a number of communities.

14. See Gillis (1974) and Hollingshead (1949) for socioeconomic and historical analyses of differences. Schwartz and Merten (1968) argue that differences in peer group styles are greater than just socioeconomic and historical differences.

15. See Fine (1979) and Schwartz (1972) for expositions of similar positions.

16. See Berger and Luckman (1966), McCall and Simmons (1966), Maines (1977), Mead (1964), Stone and Farberman (1970), and Strauss (1959).

17. Cf. Peterson (1979).

Chapter 3. Marginality and the American Dream

1. This ranking was constructed by the *Chicago Sun-Times* (October 22, 1972) using 1970 census data.

2. The focus of this book is the Spanish-speaking population of the community, especially the youths, although many of the demographic statistics in this chapter encompass all the ethnic groups. Most of the activities and the character of the neighborhood now center on the Spanish-speaking population, though other ethnic influences on the community should not be forgotten. The Middle Europeans are an even smaller fraction of the youth population than of the community's population, as many of the Middle Europeans are older couples whose children have moved out of the neighborhood.

3. A survey conducted by anthropologist Steven Schensul (1972) for the local social service agency revealed these figures.

4. The estimate of 70,000 was made by the director of a local youth agency, who spends much of his time in the streets. He was brought up in the community and has long been active as a resident and worker. He is aware that undercounting stems from the large number of illegally subdivided apartments that are never located by the census bureau, the large number of illegal aliens, the language barriers between the census takers and the residents, and the fears residents have of answering questions. Some of these problems and the problems of defining "Spanish speaking" in the census data have been documented (see, for example, Hernandez, Estrada, and Alvirez, 1973).

5. The youths describe some of these activities as "rapping" (talking) to "chicks" (young women) or "dudes" (young men) and "gang banging" (any kind of intergang conflict). "Gang banging" does not refer to a gang rape, which is a "gang bang." A "gang banger" is a gang member, not necessarily a rapist.

When I accompanied several neighborhood "chicks" on a tour of a local college, our guide referred to the young women as "kids." Connie whispered to me, "If she calls us "kids" one more time, I'm going to belt her." Other terms used for females are "whores" and "ladies." A "lady" is someone's mother, someone older, or someone from a higher social class. Early in my research I was walking with a gang member when we bumped into the gang member's "old lady" (wife or steady girl-friend), and I quickly said, "You better explain who I am." "That's okay," he replied, "She can see you're a lady." Some of the young women who associate with gangs started talking about their first impressions of me. "At first we thought you were a lady and wouldn't talk to us. We were hoping you would. Then we found you weren't like that at all. Now you're a chick like us."

6. Evidence was gathered by a community resident participating in a seminar in a local college program.

7. I walked many times to this chain store supermarket and found the products to be of inferior quality and the shelves often empty. I calculated that I could save money and eat better by spending ninety cents for transportation and using another supermarket on 36th Street. But I did not have to carry groceries to feed a large family.

8. All data presented on 32nd Street are based on United States census figures and include both Spanish-speaking and other residents except where indicated. In 1969 the median income for Spanish-speaking families was $7,534 nationwide (lower than for 32nd Street in 1970) and $8,369 in Chicago, while the median for non-Spanish-speaking families in Chicago was $10,394 (Chicago Department of Development and Planning, 1973).

9. In 1970 almost 50 percent of whites nationwide made over $10,000, while only 26 percent of blacks did so. In Chicago 24 percent of the non-Spanish-speaking families earned $15,000 or more.

10. A survey conducted in Los Angeles in 1964–1965 (Grebler, Moore, and Guzman, 1970) found that 22 percent of Chicanos were on welfare, and 28 percent

received social security and other federal pensions, while only 54 percent received a regular income. However, in Chicago in 1970, 32 percent of the Spanish-speaking families below the poverty level received public assistance while 37 percent of the non-Spanish-speaking did (Chicago Department of Development and Planning, 1973).

11. In 1970, 17 percent of Chicago Spanish-speaking families were single-parent families, compared with 23 percent of non-Spanish speaking families. In addition, 20 percent of the Spanish-speaking children under eighteen were living with one or no parent, compared with almost 30 percent of the non-Spanish-speaking children (Chicago Department of Development and Planning, 1973).

12. The 1969 median income was $4,039 for Chicago Spanish speaking females and $4,744 for non-Spanish speaking (Chicago Department of Development and planning, 1973). For Chicago families with female heads, in 1970 the median income for blacks was $3,800; Latins, $3,426; and other whites, $4,322 (*Chicago Sun-Times*, February 15, 1973).

13. Included in this category are men who did not look for work in the four weeks before the census was taken, either because they were tired of looking for work or because they were sick. There is no way of knowing how many fit into each of these two categories, but one can speculate that many men had given up looking for work because they were unskilled and there were few jobs available to them. In Chicago 84.3 percent of the Spanish speaking males over sixteen were in the labor force while only 76 percent of the non-Spanish speaking were. The unemployment rate was 5.3 percent and 4 percent, respectively (Chicago Department of Development and Planning, 1973). Nationally, the 1970 unemployment figures were 3.7 percent of white males and 4.9 percent of white females, as compared with 6.4 percent of black males and 7.8 percent of black females.

14. Nationally, those of Mexican origin have not done as well as Anglos in the occupational sphere. As reported by Lopez y Rivas (1973), the 1960 census indicated that less than 20 percent of those of Mexican origin held white-collar jobs, while 50 percent of Anglos did. This had not changed significantly by 1972.

15. The figure of 70 percent is the number community groups employ when discussing the educational situation of 32nd Street. It is reasonably accurate. Educational attainment for those of Mexican origin is generally lower than for Anglos or blacks throughout the country. In the Southwest, for example, where most Spanish-surname people live, the average number of years of school completed for Anglos was 10.6 in 1950 and 11.6 in 1960; for nonwhites, 7.8 in 1950 and 9.0 in 1960; and for Spanish-surname people, 5.4 in 1950 and 7.1 in 1960 (Moore, 1970: 66). In 1970 in Chicago the median number of years of school completed for those over twenty-five was 8.7 for the Spanish speaking compared with 11.3 for the non-Spanish speaking. Only 27 percent of the Spanish speakers over twenty-five had completed high school as compared with 45 percent of the non-Spanish speakers (Chicago Department of Development and Planning, 1973). In Chicago 5 percent of the seven-to-thirteen year olds, 7 percent of the fourteen and fifteen year olds, 22 percent of the sixteen and seventeen year olds, and 60 percent of the eighteen and nineteen year olds were not enrolled in school.

16. The reading achievement scores for schools that the residents of 32nd Street attend were not only well below the national average for 1970–1972 but were significantly below the city averages for all grades and decreased relative to the national average with each additional grade. For example, the Tudor High eleventh grade class score was 13 (1971–1972) while the ninth grade score was 20; the national average was 50.

17. The problems experienced by Mexican-Americans with the educational system are not particular to this community. Using data from the United States Civil Rights Commission's Mexican-American Education Study, Navarro-Uranga (1973) found that in the Southwest, Mexican-Americans did worse in schools than blacks or Anglos. She found the dropout rates to be higher for Mexican-Americans than for blacks or Anglos, reading comprehension lower, and grade repetitions more frequent. There were no classes in cultural history and few Mexican-American teachers. The Mexican-American community was excluded from participation in school affairs. Moreover, less money was spent per pupil in schools with a high percentage of Mexican-Americans. In addition, Wright, Salinas, and Kuvlesky (1973) found that Mexican-Americans had a strong commitment to educational and occupational goals despite the lack of opportunities.

18. I also felt that the diagnosis was incorrect and that because she was sometimes difficult to handle in school, school authorities wanted her out of the normal classroom.

19. Of the present population of 32nd Street of Mexican origin, approximately half were born in the United States of parents born in the United States and half were born in Mexico or had at least one parent born in Mexico. Many of the third generation Chicanos do not speak much Spanish, but there has been increasing interest in learning Spanish and learning about Mexico. Most youths, even if they speak little Spanish, understand it when they hear their parents or the parents of their friends conversing. Classes in Spanish and in Mexican culture are being offered, and bilingual, bicultural programs are emphasized by most community groups. More links are being developed with national Chicano groups: the Raza Unida party (a national political party of Chicanos, which held its first national convention in 1972), the Brown Berets (a national organization for Chicano rights), and community members have represented Chicago Chicanos at many national conferences. Four chartered buses and many carloads, including many gang youths and other street people who were never before interested in Chicano affairs, went to the Midwest Chicano Conference in Iowa in 1973. From 1971 to 1974 I saw a large number of young people learn Spanish and become involved in their community. In the fall of 1971 I was doing Merida's Spanish homework for her, and by the fall of 1973, at age seventeen, Merida often acted as translator, wrote her own Chicano newspaper, and was involved in many Chicano political activities in the area.

20. Pinkney (1963) compared white attitudes concerning Mexicans and blacks living in integrated neighborhoods, joining social clubs, being served in integrated facilities, and so forth. He found much less prejudice against Mexicans than blacks.

In his study of a Texas community Simmons (1961) found inconsistencies in the views that Anglos held of Mexican-Americans and vice versa. He argued that

Anglos viewed Mexican-Americans as their potential peers but assumed they were inferior and attributed negative characteristics to them in order to treat them differently. This finding further supports the ambiguous status of Mexican-Americans in today's society.

21. A study of voter turnout in Michigan found that Chicanos did not differ significantly from other American groups and that the Mexican-American subculture did not discourage voting (Buehler, 1977). On 32nd Street, however, a disproportional number fail to vote because they are not citizens or are in the United States illegally.

22. In the first weeks of my research I met several of the community organizers. They contrived to meet me by getting me into a settlement house. One was very rough and demanded to know in no uncertain words what an "Anglo chick" was doing in their community. He terrified me though I tried not to show it. I later found that this was often his style. I told them about my student status and my wish to focus my dissertation on youths. A female anthropology graduate student was already in the community, so that extensive explanations were unnecessary. Over the next week I noticed them circling the park in a car several times to check on me while I was talking with the Lions. On the one hand, the organizers thought I would not last very long and, on the other, they thought I might be useful in writing proposals and posed no threat to anyone.

23. For an excellent analysis of community organizations and the manipulation of ethnic identity see Stern (1976). The following are some of the programs started by local residents. The Mental Health Training Center received $102,000 from the National Institute of Mental Health to train badly needed social service and mental health workers in the community. This program placed its students in many of the existing social service programs for on-the-job training to supplement their classroom work, for which they were getting college credit. It was ranked by the federal government as the best new careers program and was funded for a second year. Many of the students planned to transfer at the end of their second year to four-year colleges to get their bachelors degree.

The social service program received $75,000 from the Department of Health, Education and Welfare and the Law Enforcement Assistance Administration to develop services for families and youths. They conducted a survey of youths and started working through the schools. The agency had four street workers funded by Catholic Charities. These men, in their midtwenties, were all former street gang members. They spent their time on the street negotiating between the gangs, the police and the gangs, and the gangs and the court. Other programs specialized in getting students into college or in improving reading.

The Latin American job center (funded in 1972–1973 for $225,000 from government and private sources) had its own board of directors. Its objective was to train people for unions and to help small Latin contractors get started.

The heroin addiction center had an independent contract for a methadone maintenance clinic funded for $204,000. This organization existed for two years before it was federally funded.

24. The Brown Berets are a national organization for Chicano rights. Their

strength lies largely in California (where the group was founded in 1967 to protest racism in the schools and police brutality and to open a clinic for the Chicano people), Texas, and elsewhere in the Southwest. While a group did attempt to organize and recruited members on 32nd Street, it never became a powerful organization. They organized the free medical clinic and brought some national figures to 32nd Street.

Chapter 4. The Expanded Family and Family Honor

1. A *quinceanera* is a young woman's fifteenth birthday celebration and is often referred to as a cotillion. It is a special birthday for a young girl in both Mexico and the United States and symbolizes her transition from childhood to adulthood. Traditionally, she then had to be chaperoned and guarded in her behavior. In the small villages of Mexico she is often given some new clothes, while on 32nd Street some of the girls have affairs for several hundred guests, such as the one described in the text.

2. See, for example, Diaz (1966), Foster (1967), Nelson (1971), and Romanucci-Ross (1973).

3. Several empirical studies support Bott's hypothesis. In England, Young and Willmot (1957) studied the problems of wives who moved from the Bethnal Green neighborhood where many of their kin lived and found that only forty years later networks of friends and kin developed again in Dagenham (Willmott, 1963). Studies of the United States such as Handel and Rainwater (1964) and Rainwater and Handel (1964) found that geographic mobility brought an increase in home-centeredness and less sex role segregation between husband and wife in working-class families.

Mobility has not affected familial sex roles in this way in the 32nd Street community, nor have lack of propinquity and urbanization affected the strength and importance of family ties. There is evidence that propinquity is not necessary to maintain the cohesion of extended kinship, and urbanization does not entirely destroy it (Coult and Habenstein, 1962; Litwak, 1960). Both studies found extended kinship among people who lived in different places and in urban areas.

4. For similar findings in other Chicano communities see Alvirez and Bean (1976), Murillo (1971), Sena-Rivera (1979), Sotomayor (1972), and Temple-Trujillo (1974).

5. Mintz and Wolf (1950), in an historical analysis of *compadrazgo*, have documented its changes of function and content since the sixth century. According to Gibson (1966) *compadrazgo* was widely adopted in Mexico during the colonial period, when an epidemic caused significant depopulation and *compadres* became accepted as substitute parents.

Lomnitz (1977), in her study of a Mexico City shantytown, found that the function of the *compadre* relationship from the rural situation and from the "ideal model" had been strengthened and broadened in the shantytown. Rural *compadres* were never cited as necessary for emergency help and close friendship but were "respected" persons. However, through participant-observation, Lomnitz found in the shantytown that not only has the number of *compadre* relationships increased (for example, *compadres* are chosen for saint days, upon graduation from primary school, and so on), but *compadres* are frequently picked from neighbors and friends and are part of the reciprocal obligation network which is necessary for economic survival:

> The *compadrazgo* institution is being used in the shantytown to make pre-existing reciprocity relations more solid and permanent. . . . I agree with Safa (1974: 61–64) in that cooperation between equals is a result of neces-sity born of the social structure. If one lacks a powerful godfather one must make do with *compadres* (Lomnitz, 1977: 162).

Compadrazgo is a way of legitimizing mutual assistance among neighbors and is judged in its "intensity and trustworthiness of reciprocal exchange" (Lomnitz, 1977: 173).

6. Keefe, Padilla, and Carlos (1979) and Sena-Rivera (1979) argue that *com-padrazgo* is decreasing; however, Carlos (1973) has found that with urbanization and modernization that *compadres* still play an important role in Mexico and the relationship remains strong.

7. See Madsen (1964), Moore (1970), and Rubel (1966) for illustrations of its continued importance.

8. See Keefe, Padilla, and Carlos (1979), Murillo (1971), Rubel (1966), and Sena-Rivera (1979) for similar findings in other studies of Chicanos.

9. This "familism" in which individuals subordinate their needs to the collective can be traced back to Aztec culture (Mirande and Enriquez, 1979).

10. Alvirez and Bean (1976) argued that many Chicano families pool their re-sources, and Carlos (1973) has found that fictive kin help each other by finding jobs, lending money, and giving preferential treatment in business.

11. On some occasions, such as a fire or death, it might be permissible to accept emergency public aid, but it is still better if friends and family help out.

12. A fourteen-year-old girl explained:

> I stay home until at least one o'clock in the summer every day to wash the kitchen and bathroom floors, otherwise they get dirty and sticky and the little kids crawl around on them all the time. In the winter during school, I do it before I go in the morning. Sometimes I'm late from school. We clean the whole house twice a week and my other sisters do the cooking and the washing.

13. See Pitt-Rivers (1966) for an analysis of male honor in Spain.

14. See Hayner (1966) and Paz (1961), who argue that Aztec women were sub-missive to men. However, Mirandé and Enríquez (1979) argue that Aztec women had roles beyond wife and mother and that complete male domination occurred through external forces such as those imposed by colonialization (Baca Zinn, 1975; Sosa Riddell, 1974).

15. Similar patterns have been found in other Chicano communities (Flores, 1971; Nieto-Gomez, 1974; Vidal, 1971).

16. Nelson (1971: 51) describes this phenomenon in her study of a Mexican

village. In his analysis of psychological studies of the Mexican, Peñalosa (1968) found that they described the father-son relationship as distant and respectful and the father-daughter relationship as distant and conflict-free.

17. Diaz (1966), Fromm and Maccoby (1970), and Nelson (1971) so describe the fathers in the Mexican villages they studied. Rubel (1966) and Goodman and Beman (1971) describe similar findings in Chicano communities.

18. Diaz (1966) found that mothers expected their sons to become independent early in their lives in Tonalá, Mexico.

19. See Pitt-Rivers (1966) for an elaborate analysis of a similar situation in Spain.

20. A parent's problem in dealing with a son's or, for that matter, a daughter's education is exacerbated by problems in dealing with educational institutions and personnel. This is evident in the manner in which parents criticize their children's performances and in their fear of confronting school personnel, because the parents themselves lack education or feel unable to communicate in English. One teacher explained that he saw less than one-half of the parents of his students and felt that these parents were immediately on the defensive when they came in. Typically a parent is called only if the teacher thinks there is something wrong with the student. Parents do not know that they can take the initiative, as many middle-class parents do, and demand things for their child, such as remedial aid or placement in a different class.

21. For a similar view of Mexican villages see Diaz (1966), Hayner (1966), and Nelson (1971).

22. The Virgin of Guadalupe symbolizes piety, virginity, and saintly submissiveness. She is the supreme good (Mirandé and Enríquez, 1979). Peñalosa (1968) argues that "guadalupanismo," that is, the highly emotional, devout veneration of the Virgin of Guadalupe, is very strong in Mexican culture (see Bushell, 1958; Madsen, 1960).

23. See Fromm and Maccoby (1970) and Nelson (1971) for analyses of the Virgin Mother.

24. This traditional Mexican situation is similar to that of the Aztecs, who considered the mother the heart of the house, solely responsible for child rearing and cleaning, dedicated to her husband, and remaining respectable in the eyes of the community (Mirandé and Enríquez, 1979: 14).

25. Gans (1962) describes a very similar situation among Italians living in the United States.

26. This has been documented in other Chicano communities (Murillo, 1971).

27. In the modern media, concern for form and style is often linked to the violence of the cowboy in the movies.

> The gun tells us that he lives in a world of violence; and even that he "believes in violence." But the drama is one of self-restraint, the movement of violence must come in its own time and according to its special laws, or else it is valueless . . . it is not violence at all which is the "point" of the western movie, but a certain image of a man, a style, which expresses itself most clearly in violence (Warsow, 1963: 239).

28. One rule of standard etiquette may place a man in a situation in which a claim to precedence is questioned, namely, apologizing profusely for an action already completed. An apology for an act committed is seen as an act of "gripping." If an individual attempts to place another in a demeaning situation, he must follow through on his claim. If a member of the Lions gang shouts "The Nobles suck" and there is by chance a Noble within hearing distance, the Noble will interpret the act as demeaning to his gang's honor and will follow through on the challenge. If the Lion apologizes, asking for forgiveness, he is "gripping," that is, placing himself in a subordinate position to the Noble, because only someone of higher status may grant forgiveness. Consequently, if the original challenger "grips," he loses his claim to precedence in that situation.

Chapter 5. Young Men in the Streets: Honor and Reputation

1. The Lions got the sweater back a week later when several Lions jumped a group of Greeks who had it. Their claim to precedence as one of the toughest gangs on 32nd Street was reestablished.

2. Gilberto was well known as a tough fighter and the Greek was not. Gilberto could say to himself that this youth could not possibly put up a good challenge because he was not nearly an equal. Few would have questioned his decision. He would have gained nothing by fighting someone so far below him in reputation.

3. Most join for a year or less and are largely fringe members who become involved in only a few incidents (Klein, 1971). Others join short-lived gangs and never get to the state where they invest in sweaters with emblems or engage in fights that make their reputations public.

4. Much of my data comes from the Lions gang and to a lesser extent the Senior Greeks. While I had contact with a number of other gangs, because of the risks of moving back and forth and the trade-off between breadth and depth, I chose to focus my attention on those two gangs. This was necessary as many gangs changed allegiances and, given the high tensions frequently created by gang war, a researcher could easily be accused of giving information to a rival gang. It was clear that gangs had turned on outsiders in the past. For example, one outside organizer was beaten and the Lions broke the camera of a news photographer.

5. Miller's (1958) focal concerns model argues that the values of delinquent gang members are a product of the lower-class community, which has traditions distinct from and in conflict with those of the middle-class law-making segment of the population.

6. Cloward and Ohlin (1960), for example, argue that a person who accepts the goals of society but finds no means of achieving them through legitimate channels will choose illegitimate means to resolve status problems. If few illegitimate means are available, conflict or fighting groups may be the collective resolution to the lack of an alternative status universe.

7. Social control or containment theories illustrate a modern version of social disorganization theories. These explanations focus on the bonds that keep people from deviating. The more disorganized and the fewer the institutions that affirm the

importance of the moral order, the more likely people will deviate. See Hirschi (1969) or Kornhauser (1978) for an excellent analysis of control, conflict, and strain explanations.

8. There is substantial disagreement about the degree to which "delinquent" norms are at variance with the norms of the conventional society, ranging from oppositional to rather small variations. The subcultural perspective assumes a lack of overall consensus in society (Miller, 1958); the contracultural perspective assumes the rejection of societal norms and the development of oppositional norms (Cloward and Ohlin, 1960; Albert Cohen, 1952); and the subterranean perspective assumes that delinquent norms are extensions or exaggerations of a generally consensual normative system (Matza, 1961).

9. See, for example, Jansyn (1966), Klein (1971), and Klein and Crawford (1968), who acknowledge the importance of group cohesion in gang delinquency and argue that there is a relationship between cohesion and violence. Jansyn argues that as cohesion increases, the number of violent incidents decreases, while Klein and Crawford argue that as cohesion increases, violence increases.

10. Short and Strodtbeck (1965) argue that violence is linked to the lack of verbal and interpersonal skills that constitute social competence in our society. Decreased status of the leader is the critical variable in the precipitation of violent incidents.

11. Matza (1964) argues that most delinquency is collective (situation of company) and that each gang member shares in a collective misunderstanding that all the others are committed to delinquency and that delinquent acts are good evidence of their masculinity.

12. See Lofland (1969) for a detailed examination of the nature of insult.

13. Moreover, the sensitivity to others' actions as not sufficiently deferential is increased for many youths by their lack of educational success and meaningful jobs.

14. The movie was Sam Peckinpah's *Straw Dogs*. Other favorites were the *Billy Jack* movies, where fights and violence are the means of achieving personal justice.

15. Gathering data on fights and reputations was relatively easy because my book was seen as an adventure story of fights and violence. In collective discussions gang fights were often described as more successful than they really were (to enhance the group's reputation), but no individual was allowed to exaggerate his part. When I talked to individuals, however, they often exaggerated their own roles in the fight but minimized the success of the group. In addition, I often talked with fairly impartial observers. As I was frequently at the park after an event, I observed the wounds sustained. Moreover, reputations were generally maintained by rumors, not by the actual numbers of bruises, cracked heads, or skinned knees. As the rumors were spread all over the community, they would be reported to me by a variety of sources so that I learned the whole story. Data from discussions by former gang members of their past activities were also useful but had to be carefully interpreted because these men were examining their pasts through new frameworks.

16. These youths took a woman's arm as she crossed the street, always walked on the curb side, and skillfully ordered dinner in restaurants. Whenever they were introduced to others, they always shook hands and made polite conversation.

17. This is unlike the situation at Jelly's Bar (Anderson, 1978), where the

ranking takes place between, not necessarily within, orientations. Jelly's is a bar in a low-income black community. The groups that frequent the bar and liquor store are the regulars, who strive for a regular means of support; the winos, who search for fun and more wine; and the hoodlums, who try to be tough.

18. Anderson (1978: 192) describes this volatility: "identity and place are not simply achieved once and for all, but are subject to changing situational factors and emergent definitions."

19. This supports Elliott and Voss's (1974) findings that delinquency tends to be an antecedent to having delinquent friends, but on 32nd Street there were also cases in which friends became gang members together.

20. The phenomenon of partners parallels the idea of *cuatismo* (from the Nahautl *cualt* [twin brother] [Lomnitz, 1977: 175]), which is the very strong social relationship of male friendship in Mexico. Most *cuates* drink together, which represents a high degree of trust and allows the exchange of secrets. It is also similar to "going for brothers" (Liebow, 1967), or "going for cousins" (Anderson, 1978), relationships that imply trust, close friendship, and mutual obligations.

21. This dominant-subordinate relationship can be one of trust in some cultures where there are distinct classes of people. There are many trusting and close relationships between a man and his servant, but that difference is structured into the class system and not precarious, as are the relationships among gang members, where any hierarchy is tenuous.

22. Gilberto started his reputation at age twelve when he arrived on 32nd Street. One evening he talked about his early days in Chicago. He said he ended up in jail eight months after he arrived in the city because he shot at someone. He did not want to fight and liked school except that he felt better on the streets. He said he had his first fist fight with a gang member a few months after he got to school. Somebody came through a door and started punching him and he beat up the intruder, he claimed. Gilberto admitted that he was a little "punk" then, short and slightly built, but he was tough and the Lions asked him to join. He agreed because he had many enemies. After you see a few of your friends killed, he said, you stay and fight for them. That is why the Senior Greeks are still fighting—"They're stuck," he said.

Chapter 6. Femininity and Womanhood: Virginity, Unwed Motherhood, and Violence

1. Many young women felt sorry for me because they never saw me in nice clothes or in any makeup and my hair hung limply down my back. They frequently offered to lend me clothes, fix my hair, and make up my face. I was a disaster in their eyes and would never "catch a man."

2. As Pitt-Rivers (1966) argues about Spain, a man never knows who has been with a nonvirgin. By linking himself to her through marriage, he automatically becomes the protector of her sexual purity, which she has already lost, making him a retroactive cuckold.

3. Safilios-Rothschild (1969) found a similar phenomenon in modern Greece. Few transgressions of honor of this type are actually redressed today. While an attempt at murder did occur on 32nd Street, in most cases revenge is merely a fist fight or, more often, a series of verbal threats by a young woman's brother. I frequently heard the comments "If I had been there" or "If I had known about it sooner, I would have beat his ass." Moreover, young men also realize that they could be on the other side.

4. Goffman (1963) argues that checking a biography is how others discover who the person really is, his actual social identity.

5. There is evidence that virginity has lost some of its significance in many sectors of this society. As Vincent (1961) points out, messages from many sectors of the society indicate that sex is fun and exciting and that fewer women than ever before are virgins at marriage. Reiss (1967) has shown that with the increasing autonomy of the courtship group from family adults, there is increasing tolerance of premarital sex. LeMasters (1975: 94) found that blue-collar men did not expect their future wives to be virgins: "If a girl is a virgin, a man should try to seduce her. If you don't, some other guy will—and then you'll be sorry you didn't." LeMasters feels that this statement implies that few women remain virgins after they start dating. He also found that men were afraid to marry virgins because they might not be "passionate"; however, they draw a strong line between women who are non-virgins and those who are "promiscuous," and fathers worry about the kind of men their daughters are sleeping with. LeMasters claims that Whyte's (1955) street corner men were much more insistent about the importance of marrying a virgin; however, Whyte's work was carried out thirty years earlier. Both groups studied were of working class origin, Italian, and predominantly Catholic. While these studies indicate that change is likely to take place, as yet the importance of virginity on 32nd Street remains, even if behavior has changed.

6. Failure to use birth control is frequently blamed on lack of knowledge or the unavailability of birth control devices (Bumpass and Westoff, 1970; Furstenberg, 1971). These explanations do not apply here. There is also increasing evidence that motherhood is an intentional outcome of premarital sex (Kantner and Zelnik, 1974; Presser, 1974).

7. According to Lyman and Scott (1963: 46), an account is "a linguistic device employed whenever an action is subjected to valuative inquiry." It is standardized within the local culture and used to bridge the gap between action and expectation.

8. Justifications are "accounts in which one accepts the responsibility for the act in question, but denies the pejorative quality associated with it" (Lyman and Scott, 1963: 47).

9. On the one hand, this explanation of unwed motherhood contrasts with that of Goode (1960, 1961), who views unwed motherhood as an illegitimate means to obtain a legitimate end, marriage, because of lack of other options. On the other hand, a set of values states that unwed motherhood is the correct way of doing things (Henriques, 1953), and none says it is almost as good as conventional methods (Rodman, 1963).

10. Even the Spanish unmarried mothers were not treated as shameless,

though they were disgraced (Pitt-Rivers, 1966). Unlike 32nd Street women, they usually find it difficult to marry

> since the man who wished to marry such a girl would be dishonoured—
> honour requires that one marry a virgin, since otherwise one becomes a
> retroactive cuckold—yet if their conduct gives no cause to scandal, they
> are distinguished from the loose women who come within the category of
> the shameless (Pitt-Rivers, 1966: 50).

11. Pitt-Rivers (1966) argues that the premise of an honor-based subculture is sex role segmentation. Honor hinges on a woman maintaining her shame (sexual purity) and a man protecting that shame.

12. Several potentially difficult situations arose through my relationship with these young women. I was asked to be a sponsor for a female gang, a position usually reserved for someone who is older and often an ex-member. It was difficult to refuse; however, because the groups fight I had no desire either to ally myself with one group, which would have meant exclusion from others, or to risk being dragged into a fight. One of the times I really became frightened was when some of the young women tried to get me to fight. Some very tough-looking women I did not know came to the park. When they approached the bench where I was sitting, they demanded to know if I were a Blue Dolphin. They did not seem convinced by my answer, but the Lions supported my statement. There was a fairly bloody fight between the two gangs later, but not at the park, where I remained.

Chapter 7. Education and School Authority

1. Explanations based on the culture of poverty consider the home and community, as not the school itself, the major causes of school failure of poor children. Children's learning is held back by poor stimulation prior to school entrance and cannot really be repaired by the school system. The students lack motivation, language, and self-esteem. See Rist (1973) for a critique. This type of analysis is used by Jensen (1969), who argues that blacks have consistently lower intelligence quotients (IQ's) than whites.

2. These studies focus on how the socialization mechanisms shape student motivations and values in order to explain how status origins affect educational attainments (Sewell, Haller, and Ohlendorf, 1970).

3. Studies of the educational system focus on organizational and structural variables such as teacher-pupil ratio, tracking, and funding (Alexander, Cook, and McDill, 1978; Heyns, 1974; Rosenbaum, 1975). Whether variables at the school district level affect individual levels of achievement is an open question. It has been argued that pupil-teacher ratio and administrative intensity at the district level affect median levels of achievement, and that a staff with high qualifications leads to student achievement. Resources have an indirect effect on achievement because resources affect the structure of school districts and staff qualifications (Bidwell and Kasarda, 1975). There have been a number of criticisms of such studies, but it is

beyond the scope of this chapter to enumerate them. Jencks (1972) found no effect at the district level.

4. The following scene provides an example of the problems parents face when they do not have the necessary skills to help their children. One father was unable to communicate to his seventh grade daughter that he was equally upset with her failing reading and gym. An articulate man who speaks both Spanish and English well, could easily say, "You must wear your shorts to gym so that you do not fail again," but although he was aware that reading was much more important, he felt unable to do or say anything about it. His daughter was also aware of the relative importance of reading skills and wearing shorts to gym, but she failed to understand why her father seemed more angry about the gym class. "Dad yelled and hit me because I got a "U" [unsatisfactory] in gym, but he didn't even say anything about my reading class."

5. There is evidence that the better students tend not to be delinquent (Frease, 1973; M. Gold, 1970; Hirschi, 1969; Jensen, 1976; Polk, 1969). Elliot (1966) and Elliot and Voss (1974) found that the rate of delinquency was highest for those who later dropped out, and this group's rate was lowest *after* they dropped out. They attributed the decrease in delinquency to the alleviation of status frustration by the act of dropping out.

6. Several studies have examined the relationship between tracking and delinquency in both the United States and England (Hargreaves, 1968) and have found that tracking into the lower strata is a good predictor of delinquency (Kelly, 1974; Kelly and Balch, 1971). Schaefer, Olexa, and Polk (1972) found that assignment to noncollege tracks not only had a negative effect on grades but decreased extracurricular involvement, increased dropouts, and created discipline problems.

7. Social control or bonding theorists have argued that attachments to teachers and schools are important barriers to delinquency (Hindelang, 1973; Hirschi, 1969; Jensen, Erickson, and Gibbs, 1978).

8. See Rist (1970, 1973) and Rosenthal and Jacobson (1968) for detailed analyses of this process.

9. See Weber (1964) and Eckstein and Gurr (1975) for similar definitions of legitimacy and authority.

10. For a comparative analysis of a similiar phenomenon see Schwartz et al., (n.d.)

11. Only 35 to 40 percent of Tudor High School students (tenth through twelfth grades) are from 32nd Street. There is no way to differentiate their grades or their dropout rate from others.

12. While school was a natural topic of conversation among the upwardly mobile youths, others had to be asked about school activities. Occasionally, the topic arose naturally among the Lions when an event such as a fight, a graduation, or a suspension occurred, but I often extended the discussions. Recognized as an educated person (a reporter), I was asked for advice about school and jobs.

I spent time in the public and parochial high schools and the Marsh Upper

Grades Center. In the public high school I attended classes, graduation, and several school events. My presence in the classes of Tudor High went largely unnoticed by teachers. In 1973 I was a guest lecturer in some sociology classes. At Marsh I attended classes, a graduation dinner-dance, and a number of ceremonial occasions, including graduation. I also gave an in-service lecture to the teachers, spoke with them afterward, and interviewed several of them.

My position in St. Catherine's Catholic high school was different. I was invited with a drug counselor by the principal of the school to talk to the students about the dangers of drug usage. For six months we spent one day a week, several hours a day, in the school. I was invited by the students to attend graduation, freshman initiation ceremonies, the senior play, and a number of other school activities. These observations, experiences, and discussions with the teachers in the three schools allowed me to verify the youths' descriptions.

13. The statistics on employment of males age sixteen to twenty-one in Chicago in 1970 support the 32nd Street youths' experiences. The unemployment rate for Spanish-speaking high school graduates was 26.2 percent and for nongraduates, 27.9 percent. For non-Spanish speaking graduates it was 25.2 percent and for nongraduates, 46.8 percent (Chicago Department of Development and Planning, 1973).

14. See Bossert (1978) for an analysis of the relationship between classroom organization and student relationships. The male-female competition also may be exacerbated by the generally cooperative cognitive styles of learning found among Mexican-Americans rather than competitive Anglo styles (Ramirez, 1976).

15. Coleman (1961) argues that youths judge each other in terms not of academic achievement but of expressive activities and relationships (popularity with peers, sexual attractiveness, and athletics) that have little function in life and are contrary to what their parents expect and what school is supposed to do.

16. Jesús later passed the GED exams, received a college diploma from the University without Walls program, and attended a graduate program in the social sciences.

17. Some youths are identified as smart or nice or good early in elementary school and word is passed along through formal and informal channels. For example, one seventh grade teacher told me how pleased he was to have a particular student in his class. A sixth grade teacher had called him at home and spent half an hour extolling the virtues of this student. On the other hand, negative information is passed along about the troublemakers. Consequently, those at the top and at the bottom have preexisting identities to step into.

18. Most of the examples are from girls' schools. Life at St. Catherine's seems to be similar to life at the boys' schools from what the boys say. Several of the boys attended a very prestigious parochial college preparatory school. They were well motivated, did well, and most went on to college.

19. During discussions about drugs, it became evident that over half of the juniors and seniors used drugs extensively. Marijuana, the most popular, was followed quite closely by acid, "uppers," and "downers." The nuns were not aware of the heavy drug use until one student passed out after sniffing cleaning fluid in the cloakroom.

Chapter 8. Earning a Living

1. The work situation on 32nd Street is not as bad as the one portrayed in Liebow (1967), where the men have given up looking for work and only occasionally engage in day labor. The situation is more similar to that of the regulars at Jelly's Bar (Anderson, 1978), who generally have a visible means of support and who continue to value work. There is some evidence that work orientations for poor and more affluent youths are similar and that differences in attitudes can be attributed to different work experiences encountered (Goodwin, 1980).

The situation found on 32nd Street seems consistent with the findings of Sewell and Hauser (1975) in that early background appears to be a better predictor of occupational attainment than does education. Whereas black youths have a higher educational level than Chicanos, their rate of unemployment is higher even when high school dropouts are compared. Discrimination probably accounts for much of the difference; however, the commitment to the American dream and the importance of work for men of honor contribute to the relatively low unemployment rate of the Chicanos despite the low level of educational attainment.

2. Researchers have found that in inner-city labor markets there is little positive relationship between education and earning, especially among nonwhite workers, which led them to conceptualize the job market as a dual labor market (Marshall, Cartter, and King, 1976). The primary market has steady, well-paying jobs with on-the-job training for upward mobility, which fosters long-term employment for certain types of employees. The secondary labor market is composed of jobs with low wages, no training necessary, no expectations of stable work habits or commitments to the firm, no grievance procedures, and no possible advancement. Most jobs that the 32nd Street residents obtain are of the latter variety. From interviews of out-of-school young men, Buchele (1976) found that work experiences were determined more by a job's characteristics than by a worker's personal attributes. Job characteristics have an important bearing on employment turnover, income, and job satisfaction.

3. A similar type of economic exchange is described as the irregular or hidden economy (Henry, 1978). All exist outside the official, taxable economy. Mutual obligations differ from the irregular economy in that they generally arise from a pre-existing social relationship, feature cashless exchanges, and are not merely a single transaction. The irregular economy system may or may not arise among a group of friends and continue beyond a single transaction.

4. According to Anderson (1978: 208) the regulars feel that working is a primary value and gives them a sense of decency that those who do not work do not have. Failure to have a visible means of support usually means that the residual values of toughness, drinking, and getting rich become more salient. The hoodlums have a different orientation toward work.

5. Among the gang members, work was not a frequent topic of general conversation. On a number of occasions I either initiated the topic or greatly prolonged what probably would have been a very short conversation. The young women who worked liked to discuss what they would buy with their earnings, so that work was discussed more frequently. Occasionally a youth would ask for my advice.

6. This is different from the situation among blacks studied by Goodwin (1980), in which people were less likely to go off welfare and take a $200-a-week job if they earned money illegally. On 32nd Street, it is considered wrong to do so and more people work legitimately in addition to earning money illegally.

7. The value of the absence of supervision is not particular to this community or country. Carter (1966: 165) describes the case in England: "Children in interesting jobs can be made miserable by an inconsiderate boss, or one who is constantly underlining authority."

8. Youths frequently referred to my job as a researcher as a "good hustle." All I had to do was stand around and talk all day and go to parties at night. While they knew I wrote notes every night and had even examined them several times, that was not considered work no matter how hard I protested.

9. In a study of ABCD's (Boston's Community Action Program) Doeringer (1969) found that marital status has little distinct influence upon job tenure. On 32nd Street working was viewed as increasingly important, but I have no statistical data on whether job tenure increased with additional responsibilities. Buchele (1976) found that married men earned 26 percent more than single men.

10. Rosenberg (1975) found in his analysis of labor statistics of low-income neighborhoods in four major cities that mobility out of the secondary labor market is particularly difficult for minorities and is complicated by lack of education and vocational training. But a start in the secondary labor market does not completely rule out movement into the primary market.

Chapter 9. Adult Juvenile Gang Membership

1. Komarovsky (1962) found in her study of marriage that working-class men and women socialized separately, as did Liebow (1967) in his studies of lower-class street corner men. Anderson (1978) found the same phenomenon among the men in or near Jelly's Bar whether they were the regulars who had jobs and steady female relationships or the winos and hoodlums who had neither. Bott (1971) found similar patterns in British working-class families.

Studies of Italian communities (Gans, 1962; Whyte, 1955) have found sex-segregated peer groups, as do all studies of honor-based subcultures (see, for example, Peristiany, 1966). Suttles (1968) found the same phenomenon among the four ethnic and racial groups he studied in an inner-city community.

2. Matza (1964) argues that delinquents are not committed to delinquent norms but mistakenly believe that others are. When the obvious indicators of adulthood (full physical size, marriage, fatherhood, and employment) are attained, they no longer feel the need to demonstrate their manhood through aggressive delinquent acts and leave the gangs.

3. Both Erlanger(1979) and Moore (1978) found many older members in Chicano gangs.

4. I was convinced that I would not find anyone I knew when I returned to 32nd Street in 1977 and I was nervous about my reception by the Lions. To my surprise,

within five hours of my return I had located many of the youths I had known previously. Many of the Lions were sitting on the same bench, in the same park, talking about many of the same things as they had in 1971. They behaved as though I had been away several months rather than years. They immediately noticed that my hair was grayer and that I was dressing slightly better (respectable, well-pressed pants rather than jeans). They laughed at what they viewed as my economic failure. They could earn as much money driving trucks, they claimed.

Unless noted otherwise, the data in this chapter concern the Lions.

5. Jacobs (1978) has demonstrated the importance and strength in Illinois prisons of gangs based largely on ethnic rather than territorial divisions.

6. Suttles (1968) argues that gangs as fighting groups end when the members reach eighteen or nineteen. Later new groups, social athletic clubs, form with new memberships and new names. They do not engage in criminal activities and do not fight in the name of the group.

7. Confidence has been described by Simmel (1950) as a state between full knowledge and ignorance that, developing over time, allows a group with some social distance unhesitatingly to exchange goods, services, and information about each other. The exchange of personal information is necessary to develop confidence and certifies that the members have confidence in each other.

8. Most of my discussions of family, girlfriends, and the future occurred toward the end of my first year and continued after I stopped spending much of my time on the streets. Not all of the street males or the Lions would talk to me. Occasionally the street-oriented males asked my advice about their girlfriends, work, or school. Sometimes drugs or alcohol helped them open up. I tried not to give advice but asked questions concerning their wishes, beliefs, and activities. It was very difficult not to give advice to stay in school or get some sort of training or the like. On one occasion, when I was talking to a Lion whose girlfriend had just told him she was pregnant, I made the mistake of asking why they did not use birth control in a tone that he took as an indictment of his behavior. With that comment, what had been a fascinating conversation about his intimate life turned into a discussion of sports and fights. I had many private conversations with more than half of the Lions and other street males, but others never felt close enough to me to engage in such conversations. When I returned several of the Lions continued to talk about personal issues but others would not.

9. For similar descriptions of male street interaction see Liebow (1967), Matza (1964), Miller (1958), and Rainwater (1970).

Chapter 10. The Consequences of Being Different

1. Adherents to a Mertonian perspective (Merton, 1957) argue that everyone aspires to achieve the American dream of economic and social success, which implies obtaining a good job and being evaluated on the basis of job skills, technical competencies, and material objects in "good taste," but does not specify what is right or wrong, good or bad, in most other areas. It is assumed these values exert pressure

on individuals to do better, and failure is caused by situational exigencies (lack of opportunities). Daily conduct at variance with achievement of the American dream is beyond the individual's control, an ad hoc adaptation that should not claim allegiance and that is not part of an integrated cultural system. Therefore movement away from the group should be relatively easy if opportunities arise. Others, who trace lower-class behaviors to a long history of exclusion and view norms as reflecting social attitudes and activities at variance with those of the wider society to which members are socialized, argue that movement out of these groups is extremely difficult (Lewis, 1965; Miller, 1958).

2. It was difficult for me, as a single woman with no children, to rent an apartment in the community. Only if I brought a young child along would people consider renting me an apartment in their homes. As a mother, I was respectable. As a woman alone, I was suspect. I should have been living with relatives. They were concerned not about my ability to pay but about my moral character.

3. While Chicanos may also have problems finding wives, many of them do not place importance on the need for equality between the sexes and can find women from 32nd Street who will make traditional wives.

4. For an historical analysis of the start of the local activist movement see Stern (1976).

5. Stern (1976) has made an interesting analysis of the different uses of ethnicity.

Bibliography

Alexander, Karl, and Edward McDill
  1976 "Selection and allocation within schools: Some causes and consequences of curriculum placement." *American Sociological Review* 41:963–980.
Alexander, Karl, Martha Cook, and E. L. McDill
  1978 "Curriculum tracking and educational stratification: Some further evidence." *American Sociological Review* 43:47–66.
Alvirez, David, and F. D. Bean
  1976 "The Mexican American Family." In C. H. Mindel and R. W. Habenstein (eds.), *Ethnic Families in America*, pp. 271–292. New York: Elsevier.
Anderson, Elijah
  1978 *A Place on the Corner*. Chicago: University of Chicago Press.
Anderson, Nels
  1923 *The Hobo*. Chicago: University of Chicago Press.
Baca Zinn, Maxine
  1975 "Political familism: Toward sex role equality in Chicano families." *Aztlán: Chicaco Journal of the Social Sciences and the Arts* 6:13–26.
  1976 "Chicanas: Power and control in the domestic sphere." *De Colores* 2(3):19–21.
Berger, Bennett
  1963 "On the youthfulness of youth cultures." *Social Research* 29:319–342.
  1968 *Working-Class Suburb*. Berkeley: University of California Press.
Berger, P., and Thomas Luckman
  1966 *The Social Construction of Reality*. Garden City, N.Y.: Doubleday.
Berger, Peter, Brigette Berger, and Hansfried Kellner
  1973 *The Homeless Mind*. New York: Random House.
Bidwell, Charles E., and John D. Kasarda
  1975 "School district organization and student achievement." *American Sociological Review* 40:55–70.
Blake, Judith
  1972 "Coercive pronatalism and American population policy." *International*

Population and Urban Research. Berkeley: University of California Press.

Bloch, Herbert, and A. Niederhoffer
1958 *The Gang: A Study in Adolescent Behavior*. New York: Philosophical Library.

Blood, R., and D. Wolfe
1960 *Husbands and Wives*. Glencoe, Ill.: Free Press.

Bossert, Steven T.
1978 "Classroom structure and teacher authority." *Education and Urban Society* 11:49–59.

Bott, Elizabeth
1971 *Family and Social Network*. New York: Free Press.

Bradshaw, B. S., and F. D. Bean
1972 "Some aspects of the fertility of Mexican-Americans." In C. F. Westoff and R. Parke, Jr. (eds.), *Demographic and Social Aspects of Population Growth*, pp. 140–164. Commission on Population Growth and the American Future, Research Reports, vol. 1. Washington, D.C.: U.S. Government Printing Office.

Buchele, Robert K.
1976 "Jobs and Workers: A Labor Market Segmentation Perspective on the Work Experience of Young Men." Ph.D. dissertation, Harvard University.

Buehler, Marilyn
1977 "Voter turnout and political efficacy among Mexican-Americans in Michigan." *Sociological Quarterly* 18:504–517.

Bullock, Paul
1972 "Employment problems of the Mexican Americans." In Rudolph Gomez (ed.), *The Changing Mexican American*, pp. 90–105. El Paso: University of Texas Press.

Bumpass, L., and C. Westoff
1970 "The perfect contraceptive population." *Science* 169:1177–1182.

Burgess, Ernest
1967 "The growth of the city." In R. Park and E. Burgess (eds.), *The City*, pp. 47–62. Chicago: University of Chicago Press.

Bushnell, John H.
1958 "La Virgen de Guadalupe as surrogate mother." *American Anthropologist* 60:261–265.

Campbell, J. K.
1966 "Honour and the devil." In J. G. J. Peristiany (ed.), *Honour and Shame*, pp. 131–171. Chicago: University of Chicago Press.

Carlos, Manuel L.
1973 "Fictive kinship and modernization in Mexico: A comparative analysis." *Anthropological Quarterly* 46:75–91.

Carter, Michael
1966 *Into Work*. Baltimore: Penguin Books.

Casavantes, Edward
  1976 "Pride and prejudice: A Mexican American dilemma." In C. A. Hernán-
    dez, M. J. Haug, and N. N. Wagner (eds.), *Chicanos*, pp. 9–14. Saint
    Louis: C. V. Mosby.
Chicago Department of Development and Planning
  1973 *Chicago's Spanish Speaking Population: Selected Statistics.*
Cloward, R., and L. Ohlin
  1960 *Delinquency and Opportunity.* New York: Free Press.
Cohen, Abner
  1974 *Two-Dimensional Man.* Berkeley: University of California Press.
Cohen, Albert
  1952 *Delinquent Boys.* Glencoe, Ill.: Free Press.
Coleman, James
  1961 *The Adolescent Society.* New York: Free Press of Glencoe.
Cotera, Marta
  1976 *Profile of the Mexican American Woman.* Austin: National Educational
    Laboratory.
Coult, Allen, and R. Habenstein
  1962 "The study of extended kinship in urban society." *Sociological
    Quarterly* 3:141–145.
DeHoyos, Arturo and Genevieve
  1966 "The amigo system and alienation of the wife in the conjugal Mexican
    family." In Bernard Farber (ed.), *Kinship and Family Organization*, pp.
    102–115. New York: Wiley.
Diaz, May N.
  1966 *Tonalá: Conservatism, Authority and Responsibility in a Mexican
    Town.* Berkeley: University of California Press.
Doeringer, Peter
  1969 "Programs to employ the disadvantaged: A labor market perspective."
    In P. Doeringer (ed.), *Programs to Employ the Disadvantaged*, pp.
    245–261. Englewood Cliffs, N.J.: Prentice-Hall.
Douglas, Jack
  1971 *American Social Order.* New York: Free Press.
  1976 *Investigative Social Research.* Beverly Hills: Sage.
Durkheim, Emile
  1964 *Division of Labor in Society.* Trans. by G. Simpson. New York: Free
    Press.
Eckstein, Harry, and Ted Gurr
  1975 *Patterns of Authority: A Structural Basis for Political Inquiry.* New
    York: Wiley.
Elliott, D. S.
  1966 "Delinquency, school attendance and dropout." *Social Problems*
    13:306–318.
Elliott, D. S., and H. L. Voss
  1974 *Delinquency and Dropout.* Lexington, Mass.: D. C. Heath.

Erlanger, Howard
    1979 "Estrangement, machismo and gang violence." *Social Science Quarterly* 60:235–248.

Farmer, George
    1972 "Education." In Rudolph Gomez (ed.), *The Changing Mexican American*. El Paso: University of Texas Press.

Ferree, Myra Marx
    1979 "Employment without liberation: Cuban women in the United States." *Social Science Quarterly* 60:35–50.

Fine, Gary
    1979 "Small groups and culture creation." *American Sociological Review* 44:733–745.

Fine, Gary, and S. Kleinman
    1979 "Rethinking subculture: An interactionist analysis." *American Journal of Sociology* 85:1–20.

Fischer, Claude
    1976 *The Urban Experience*. New York: Harcourt Brace Jovanovich.

Foster, George
    1967 *Tzintzunztán*. Boston: Little, Brown.

Frease, D. E.
    1973 "Delinquency, social class and the schools." *Sociology and Social Research* 57:443–459.

Frisbie, W. P., F. D. Bean, and I. W. Eberstein
    1980 "Recent changes in marital stability among Mexican Americans." *Social Forces* 58:1205–1220.

Fromm, Erich, and Michael Maccoby
    1970 *Social Character in a Mexican Village*. Englewood Cliffs, N.J.: Prentice-Hall.

Furstenberg, Frank F., Jr.
    1971 "Birth control experience among pregnant adolescents: The process of unplanned parenthood." *Social Problems* 19:192–203.

Gans, Herbert
    1962 *The Urban Villagers*. New York: Free Press.
    1968 "Culture and class in the study of poverty: An approach to anti-poverty research." In D. P. Moynihan (ed.), *On Understanding Poverty*, pp. 201–228. New York: Basic Books.

Garfinkel, Harold
    1956 "Conditions of successful degradation ceremonies." *American Journal of Sociology* 61:420–424.

Geertz, Clifford
    1973 *The Interpretation of Cultures*. New York: Basic Books.

Gibson, Charles
    1966 *Spain in America*. New York: Harper and Row.

Gillis, John
    1974 *Youth and History*. New York: Harcourt Brace Jovanovich.

Goffman, Erving
  1959 *Presentation of Self in Everyday Life*. New York: Doubleday Anchor.
  1963 *Stigma*. Englewood Cliffs, N.J.: Prentice-Hall.
  1967 *Interaction Ritual*. New York: Doubleday Anchor.
  1971 *Relations in Public*. New York: Basic Books.
  1974 *Frame Analysis*. New York: Harper and Row.

Gold, M.
  1970 *Delinquent Behavior in an American City*. Monterey, Calif.: Brooks/Cole.

Gold, Raymond
  1969 "Roles in sociological field observations." In G. McCall and J. L. Simmons (eds.), *Issues in Participant Observation*, pp. 30–38. Reading, Mass.: Addison-Wesley.

Goode, William J.
  1960 "A deviant case: Illegitimacy in the Caribbean." *American Sociological Review* 25:21–30.
  1961 "Illegitimacy, anomie and cultural penetration." *American Sociological Review* 26:910–925.

Goodenough, Ward
  1963 *Cooperation in Change*. New York: Wiley.

Goodman, M. E., and A. Beman
  1971 "Child's-eye-views of life in an urban barrio." In N. Wagner and M. Haug (eds.), *Chicanos: Social and Psychological Perspectives*, pp. 109–122. Saint Louis: C. V. Mosby Company.

Goodwin, Leonard
  1980 "Poor youth and employment: A social psychological perspective." *Youth and Society* 11:311–351.

Gordon, Robert
  1967 "Social level, disability, and gang interaction." *American Journal of Sociology* 73:42–62.

Grebler, Leo, J. W. Moore, and R. C. Guzman
  1970 *The Mexican-American People*. New York: Free Press.

Grønbjerg, Kirsten, David Street, and G. Suttles
  1978 *Poverty and Social Change*. Chicago: University of Chicago Press.

Gusfield, Joseph
  1967 "Tradition and modernity: Misplaced polarities in the study of social change." *American Journal of Sociology* 72:351–362.
  1975 *Community: A Critical Response*. New York: Harper and Row.

Handel, G., and L. Rainwater
  1964 "Persistence and change in working-class life-styles." In A. B. Shostak and W. Gomberg (eds.), *Blue-Collar World*, pp. 36–41. Englewood Cliffs, N.J.: Prentice-Hall.

Hannerz, Ulf
  1969 *Soulside*. New York: Columbia University Press.

Hargreaves, D.
   1968 *Social Relations in a Secondary School*. New York: Humanities Press.
Hayner, Norman
   1966 *New Patterns in Old Mexico*. New Haven: College and University
         Press.
Henriques, Fernando
   1953 *Family and Colour in Jamaica*. London: Eyre and Spottiswoode.
Henry, Stuart
   1978 *The Hidden Economy*. London: Martin Robertson.
Hernandez, J., L. Estrada, and D. Alvirez
   1973 "Census data and the problem of conceptually defining the Mexican
         American population." *Social Science Quarterly* 53:671–687.
Heyns, Barbara
   1974 "Social selection and stratification within schools." *American Journal
         of Sociology* 79:1434–1451.
Hindelang, M. J.
   1973 "Causes of delinquency: A partial replication." *Social Problems*
         21:471–487.
Hirschi, Travis
   1969 *Causes of Delinquency*. Berkeley: University of California Press.
Hollingshead, August B.
   1949 *Elmtown's Youth*. New York: Wiley.
Horowitz, R.
   1982 "Masked intimacy and marginality: Adult delinquent gangs in a
         Chicano community." *Urban Life* 11:3–26.
Horowitz, R., and G. Schwartz
   1974 "Honor, normative ambiguity and gang violence." *American Sociologi-
         cal Review* 39:238–251.
Hunter, Albert
   1975 *Symbolic Communities*. Chicago: University of Chicago Press.
Jacobs, James
   1978 *Statesville*. Chicago: University of Chicago Press.
Janowitz, Morris
   1967 *The Community Press in an Urban Setting*. Chicago: University of
         Chicago Press.
Jansyn, Leon
   1966 "Solidarity and delinquency in a street corner group." *American Socio-
         logical Review* 31:600–614.
Jencks, Christopher, M. Smith, H. Acland, M. J. Bane, D. Cohen, H. Gintis, B.
Heyns, and S. Michelson
   1972 *Inequality*. New York: Basic Books.
Jensen, A.
   1969 "How much can we boost I.Q. and scholastic achievement?" *Harvard
         Educational Review* 39:273–274.

Jensen, Gary F.
  1976 "Race, achievement and delinquency: A further look at delinquency in a birth cohort." *American Journal of Sociology* 82:377–387.
Jensen, Gary F., M. L. Erickson, and J. P. Gibbs
  1978 "Perceived risk of punishment and self-reported delinquency." *Social Forces* 57:57–78.
Johnson, John M.
  1975 *Doing Field Research.* New York: Free Press.
Kantner, Melvin, and John Zelnik
  1974 "The resolution of teenage first pregnancies." *Family Planning Perspectives* 6:74–80.
Karp, David, G. Stone, and W. Yoels
  1977 *Being Urban.* Lexington, Mass.: D. C. Heath
Kasarda, John, and M. Janowitz
  1974 "Community attachment in mass society." *American Sociological Review* 39:328–339.
Keefe, S. E., A. M. Padilla, and M. L. Carlos
  1979 "The Mexican-American extended family as an emotional support system." *Human Organization* 38:144–152.
Kelly, D. H.
  1974 "Track position and delinquent involvement: A preliminary analysis." *Sociology and Social Research* 58:380–386.
Kelly, D. H., and R. W. Balch
  1971 "Social origins and school failure." *Pacific Sociological Review* 14:413–430.
Klein, Malcolm W.
  1971 *Street Gangs and Street Workers.* Englewood Cliffs, N.J.: Prentice-Hall.
Klein, Malcolm W., and L. Y. Crawford
  1968 "Groups, gangs and cohesiveness." In J. F. Short (ed.), *Gang Delinquency and Delinquency Subcultures,"* pp. 256–272. New York: Harper and Row.
Kleinman, Sherryl I.
  1980 "Learning the ropes as fieldwork analysis." In W. Shaffir, R. Stebbins, and A. Turowetz (eds.), *Fieldwork Experience,* pp. 171–184. New York: St. Martin's Press.
Kobrin, Solomon
  1951 "The conflict of values in delinquency areas." *American Sociological Review* 16:653–661.
Kobrin, Soloman, Joe Puntil, and Emil Peluso
  1967 "Criteria of status among street groups." *Journal of Research in Crime and Delinquency* (January): 98–118.
Komarovsky, Mirra
  1962 *Blue-Collar Marriage.* New York: Random House.
Kornblum, William
  1974 *Blue Collar Community.* Chicago: University of Chicago Press.

Kornhäuser, Ruth
   1978   *The Social Sources of Delinquency.* Chicago: University of Chicago
          Press.
Leach, Edmond R.
   1961   *Rethinking Anthropology.* London: Athlone Press.
LeMasters, E.
   1975   *Blue-Collar Aristocrats.* Madison: University of Wisconsin Press.
Lewis, Oscar
   1965   *La Vida.* New York: Vintage Books.
   1967   *Tepoztlán.* New York: Holt, Rinehart and Winston.
Liebow, Elliot
   1967   *Tally's Corner.* Boston: Little, Brown.
Litwak, Eugene
   1960   "Geographic mobility and extended family cohesion." *American Socio-
          logical Review* 25:385–394.
Lofland, John
   1969   *Deviance and Identity.* Englewood Cliffs, N.J.: Prentice-Hall.
Lomnitz, Larissa Adler
   1977   *Networks and Marginality.* Trans. by Cinna Lomnitz. New York: Aca-
          demic Press.
Lopez y Rivas, Gilberto
   1973   *The Chicanos.* New York: Monthly Review Press.
Lyman, S., and M. Scott
   1963   "Accounts." *American Sociological Review* 33:46–62.
McCaghy, Charles H., and Skipper Lefton
   1968   *In Their Own Behalf: Voices from the Margin.* New York: Appleton-
          Century-Crofts.
McCall, George, and J. L. Simmons
   1966   *Identities and Interaction.* New York: Free Press.
Madsen, William
   1960   *The Virgin's Children.* Austin: University of Texas Press.
   1964   *The Mexican Americans of South Texas.* New York: Holt, Rinehart,
          and Winston.
Maines, David
   1977   "Social organization and social structure in symbolic interactionist
          thought." *Annual Review of Sociology* 3:235–259.
Manning, Peter
   1973   "Existential sociology." *Sociological Quarterly* 14:200–215.
Marshall, F. R., A. M. Cartter, and A. G. King
   1976   *Labor Economics.* Homewood, Ill.: Irwin, Inc.
Mason, Karen, and L. Bumpass
   1975   "U.S. women's sex role ideology, 1970." *American Journal of Sociology*
          80:1212–1219.
Matza, David
   1961   "Subterranean traditions of youth." *Annals of Political and Social
          Science* 338:103–118.

1964 *Delinquency and Drift*. New York: John Wiley and Sons.
Mead, Herbert
1964 *On Social Psychology*. Chicago: University of Chicago Press.
Merton, Robert K.
1957 Social Theory and Social Structure. Glencoe, Ill.: Free Press.
Miller, Walter B.
1958 "Lower class delinquency as a generating milieu of gang delinquency." 14:5–19.
1969 "White gangs." *Transaction* 6:11–26.
1971 "Subculture, social reform and the culture of poverty." *Human Organization* 30:111–125.
1975 *Violence by Youth Gangs and Youth Groups as a Crime Problem in American Cities*. Office of Juvenile Justice and Delinquency Prevention, United States Department of Justice. Washington, D.C.: Government Printing Office.
Mintz, S. W., and E. R. Wolf
1950 "An analysis of ritual co-parenthood." *Southwestern Journal of Anthropology* 6:341–635.
Mirandé, A., and E. Enríquez
1979 *La Chicana*. Chicago: University of Chicago Press.
Montenegro, Marilyn
1976 *Chicanos and Mexican Americans: Ethnic Self-Identification and Attitudinal Differences*. San Francisco: R and E Associates.
Moore, Joan
1970 *Mexican Americans*. Englewood Cliffs, N.J.: Prentice-Hall.
1978 *Homeboys*. Philadelphia: Temple University Press.
Morse, Nancy, and R. S. Weiss
1955 "The function and meaning of work and the job." *American Sociological Review* 20:191–198.
Murillo, Nathan
1971 "The Mexican-American family." In N. N. Wagner and M. J. Haug (eds.), *Chicanos: Social and Psychological Perspectives*, pp. 97–108. Saint Louis: C. V. Mosby.
Navarro-Uranga, Susan
1973 "The study of Mexican-American education in the Southwest: Implications of research by the Civil Rights Commission." In R. O. de la Garza, Z. A. Kruszewski, and T. A. Arciniega (eds.), *Chicanos and Native Americans*, pp. 161–172. Englewood Cliffs, N.J.: Prentice-Hall.
Nelson, Cynthia
1971 *The Waiting Village: Social Change in Rural Mexico*. Boston: Little, Brown.
Nieto-Gomez, Anna
1971 "Chicanas identify." *Regeneración* 1(10):9–13.
1974 "La Feminista." *Encuentro Feminil* 1:34–37.

Parsons, Talcott
    1951 *Toward a General Theory of Action*. Cambridge: Harvard University
           Press.

Paz, Octavio
    1961 *The Labyrinth of Solitude*. Trans. by Lysander Kemp. New York:
           Grove.

Peñalosa, Fernando
    1967 "The changing Mexican-American in Southern California." *Sociology
           and Social Research* 51:405–417.
    1968 "Mexican family roles." *Journal of Marriage and the Family*
           30:680–689.
    1973 "Toward an operational definition of the Mexican-American." In
           Gilberto Lopez y Rivas (ed.), *The Chicanos*, pp. 91–106. New York:
           Monthly Review Press.

Peristiany, J.
    1966 *Honour and Shame*. Chicago: University of Chicago Press.

Peterson, R. A.
    1979 "Revitalizing the culture concept." *Annual Review of Sociology*
           5:137–166. Palo Alto, Calif.: Annual Reviews, Inc.

Pinkney, Alphonso
    1963 "Prejudice toward Mexican and Negro Americans: A comparison."
           Phylon, 24 (winter): 353–359.

Pitt-Rivers, Julian
    1966 "Honour and social status." In J. Peristiany (ed.), *Honour and Shame*,
           pp. 19–78. Chicago: University of Chicago Press.

Polk, K.
    1969 "Class, strain and rebellion among adolescents." *Social Problems*
           17:214–224.

Presser, Harriet
    1974 "Early motherhood: Ignorance or bliss?" *Family Planning Perspectives*
           6:8–14.

Rainwater, L., and G. Handel
    1964 "Changing family roles in the working class." In A. B. Shostak and W.
           Gomberg, (eds.), *Blue-Collar World*, pp. 70–75. Englewood Cliffs, N.J.:
           Prentice-Hall.

Rainwater, Lee
    1970 *Behind Ghetto Walls*. Chicago: Aldine.

Ramirez, Manuel, III
    1976 "Cognitive styles and cultural democracy in education." In C. A.
           Hernandez, M. J. Haug, and N. N. Wagner (eds.), *Chicanos*, pp.
           196–203. Saint Louis: C. V. Mosby.

Redfield, Robert
    1960 *The Little Community*. Chicago: University of Chicago Press.

Reiss, Ira
    1967 *The Social Context of Premarital Sexual Permissiveness*. New York:
           Holt, Rinehart, and Winston.

Rist, Ray
1970 "Student social class and teacher expectations: The self-fulfilling prophecy in ghetto education." *Harvard Educational Review* 40:411–451.
1973 *The Urban School: A Factory for Failure*. Cambridge: MIT Press.
Rodman, Hyman
1963 "Lower-class value stretch." *Social Forces* 42:205–215.
Romanucci-Ross, Lola
1973 *Conflict, Violence and Morality in a Mexican Village*. Palo Alto: National Press Books.
Rosenbaum, James E.
1975 "The stratification of socialization processes." *American Sociological Review* 40:48–54.
Rosenberg, Samuel
1975 "The Dual Labor Market: Its Existence and Consequences." Ph.D. dissertation, University of California at Berkeley.
Rosenthal, R., and L. Jacobson
1968 *Pygmalion in the Classroom*. New York: Holt.
Rubel, Arthur
1966 *Across the Tracks*. Austin: University of Texas Press.
Safilios-Rothschild, Constantina
1969 " 'Honour' crimes in contemporary Greece." *British Journal of Sociology* 20:205–218.
Sahlins, Marshall
1972 *Stone Age Economics*. Chicago: Aldine-Atherton.
Schaefer, W. E., C. Olexa, and K. Polk
1972 "Programmed for social class tracking in high school." In K. Polk and W. E. Schaefer (eds.), *Schools and Delinquency*, pp. 33–54. Englewood Cliffs, N.J.: Prentice-Hall.
Schatzman, L., and A. Strauss
1973 *Field Research*. Englewood Cliffs, N.J.: Prentice-Hall.
Schensul, Steven
1972 "Action research in a Chicano community." Paper, American Anthropological Association, Toronto.
Schwartz, G., M. Ducey, F. Behan, R. Horowitz, and P. Langer
n.d. "Youth and Community: A Comparative Perspective." Manuscript, Illinois Institute for Juvenile Research.
Schwartz, Gary
1972 *Youth Culture: An Anthropological Approach*. Reading, Mass.: Addison-Wesley Modular Publications.
n.d. "Culture Process." Paper, Illinois Institute for Juvenile Research. Mimeographed.
Schwartz, Gary, and D. Merten
1968 "Social identity and expressive symbols: The meaning of an initiation ritual." *American Anthropologist* 70:1117–1131.

Seña-Rivera, Jaime
  1979 "The extended kinship of the United States: Competing models and the case of la familia chicana." *Journal of Marriage and the Family* 41:121–129.
Sennett, Richard, and Jonathan Cobb
  1972 *The Hidden Injuries of Class*. Random House: New York.
Sewell, W. H., and R. M. Hauser
  1975 *Education, Occupation and Earnings: Achievement in the Early Career*. New York: Academic Press.
Sewell, W. H., A. D. Haller, and G. W. Ohlendorf
  1970 "The educational and early occupational attainment process: Replications and revisions." *American Sociological Review* 35:1014–1027.
Shaffir, W.
  1974 *Life in a Religious Community*. Toronto: Holt, Rinehart, and Winston.
Shaw, Clifford
  1931 *Natural History of a Delinquent Career*. Chicago: University of Chicago Press.
  1966 *The Jackroller*. Chicago: University of Chicago Press.
Shaw, Clifford, and Henry McKay
  1966 *Juvenile Delinquency in Urban Areas*. Chicago: University of Chicago Press.
Short, James F., Jr.
  1965 "Social structure and group processes in explanation of gang delinquency." In M. and C. Sherif (eds.), *Problems of Youth*, pp. 155–188. Chicago: Aldine.
Short, James F., and F. Strodtbeck
  1965 *Group Process and Gang Delinquency*. Chicago: University of Chicago Press.
Simmel, Georg
  1950 *The Sociology of Georg Simmel*. Trans. and ed. by Kurt Wolff. New York: Free Press.
Simmons, Ozzie G.
  1961 "The mutual images and expectations of Anglo-Americans and Mexican Americans." *Daedalus* 90:286–299.
Sosa Riddell, Adaljiza
  1974 "Chicanas and el movimiento." *Aztlán: Chicano Journal of the Social Sciences and the Arts* 5:155–165.
Sotomayor, Marta
  1972 "Mexican American interaction with social systems." *Social Casework* 52:316–322.
Spady, W. G.
  1970 "Lament for the letterman: Effects of peer status and extracurricular activities on goals and achievements." *American Journal of Sociology* 75:680–702.
Stein, Maurice R.
  1960 *The Eclipse of Community*. Princeton: Princeton University Press.

Stern, Gwen
  1976 "Ethnic Identity and Community Action in El Barrio." Ph.D. disser-
        tation, Northwestern University.
Stone, G., and H. Farberman, eds.
  1970 *Social Psychology through Symbolic Interaction.* Waltham, Mass.:
        Ginn-Blaisdell.
Strauss, Anselm
  1959 *Mirrors and Masks.* New York: Free Press.
Stycos, J. Mayone
  1955 *Family and Fertility in Puerto Rico.* New York: Columbia University
        Press.
Suttles, Gerald
  1968 *The Social Order of the Slum.* Chicago: University of Chicago Press.
  1972 *Social Construction of Communities.* Chicago: University of Chicago
        Press.
  1978 "Culture and life-style among the minority poor." In K. Gronbjerg, D.
        Street, and G. Suttles (eds.), *Poverty and Social Change.* Chicago: Uni-
        versity of Chicago Press.
Temple-Trujillo, Rita E.
  1974 "Conceptions of the Chicano family." *Smith College Studies in Social
        Casework* 45:1–20.
Thomas, W. I., and F. Znaniecki
  1918 *The Polish Peasant in Europe and America.* Boston: Badger.
Thrasher, Frederick
  1927 *The Gang.* Chicago: University of Chicago Press.
Toch, Hans
  1969 *Violet Men.* Chicago: Aldine.
Toennies, Ferdinand
  1957 *Community and Society.* Trans. and ed. by C. Loomis. New York:
        Harper and Row.
Vidal, Mirta
  1971 *Women: New Voice of La Raza.* New York: Pathfinder.
Vidich, A. J.
  1969 "Participant observation and the collection and interpretation of data."
        In G. McCall and J. L. Simmons (eds.), *Issues in Participant Observa-
        tion,* pp. 78–86. Reading, Mass.: Addison-Wesley.
Vincent, Clark
  1961 *Unmarried Mothers.* New York: Free Press.
Warsow, Robert
  1963 "The gentleman with a gun." In M. Lusky (ed.), *An Anthology of
        Encounter Magazine.* New York: Basic Books.
Wax, Rosalie
  1971 *Doing Field Work: Warnings and Advice.* Chicago: University of
        Chicago Press.

Weber, Max
    1964 *The Theory of Social and Economic Organization.* Trans. and ed. by T.
          Parsons. New York: Free Press.
Welfare Council of New York City
    1950 "Working with Teen-age Gangs." A report on the Central Harlem
          Street Clubs Project.
Welfare Planning Council, Los Angeles Region, Research Department
    1967 "Mexican-American Survey Project: Summer Youth Program." Venice,
          Calif.
Werthman, Carl
    1967 "The function of social definitions in the development of delinquent
          careers." In *Task Force Report: Juvenile Delinquency and Youth
          Crime,* pp. 155–170. Washington, D.C.: U.S. Government Printing
          Office.
Whyte, W. F.
    1955 *Street Corner Society.* Chicago: University of Chicago Press.
Williams, Robin
    1960 *American Society.* New York: Knopf.
Willmott, P.
    1963 *The Evolution of a Community.* London: Routledge and Kegan Paul.
Willmott, P., and M. Young
    1960 *Family and Class in a London Suburb.* London: Routledge and Kegan
          Paul.
Wirth, Louis
    1938 "Urbanism as a way of life." *American Journal of Sociology* 44:3–24.
    1964 *On Cities and Social Life.* Ed. by Albert Reiss, Jr. Chicago: University
          of Chicago Press.
Wright, David E., E. Salinas, and W. P. Kuvlesky
    1973 "Opportunities for social mobility for Mexican American youth." In R.
          O. de la Garza, Z. A. Kruszewski, and T. A. Arciniega (eds.), *Chicanos
          and Native Americans,* pp. 43–60. Englewood Cliffs, N.J.: Prentice-
          Hall.
Yablonsky, Lewis
    1970 *The Violent Gang.* Baltimore: Penguin Books.
Yancey, W. L., E. P. Ericksen, and R. N. Juliani
    1976 "Emergent ethnicity: A review and reformulation." *American Socio-
          logical Review* 41:391–402.
Young, M., and P. Willmott
    1957 *Family and Kinship in East London.* London: Routledge and Kegan
          Paul.
Zorbaugh, Harvey Warren
    1929 *The Gold Coast and the Slum.* Chicago: University of Chicago Press.

Index

Absenteeism (school), peer group ties and, 171

Academic achievement: self-perception of pupils and, 145; struggle for, by Chicanos, 32; of study group youths, 30

Actions: meaning of, and social identity, 28. *See also* Behavior; Conduct

Activists. *See* Feminists; Political activists

Adulthood, steady job and, 160, 169

Adults, norms and values of, 26

Age-segmented groups, 226, 229

American dream: codes and expectations and, 21, 24; failure to finish school and, 158; limits on, 223–224; persistence of, 41–51; pursuit of, and violation of local standards, 229; valued in community, 24

Anglo world: friends in, 209; moving into, 198–209

Apartments in study community, size of, 39

Apologizing, 246 n.28

Behavior, culture and, 20. *See also* Actions; Conduct

Birth control, 123–125, 205, 228; failure to use, 249 n.6; meaning of, 206; by single women, 128–129

Blacks: Chicanos' view of, 48; comparative dropout rates of, 241 n.17; discrimination against, 46; incomes of, 239 n.9, 240 n.12; prejudice against, 241 n.20; unemployment of, 240 n.13

Blood ties, motherhood and, 71

Brown Berets, 241 n.19; 242 n.24

Bureaucracies, dealing with, 49

Business district, distance from, 33

Career goals, 151, 153

Careers program in mental health, 242 n.23

Career women, acceptability of role of, 70

Catholic priests, community activities of, 49

Catholic schools, 36, 44, 153–156. *See also* Education

Census data, problems with, in study community, 239 n.4

Chaperones, 67, 117

Chastity, submission and, 121. *See also* Virginity

Chicago Transit Authority, 43

Chicanismo, 219; future of, 234–235

Chicano community; leaving, 198–209; segmentation in, 225–231; stability of, 254 n.4; urban renewal and, 235; wider society and, 222–231. *See also* Feminists; Fieldwork in Chicano community; Political activists

Chicano cultural history classes, 241 n.17

Chicano national political party, 240 n.19

271

Economic support, cohesive family and, 75

Education, 198–200; American dream and, 21, 138; community achievement in, and slum status, 44; dropout rate and, 44; earnings and, 43, 253 n.2; explanations of failure in, 139–140; grades of pupils in study area, 44; as major concern in study community, 30; parents' views of special, 46; parochial school, 44; residents' views of importance of, 46; styles of learning in, 252 n.14; teen pregnancy and, 36, 44. *See also* Schools; Teachers

Educational success, 198–209; 240 n.15

Elders, treatment of, 74

Emotional support from family, 58, 59, 75

Employment, marriage and, 171–172. *See also* Unemployment

Employment situation in study area, 42

Ethnicity, 46–48; dating and, 207–208

Etiquette: apologizing and, 246 n.28; convention and, 86–88; expected, 74; honor and, 23, 73. *See also* Insults; Social blunders

Exchanges: expanded family and, 58; of goods and services in gangs, 227–228; hidden economy and, 253 n.3

Expectations, codes and, 21, 24

Extracurricular activities, 148–149, 158; sense of self-worth and, 152

Extramarital affairs, 61–62

Families, single-parent, 240 n.11

Family: Chicano, 55–59; cohesive, 55–59, 75; disadvantage of close ties with, 58–59; exchange of aid and, 160; expanded, 55, 56, 160, 230–231, 235; honor and, 23; importance of network of friends and, 38, 160; symbols of expanded, 54; values of Chicano, 54

Family finances, 42, 57

Family honor: revenge to uphold, 118; virginity and, 117

Family life, symbols of, 75

Family relationships, success and, 208

Fathers: authority of, 64; honor of, 66–67; role of, 60; sons and, 63–66

Federal bureaucracies, dealing with, 49

Federal government, resources from, 50

Females: academic superiority and relationships with males, 142; income of Spanish- and non-Spanish-speaking, 240 n.12; terms used for, 239 n.5

Femininity, work and, 159–160

Feminists, 11

Fieldwork in Chicano community, 5–6, 7; appearance of researcher and, 6, 9; gathering data on fights and reputations, 247 n.15; relationship with families and, 10; relationship with parents and, 11; relationship with women and, 9, 10; subjects' view of researchers and, 6, 9–10. *See also* Research

Fighting: age and, 194; meaning of, 90; reputation as gang member and, 183; selectivity in, 103, 105

Fighting gangs, death rates in, 4

Friends, mutual obligations and, 160, 169. *See also* Peer groups

Friendship, 22, 38, 99–100; gangs and, 196; lack of, between the sexes, 191; reputation hierarchy and, 101–102

Gang leaders, 98

Gang members: close ties among, 190–191; compassion among, 190; confidence among, 186–187; evolution of activities of, 185; exchanges of personal information among, 189; highly valued, 187; identifying, 28; length of membership in gangs, 227; mutual obligations among, 186–187, 188; names of, 189, 195–196; older, 254 n.3; punishment of, 190; reputation of, and fighting, 183; trust among, 186–187, 188. *See also* Gangs

Gang reputations, 94–97

and, 132–136; lack of verbal and interpersonal skills and, 247 n.10; reputation and, 89–90; status of leader and, 247 n.10; style and situational legitimacy of, 83; among women, 114–115, 132–136. *See also* Fighting; Fighting gangs; Guns
Virgin, maintaining identity as, 119–121. *See also* Marriage
Virginity, 66–70; 249 n.5; by choice, 205; femininity and, 228; freedom and, 116–118, 205; loss of significance of, 249 n.5; marriage and, 120–121; *quinceañera* as affirmation of, 53; rarity of, 228; respect for, 125–127
Virgin Mother symbol, 66, 71
Voting, 48

Wages, 162–163; low, 161; supplementing, 160, 161, 163–165
Welfare. *See* Mutual obligation networks; Public aid
Wife: role of, 60; working, 63
Women: behavior of unmarried, 125–130; best jobs for, 173; cultural constraints and, 136; defending honor of, 111–113; evaluation of identity of, 116; femininity of, work and, 159–160; freedom from supervision and, 117; gangs of, 132–133; honor and, 23; independence and work by, 160, 174–175; independent, 204–205; insult and violence and, 132–136; jobs and independence for, 174–175; office work and, 173–174; as political activists, 213–214; researcher's relationship with, 9–10; role expectations of, 135; self-defense of honor in school, 150; socializing of, 191; violence among, 114–115, 132–136; work and, 173–176, 204; work of, 61; working vs. nonworking, 160. *See also* Career women; Daughters; Females; Wife
Work: age status and, 160; education and, 24; femininity and, 159; independence of women and, 174; marginal expressive value of, 224; marital status and, 254 n.9; meaning of, 175, 224; orientation toward, 253 n.4; peer group affiliation and, 170; self-worth and, 165–169; as topic of conversation, 253 n.5; women's and men's, 61
Work life, separation of, from street life, 170

Youths: effect of gossip on, in study community, 39; inconsistency between self-perceptions of, and school personnel's perceptions of, 145; norms and values of, 25; school atmosphere and behavior of, 150–151. *See also* Pupils

Printed in the United States
35823LVS00003B/187-210

9 780813 509914